Helping Families to Change

Helping Families to Change

by
Virginia Satir
James Stachowiak
Harvey A. Taschman

Prepared and Edited by
Donald W. Tiffany, Ph.D.
Julius I. Cohen, M.S.W.
Analee M. Robinson, M.S.
High Plains Comprehensive Community Mental Health Center
Keith C. Ogburn, M.S.
Hutchinson Public School System, Hutchinson, Kansas

Illustrations by Marilyn Ybarra

Jason Aronson, Inc.   **New York**

This project was partially supported by federal funds provided for mental health center projects under PL 89-749, Sec. 314 (d), Grant No. MHC 37-71-39-03, administered by the Kansas State Department of Social Welfare.

Third Printing . . . . . January 1977

ISBN: 0-87668-238-7

Library of Congress Catalog Number: 75-33584

CONTENTS

ACKNOWLEDGMENTS

The editors wish to express their appreciation to all who contributed to the preparation of this volume. In particular, our thanks go to Virginia Satir, M.A., James Stachowiak, Ph.D., and Harvey Taschman, Ph.D., for permitting us to edit and publish their material. Providing support, organizational skill, and consultation throughout the original workshop that fathered this publication was Don Klein, Ph.D. His presence was strongly felt, and we are grateful to him for taking time from his busy schedule to be a part of our effort.

Since the workshops and seminars that provided the substance for this book were partially funded by a Federal Public Health Service grant-in-aid, many staff members in the Region VII office were involved with the review and facilitation of our project. In particular, we want to acknowledge the involvement of Elizabeth Ossorio, Ph.D., our regional consultant, who took time to attend our workshop and whose encouragement we especially valued.

At the state level, we received substantial assistance from the community mental health service staff of the Kansas Division of Mental Health and Retardation, State Department of Social and Rehabilitation Services. Not only were they gracious enough to give us the benefit of their consultation, but their active participation in the workshop helped assure its success. In particular, we are indebted to Howard Williams, M.D., whose warmth, humor, and leadership as master of ceremonies kept everyone at ease and provided them with a sense of order and continuity. To Mary Grohmann, Ph.D., his assistant, we are also grateful for her participation as a resource person.

At the administrative level, we wish to express thanks to our governing board, who saw the value of our undertaking and whose pride in and support of our efforts has been a major morale builder. To our Center Director, John Cody, M.D., we also say thanks for his encouragement, interest, and cooperation in providing the resources needed for the project's completion.

Necessary for this undertaking was the backing and involvement of a dedicated Mental Health Center staff committed to the principles underlying our objectives. The staff members were with us all the way in making this project go. They served as leaders of small discussion groups and later as seminar leaders. Their participation went beyond routine responsibilities and deserves special commendation.

The cooperation of officials and staff of Fort Hays Kansas State College must not be overlooked. To those individuals, and particularly John Garwood, Ph.D., we would like to convey our thanks for the use of campus facilities and for awarding college credit to those who completed the program. Thus the college in effect indicated that educating community gatekeepers to relate more effectively to families is an activity worthy of academic recognition and support. The opportunity to earn college credit also served as an incentive for many individuals to persevere through six months of ongoing seminars despite the travel and personal inconvenience involved.

To our secretaries, Marcelyn Herbig, De Dusin, Wanda Hake, Gayle McFadden, and Patricia Littler, we are indeed grateful for putting up with our endless requests and attending to the mass of minutia we faced in preparing for the workshop, and for transcribing and typing the ensuing manuscripts.

We also wish to especially recognize volunteers from the Ellis County Mental Health Association for their help: Aylene Beltz, Marilyn Ginther, Pat Hargrave, Nadine Leiker, Patricia Luckie, and Vonda Sanders. Not only did they confer with us in the early planning stages, but they actively assisted with the many amenities and tasks needing attention.

Above all we want to express our gratitude to the community gatekeepers who, through their participation in the project, helped shape the contents of this volume. Their dedication to becoming more effective professionals in relation to the families they serve was continually in evidence and confirmed our belief that helping families to change is a timely objective, shared by many, and in need of the development this publication is intended to foster.

PREFACE

The way we relate to other people and how we can live with other human beings are some of the things we learn as children within the family. Our perceptions, our styles of communicating, and our modes of interacting are all shaped within the confines of our own family—the laboratory of early experience.

Many studies have confirmed the importance of these early childhood learnings. The structures and dynamics of family units have been extensively studied and analyzed, until now it is almost a truism to say that an individual's problems do not exist in social isolation and that people do not suddenly "break out" with behavioral problems as they would with measles. Given that the family is crucial in shaping human behavior, it follows that for all human relations to improve, families must change their ways of functioning so they will not nurture harmful modes of interaction and perpetuate ineffective or damaging models of behavior from one generation to the next. Implicit in what we present here is the optimistic but justifiable view that such change can occur, and that there are methods for helping families replace old behavior with new, more satisfying approaches to the many demands of today's complex society.

To help families function more effectively, we devised a program to develop or improve the effectiveness of people in the community who, as a part of their everyday employment, work with families in one way or another. This project was based on the belief that family therapy can often best be provided by the community helpers with whom troubled families come in contact in the natural course of events, such as welfare workers, ministers, lawyers, educators, and public health nurses. This concept is in keeping with the objectives of the community mental health movement. One major goal of that movement has been to utilize and integrate all therapeutic potentials available in the community to improve mental health and achieve a better way of life for everyone.

More specifically we had found that most community helpers have difficulty relating to families as units. They tend to view clients outside the family context and, consequently, work with distorted or limited perceptions of what the actual problems are and how those problems can be modified. Despite their own experiences of growing up in families, few community helpers regard the family as a system within which each member contributes to its characteristic interactional pattern.

We assumed that a more effective family-systems attitude could be developed in community helpers if we went about it properly. Our intent is to avoid merely "spoon-feeding" information. There are two requisites for the kind of meaningful educational experience which we believe will lead to improved community service: (1) information should be paired with experiential involvement by the readers for "carry-over" to job situations to occur; and (2) opportunities must be found for the application and practice of new skills.

The selection of the contents of this volume was based on the premise that family systems are ineffective to the degree that they rigidly adhere to ways of communicating which render them incapable of dealing with the problems facing them. The assumption was that when therapeutic intervention enables members of the family to improve their communication patterns, the ultimate result is functional family behavior.

While the main focus is on families with serious difficulties who usually come to the attention of community helpers, the knowledge and approaches for bringing about desirable changes in family functioning are universally applicable. Virginia Satir has defined a family therapist as "anyone who tries to help families." Many people, in many ways, are involved in trying to help families and could rightfully be called "therapists." This material is intended not only for the professional in his office or clinic, but for all concerned people who see the need for family change and have the opportunity for constructive intervention.

The material contained here may be of use to other mental health centers, social agencies, or any organization interested in improving family life as they plan similar programs. The exercises for awareness of interactions and improvement of perception and communication can, of course, be followed by any reader who has the cooperation of one or two other people to participate with him.

The contents mirror the two-fold purpose of the volume: to provide the basic information about family interactions and to develop the necessary skills for therapeutic intervention. Harvey Taschman's discussion of sociological foundations and investigations of family therapy which provides the historical and theoretical context for understanding family systems; James Stachowiak's research and clinical findings, which undergird the theory of conjoint family therapy as a tool for change; and Virginia Satir's techniques to cultivate personal awareness and family change, which she has developed out of a background of rich clinical experience, are an inextricably interdependent whole, considerably "greater" than the sum of its parts.

So we share with you and offer for your consideration, whoever, whatever you are—mental health program director, caseworker, nurse, minister, teacher, instructor of communication skills, family life educator, father, mother, anyone who lives in a family—what we believe are constructive guidelines for helping families. Our fervent hope is that the improvement of family functioning will ultimately lead to what all of us are vitally concerned with—the amelioration of the human condition, making life more effective, more satisfying, and more meaningful.

Donald W. Tiffany
Julius I. Cohen
Analee M. Robinson
Keith C. Ogburn

Introducing Harvey A. Taschman

As a sociologist focusing primarily on child and family mental health, Harvey Taschman has a broad background of education and experience. He graduated from the University of Wisconsin in 1946, and subsequently earned advanced degrees from Western Reserve University and the University of Pittsburgh. His early experience was with the Veterans Administration Hospital, Butler, Pennsylvania, as a medical social worker, and in St. Elizabeths Hospital, Washington, D.C., as a psychiatric social worker. In December 1955 he joined the Alamance County Health Department, Burlington, North Carolina, serving as a psychiatric social work consultant and conducting in-service training programs. From 1957 to 1960 Harvey was Chief Psychiatric Social Worker at the Mental Health Center of Raleigh and Wake County, North Carolina. From 1962 to 1967 he held the position of Social Administration Specialist at the Mental Health Center, National Institute of Mental Health, where Harvey A. Taschman was involved in research, clinical practice, consultation, and community work in mental health. After completing his doctoral program of study and receiving the Ph.D. from the University of Pittsburgh in 1967, he came to the position which he now holds as Consultant in Child Mental Health Services at the Center for Studies of Child and Family Mental Health, National Institute of Mental Health, Rockville, Maryland. He has published articles on his research, has made many public appearances furthering the community mental health cause, and has presented scholarly papers on the subject of family therapy and child advocacy at professional meetings of mental health organizations.

Chapter 1

Developments and Innovations in Family Therapy in a Changing Society

by Harvey A. Taschman

The theme of our efforts in this volume is proclaimed in the title, *Helping Families to Change.* Other contributors will address themselves specifically to techniques of working with troubled families. My basic purpose is to establish a framework for what is to follow. I am not going to tell you how to work with a family, but rather I shall trace some of the developments of family therapy, highlight different methods, and discuss the results of various research studies, some of which were supported by the National Institute of Mental Health.

Historical Development of the Family

Before doing this, however, I would like to look at the family as an institution. If we are to work successfully with families, it is important that we have some knowledge about the evolution of the family system in historical perspective and that we have an understanding of all the various social forces that impinge upon the American family today. Let me emphasize that the family is not a static system in our culture, but one which is dynamic and constantly evolving both in its structure and in its function. There are no eternal verities, and the values or system of beliefs as well as the roles played by the family members are changing today more rapidly than ever before.

The origin of the family is unknown. Some have theorized that at the beginning of man's existence, over a million years ago, human males and females procreated in the same random manner as most other animals. When man developed tools and agriculture, enabling him to spend more time in one place, it is thought that the incest taboo was invoked, which forbade mating in ascending or descending blood lines. Today the incest taboo is found among peoples and races all over the world. Some form of polygyny or polyandry was probably practiced, and the family units were households with either several wives or several husbands. These are, of course, speculations. Westermarck, who wrote *The History of Human Marriage*, published first in 1891, theorized that the family existed even before the human race, that family life was found among prehistoric man and had originated among the higher animals. [1] Regardless of how the family began, we know that every identifiable society developed some form of family life. It is likely, too, that the particular form of marriage and family unit reflected the total ecology of the civilization and constituted man's attempts to survive in that ecology.

Polygamy, for example, served to perpetuate the race at a time when infant mortality was very high, when disease, pestilence, and war threatened man's very existence. We tend to think of monogamy as the highest form of marriage and the best, but let us not forget that even in the United States polygyny was practiced among the Mormons until 1890. It is somewhat difficult, too, to distinguish the serial or progressive monogamy as practiced in our country today by way of legal divorces from the polygamy which exists in other parts of the world.

The Modern Family

Ever since the Industrial Revolution, some 200 years ago, and the rapid social and economic changes that came in its wake, we have been moving from an agrarian to an urban society. This has had a major impact upon all of our institutions, including the family. As people moved from the farm to the city, the extended family and elaborate kinship ties gradually gave way to new values in family living. The *nuclear family*, living in its own home and making its own decisions, became the ideal. The pediatrician, the psychiatrist, and the child-guidance clinic have replaced the grandmother in giving advice to the young parents on child-rearing practices, while the grandparents have been relegated to the role of baby-sitter. The *institutional family* of rural society, with its subordination of the wife to the husband and with parental authority firmly established, was challenged by the new industrial society in which women became emancipated, and the new *companionship family* emerged which placed its values on democracy, personality development, and self-expression in family living.

These changes took place gradually, and only after much struggle and anxiety. There were some who predicted dire consequences for these new values and the direction in which the American family was moving. In 1941 Pitirim Sorokin, a noted sociologist, wrote the following:

> The family as a sacred union of husband and wife, of parents and children, will continue to disintegrate. Divorces and separations will increase until any profound difference between socially sanctioned marriages and illicit sex relationships disappears. Children will be separated earlier and earlier from their parents. The main socio-cultural functions of the family will further decrease until the family becomes a mere incidental cohabitation of male and female while the home will become a mere overnight parking place, mainly for sex-relationship. [2]

Six years later Carle Zimmerman, another sociologist, predicted that the American family was doomed unless it returned to what he called the "domestic" type of family our grandparents lived in.[3] Were they right? Today there are many threats to traditional monogamy and there are many who believe that we will gradually develop other forms of marriage and family patterns. Lederer and Jackson wrote that in the United States the state of marriage is a calamity.[4] As predicted, the divorce rate has been increasing steadily since about 1960, and in 1970 it was approximately the same as in 1946, which had an isolated, all-time high number of divorces at the conclusion of World War II. Rustum and Della Roy, writing in the March/April 1970 issue of the *Humanist*, claimed that traditional marriage is dead for large numbers of couples in today's world, and they suggested the possibility of legalizing bigamy and advocated training for marriage.[5] Herbert Otto has also critically examined our traditional monogamy and reported that marriage specialists estimate that between 40 and 60 percent of all marriages are in need of counseling.[6] He further reported that one-third of all first-born children in the United States from 1964 to 1966 were conceived out of wedlock, with the result that large numbers of people were coerced into unwanted, "shotgun" marriages.

In addition, Otto discussed some modern alternatives to traditional family living. The 1960s witnessed the rapid growth of communes as an alternative to the nuclear family. In 1969 the Alternatives Foundation of Berkeley, California, published a directory of intentional or utopian communes in the United States. The communes vary in their emphasis. Some are agricultural, some diversified, some religious. The movement is beginning to attract significant segments of the established population. These new styles of communal living range from the type exemplified by the "Twin Oaks" community in Virginia, where personal property and monogamous relationships are maintained, to the other extreme represented by the commune known as "The Family" near Taos, New Mexico, which encourages the sharing of husbands, wives, and children. The development of the commune, in any event, is one reaction to the dehumanization of the cities against which some people feel the single family unit is defenseless.

Problems Facing Families Today

Let us consider some of the other major developments that are bringing about changes in the social fabric of America—changes which have considerable relevance for the family, since the family after all is a microcosm of society. The life-span continues to lengthen as a result of progress in medicine. Consequently, we have an ever-increasing population of senior citizens while our nation clings tenaciously to a cult of youth. Today's grandparents and great grandparents, who would hold high status and be respected for their wisdom in another society, often find themselves alienated both from their own families and from society at large.

Paradoxically, many of our youth feel equally alienated from a society whose social institutions they believe are still based on nineteenth- and early twentieth-century values and, consequently, are not in keeping with the knowledge and scientific accomplishments of the jet age. Thus we find educational institutions at both the university and high-school level under attack from students who question the relevance of both the substance and the manner of delivery of the knowledge or information they must consume. Organized religion, too, has come under attack by the young, who are more concerned about "man's inhumanity to man" than personal salvation.

Our population has become more mobile, and while a boy still might marry the girl next door, he might just as easily marry a girl from across the seas, from some far different culture. Transportation has revolutionized our lives to the extent that the one-world idea enunciated in the 1940s is today all but a political reality. It is possible to travel to almost any part of the world in a matter of hours.

The mass media, particularly television, have produced an exquisitely informed citizenry. Every schoolboy seems to know about the intricacies of rocketry and space travel. And in the political area, it is no longer possible to fool all of the people all of the time.

The social revolution, which gained momentum in the 1960s with the demands of the minorities, continues to progress, not, however, without some pain. The eighteen-year-old vote can be expected to bring about changes even more rapidly. The prevalence of the "pill" and the easing of abortion laws lend impetus to the changing sexual mores. The women's liberation movement, which is probably a consequence of the changing role of the female in our society as well as the advocate for more rapid change, is having an effect upon our families. The roles of mother and father, and more basically of male and female, are becoming less distinct.

Adoption regulations are changing, and we have seen both interracial adoptions and adoptions by single persons. These new laws, plus the increased use of birth-control measures, have already changed the balance of the supply of white, adoptive children relative to the demand; and many more cross-cultural, cross-color adoptions are occurring.

Medical and biological progress has been nothing short of revolutionary. We are witnessing the replacement of human organs and are on the verge of creating life in the test tube. Embryo implants and organ transplants are already a reality. In his book *Future Shock*, Alvin Toffler writes:

> The ability to pre-set the sex of one's baby, or even to "program" its IQ, looks, and personality traits, must now be regarded as a real possibility. Embryo implants, babies grown *in vitro*, the ability to swallow a pill and guarantee oneself twins or triplets or, even more, the ability to walk into a babytorium and actually purchase embryos—all this reaches so far beyond any previous human experience that one needs to look at the future through the eyes of the poet or painter, rather than those of the sociologist or conventional philosopher. [7]

In Huxley's *Brave New World* a scientific elite of totalitarian "predestinators" created test-tube babies on an assembly line, predetermining their every mental and physical characteristic. [8] When Huxley wrote the book in 1932 he predicted that this revolution would occur in 600 years. It is now likely that the possibility will become reality by the end of this century.

There are, of course, numerous other social forces that are exerting or will exert an impact on the American family. To mention just a few, there is the constant threat of war, the abuse of drugs, and the threat to our ecological balance because of the pollution of the air we breathe, the water we drink, the food we eat, and the overpopulation of our society. There are the new directions in the delivery of health services, the development of the community mental health movement, the new models of education, and the more realistic approach to the problems of social welfare. Any one of these social forces would be a fitting subject for a voluminous discussion in itself.

Despite the technological, genetic, and biomedical research advances of our age, there has been virtually no change in the ability of parenting our children. While the problems are more complex than ever, the average parents are inadequately prepared for child rearing. The Joint Commission on Mental Health of Children made special note of this:

> This Nation which looks to the family to nurture its young, gives no real help with child rearing until a child is badly disturbed or disruptive to the community. The discontent, apathy, and violence today are a warning that society has not assumed its responsibility to ensure an environment which will provide optimum care for its children. The family cannot be allowed to withstand alone the enormous pressures of an increasingly technological world. Within the community some mechanisms must be created which will assume the responsibility for ensuring the necessary supports for the child and family. [9]

Toffler, recognizing this problem, suggests the possibility of developing a cadre of professional parents who would rear the children of biological parents and suggests that the latter might welcome the arrangement. [10]

The Development of Family Therapy

Against this background, then, I will briefly review the development of family therapy.

The precise point of origin in time and place of family therapy is not clear, and one reason for this is the lack of consensus that exists even today as to exactly what the term means. The literature suggests that it was first described somewhere in the mid-1950s and that a number of clinicians and theoreticians, working independently, were associated with its beginnings. By then Bateson, Jackson, and their colleagues in Palo Alto had coined the phrase "double bind," which referred to the conflicting messages which the schizophrenic patient received, usually from the mother, creating a situation in which the victim could not win regardless of what he did. This group hypothesized that the person caught in the double bind might develop schizophrenic symptoms. They later proposed that children who grow up in even relatively healthy homes are sometimes caught in the double bind. This concept has been of major importance in understanding family problems.

Wynne [11] and his colleagues at the National Institute of Mental Health used the concept "pseudomutuality" at about the same time to describe a rigid family system in which individual growth and divergence from established roles is not tolerated, the primary concern being preservation of the status quo of the family and its facade of harmony and well-being. Ackerman presented a conceptual model in his 1956 paper "Interlocking Pathology in Family Relationships," [12] and also developed a therapeutic method which he called "Family Therapy." Bowen [13] described the "undifferentiated family ego mass" and developed a therapeutic method which he called "Family Psychotherapy." During this period Virginia Satir was teaching family dynamics to psychiatric residents at the Illinois State Psychiatric Institute in Chicago, and her book *Conjoint Family Therapy*, [14] which was published several years later, was based largely on her course outlines. Meanwhile, John Bell [15] laid claim to actually being the first to use this new method as a form of treatment for the entire family. And there were many others—Clausen, Yarrow, Lidz, Sears, Bandura, to name a few—but all of them, according to Bell, were studying *individuals* who were members of families.

The Family as a System

Regardless of whether they approached family interaction from the standpoint of studying the process of interaction in families to compare those containing a schizophrenic patient with those containing a patient with a personality disorder, or whether they approached it as a specific method of treatment for the family, all of these early pioneers were agreed on at least one thing: they saw the family itself as a viable entity. They used different terminology to describe what they were seeing, but essentially what they were saying was that the family is a system, a system that is constantly changing, sometimes slowly, sometimes rapidly. It is a system that is delicately balanced and struggles to maintain that balance, or "homeostasis."[16]Sometimes the balance reflects family pathology and, in the course of therapy, the balance hopefully is changed. The system is made up of subsystems (the individual family members), and a change in one part changes the balance of the system. But the whole is not equal to the sum of its parts in a psychodynamic sense. This was the mistake made by earlier methods of treatment which assumed that by changing an individual member the entire family would necessarily benefit.

Let us imagine for a moment that a mother in a family which contains several young children enters psychoanalysis because of severe psychosomatic symptoms. During the course of her analysis it becomes clear to her that she cannot continue her sado-masochistic marriage. Her "successful" treatment ends in her obtaining a divorce. Granted, the children were probably not symptom-free before, but is the family any further ahead after the divorce? There may be serious new problems. This is not to say that individual treatment should not be used. Far from it. Individual treatment, whether it be psychoanalysis or psychotherapy, may be required for a period of time to resolve the intrapsychic conflicts of a given family member; but ethical considerations, as well as a consideration of the mental health needs of the whole family, should be taken into account.

In a chapter in the *American Handbook of Psychiatry*, Nathan Ackerman describes family therapy:

> Family treatment, although relatively new, offers promise. It gives an expanded understanding of the relations between inner and outer experience. It lends explicit emphasis to the principle of emotional contagion in family

process, the transmission of pathogenic conflict and coping from one generation to the next. . . . It is the therapy of a natural living unit; the sphere of therapeutic intervention is not a single individual but the whole family. The therapeutic interview includes all those persons who share the identity of the family and whose behavior is influenced by a circular interchange of emotion within the group. . . [17] Family psychotherapy absorbs selected features of each [of the older traditional methods of psychotherapy] but extends beyond them to evolve a new form of therapy, one that utilizes a natural group rather than the isolated individual or a contrived collection of individuals. [18]

In a Public Health Monograph on family group therapy, John Bell also succinctly describes this method as he sees it:

Family group therapy is an effort to effect behavioral and attitudinal changes within a total family through a series of conferences attended by the parents, the children nine years of age and older, and the therapist. In most instances the conferences are initiated through referral of a child who is disturbed, but from the beginning the therapeutic goals are family-centered rather than child-centered. The primary intent of the therapist is to accomplish a modification of the functioning and structure of the family as a group. It is assumed that as a consequence modifications will be effectuated secondarily in the situation of individuals within the family. The method of the therapy emerges, then, from the one basic assumption differentiating it from individual therapy: *the family is the unit to be treated.*

It is important to stress that in this method the family is not regarded as an assembly of individuals, but is recognized as a biological and social unit. One must keep in mind that here no child or parent is under treatment as an individual. Whereas in individual therapy the emphasis is on the unique person, in family therapy specific attention to the individual . . . is to be avoided as much as possible. . . .

The notion about the whole family being the patient cannot be overemphasized because it is central to this method of therapy. It is the rare family, however, who will call a clinic or a private therapist to request help because of a disturbance in family relationships. The family selects one of its members to be the patient, and frequently he is *not* the sickest member of the family.

Let us take a hypothetical illustration of a mother who calls a clinic to seek help for her twelve-year-old son who has been bullying children in school and has been caught cheating. The mother does not tell the intake worker that she is even more concerned about her husband, who is a compulsive gambler, because she is ashamed and she is certain that he would not seek help for his problem anyhow, nor does she describe her own severe symptoms of depression, nor does she say that her daughter has no friends. The clinic accepts the case at face value, for the boy meets the criteria for acceptance.

Those of us who have worked in child-guidance clinics are familiar with how parents use the child as a "ticket of admission" with the hope that their marriage will somehow be helped. Sometimes this is done without any real awareness on the part of the parent who seeks the help and at other times it seems quite deliberate. If the community happens to have a clinic identified as a child-guidance clinic and if there is no outpatient facility for adults, this would indeed be the only way the parents could get help—through the child. If the case is split, as is common practice in the child-guidance model, the astute therapist who sees the parents (and it often is only the mother) will hopefully get to the problem of the family. But it may take weeks or even months to reach the point that might be reached in but a few family sessions. Furthermore, even after it is recognized by the parents and therapist alike that the problems of one or both parents are more severe than the problems of the child who was originally brought to the clinic, the child will still be identified by all parties concerned as the patient, and the parents will remain "collaterals."

Defining Family Therapy

Let us return now to the problem of the definition of family therapy. I indicated earlier that there is no universal consensus of what it is. Some define it as a situation in which each member of the family has his own therapist; others see it as the same therapist seeing several members of the family separately; still others see it as a method in which the therapist occasionally sees other members of the family in the interest of the patient; seeing only the parents together is sometimes called family therapy; and, finally, it is defined as the whole family being seen together. But even this last definition poses problems. What is meant by the whole family? Do we mean only the nuclear family or do we include a grandparent or another member of the extended family? What about other significant members of the household who are not related? Some therapists will occasionally include household servants, significant relatives who may live in a distant town, and even a household pet when appropriate. You all know of situations, I am sure, where the dog has taken the brunt of family frustration. The way in which each family member relates to the pet dog may be of extreme significance.

The definition I would use is that family therapy is a method of treatment which generally includes the entire family living in one household. I say "generally" because there are times when it is desirable to work with different sub-parts of the family system, such as the parents or only the older siblings. However, in most instances, the family is seen together very early in the exploratory phase. Some family therapists who share this general orientation see only the parents initially, but others see the whole family right from the start. All the children are usually seen at least once, including very young ones. The family interaction patterns in the presence of even an infant (who will not directly benefit from therapy himself) will often give the therapist valuable clues to the family relationships. Incidentally, there are generally no difficulties in getting the children to take part in family sessions if the therapist himself is comfortable with this method.

In addition to the problems of definition of the method, a further source of confusion concerns the many different labels under which this method comes packaged. Some of these are: "Family Therapy," "Family Group Therapy," "Family Counseling," "Family Group Counseling," "Conjoint Therapy," "Conjoint Family Therapy," and "Family Group Casework."

Innovations in Family Therapy

Now let us turn to a consideration of some research studies in family therapy. A project supported by a grant from the National Institute of Mental Health was called "Techniques of Crisis Family Therapy."[20] Growing out of the need to find alternatives to hospitalization, the Family Treatment Unit at the University Medical Center in Denver, Colorado, explored the potential of crisis-oriented family therapy as an alternative to hospitalization. Patients judged to need hospitalization by the admitting psychiatrist were randomly assigned to the Family Treatment Unit instead. As a result, families who came to the hospital expecting to be relieved of the burden of a "crazy" relative through hospitalization found themselves returning home with the patient and perhaps a somewhat different attitude about how he could be helped.

The treatment team, consisting of a psychiatrist, psychiatric social worker, and a psychiatric public health nurse, treated the patient's trouble as a family problem. The patient's psychotic ramblings or suicidal gestures were interpreted as attempts at communication, which then appeared more logical than before. The goals were very limited and the team did not try to make the family over but, instead, focused on the accomplishment of simple specific tasks that would restore the patient's functioning and ultimately the family balance. The nurse might put a mop in a patient's hand and stay with her until the kitchen floor was clean. Instead of undergoing extensive psychotherapy, the mother might be urged to do the laundry or cook a meal, the son to weed the garden, or the daughter to return to school. On the average, treatment consisted of five office visits, one home visit, one or two telephone calls, and, when applicable, contact with a social agency. The project demonstrated that at least 84 percent of hospitalized psychiatric patients do not need psychiatric hospitalization.

Another NIMH-funded project was that of Goolishian and MacGregor, known as "Multiple-Impact Therapy."[21] It was developed at the medical center of the University of Texas in Galveston to deal with two common obstacles to therapy. One was the great distances families had to travel; some traveled as far as

450 miles to seek help for the problems of their adolescents. The other problem was the seeming impenetrability of the families' interactional patterns. The project was designed for intact families whose adolescent children were severely disturbed to the point where hospitalization was considered. The therapists regarded these problems as crisis situations and set limited goals. They believed that even small changes in the attitudes and behavior of the parents could help to bring about tremendous improvement in the behavior of their children.

The method involved working with the whole family and with various parts of the family over a two-and-a-half-day period. Numerous intensive interviews were held with the family in joint, family subgroup, and overlapping individual sessions. One-way screen observations were used, and the different therapists assigned to a family would telephone one another to check out the various stories they had heard from the different family members. This method was found to work quite well with adolescent behavioral problems, including so-called "uncontrollable" children. It also worked well with children with school phobia. It was less successful with anxious or neurotic boys and girls.

Multiple-impact therapy is being tried elsewhere now. MacGregor is using it with an urban population in Chicago, and the Family Service Association of Indianapolis is also experimenting with it.

Illustration of the Multifamily Approach

A project in which I personally took part about six years ago while employed at the Mental Health Study Center, a branch of NIMH in Prince Georges County, Maryland, involved working with adolescent, underachieving boys and their parents.[22] The boys were in their junior year of high school, were extremely intelligent (IQs above 120), and were failing. Three boys and their parents were seen by a single therapist for a series of twelve weekly sessions. We had three such groups and found, as we had suspected, that the communication patterns between the parents and their sons were poor. There were many double messages communicated to the boys, such as "We want you to do well" on the one hand, while on the other hand there was the message "You'd better not do better than your old man." The parents were anxious about extending more freedom to their sons and were fearful of a loss of control, which made parental decision-making difficult. We found the group approach to be advantageous because of the support given the parents by having other parents with similar problems interact with them. It was equally advantageous for the boys. Moreover, it was often possible for a youngster from one family to help the parents of another boy understand the meaning of their son's behavior. Likewise, a parent who seemed powerless to help his own son was able to help another by pointing out some of the real issues in the conflict that was taking place in the other family.

The following year we tried this approach with delinquent boys and found certain differences in relationships between parents and son. These parents could not set limits, and they communicated through their anxiety that they expected their sons to get into trouble; thus, unconsciously, they abetted it. For example, one mother expected her son to earn his own spending money; but if he ran short of funds, she would give him money because she was afraid if she did not he would steal it. The multifamily approach has been used since this time in mental hospitals with patients and their families, as well as in some family agencies.

Application of Technical Aids

Not too long ago therapists were reluctant to tape-record their therapy sessions. Today in some settings, particularly where there is an element of training, such recording is routine. Not only audiotapes are used but increasingly we hear of the use of videotapes. They are used for various purposes, most generally for teaching and research. In an experiment in the School of Social Work at the University of Wisconsin, Dr. Morton Perlmutter and a team of associates used videotapes in family therapy, playing back portions of the tape for the family's reaction. This was found to be particularly helpful in a number of situations. When the family is uncommunicative but still wants help, the playing back of the tapes was found to open communication networks which had been blocked by the family pathology. Another instance is when one or more members threaten others by nonverbal communication; as, for example, when a child is about to reveal a family secret and mother or father or both threaten the child by various gestures.

Still another use for recording is for self-supervision. There is nothing like playing a videotape back to see the therapist's own role. Although I have not personally had experience with video-tapes, I have used audiotape recordings. When I have played them back for my own use, they have always had an impact. If the therapist who works with individuals needs a "third ear," then surely the family therapist needs at least a "fourth" one to perceive the subvocalizations of the family members, and a second set of eyes would be helpful as well! In fact, this is why observers and a second therapist are often used.

There are times when modifications have to be made in therapeutic techniques. One such time is when working with disorganized families of the low socioeconomic population. The Philadelphia Child Guidance Clinic used an interesting technique in working with such families. Two therapists were utilized. One worked with a subgroup of the family while another took the mother behind the one-way mirror for "co-observational therapy." The aim here was to reorient the mother's observations away from her children and toward the behavior of the therapist in the room with them.[23]

Filial Therapy

Another rather interesting innovation is that of "Filial Therapy." With a grant from the National Institute of Mental Health, Guerney at Rutgers demonstrated that it is possible to teach parents to treat their own children through nondirective play therapy.[24]Training is given in groups of six to eight parents. The role that the parent is taught to take is modeled on that of the client-centered therapist. The aim is to enable the child to gain a feeling of greater self-respect and confidence, and through the medium of play to communicate to his parents feelings that he previously kept from awareness. Filial therapy is also designed to help change the child's misperceptions of his parents' feelings, behavior, and attitudes.

Home Visit Revisited

Finally, I would like to comment on what is not an innovation but a rediscovery or a reutilization of a very old method—namely, the home visit. This used to be an essential part of the social worker's role, going back all the way to Mary Richmond, and it was very effective. Somehow it became lost in the decades between 1940 and 1960 when social work looked to the psychoanalytic model of the 50-minute hour in the office, and when intrapsychic material began to have more appeal than the social environment and intrafamilial relationships. This gap was filled by the public health nurse, who became a very effective visitor and made an impact on the disordered lives of many people. When the nurse became the fourth member of the interdisciplinary team in some of the child-guidance clinics, it was she who generally made the home visit. Today, however, many of the new comprehensive mental health centers are utilizing the home visit, both for diagnostic purposes and for treatment.

A most interesting illustration of an extended home visit was described by Constance Hansen, a social worker and a clinical associate at the Mental Research Institute in Palo Alto.[25] She had used conjoint family therapy for some years when she ran into a situation with a family of six children from the lower middle class and realized she was making no progress. Miss Hansen suggested that she live with them for a week. At that point the parents had applied to a residential treatment center to have the identified patient, an acting-out boy, admitted. She told the family that she would charge no fee, but the family would provide her with the opportunity to learn more about their problems and to take notes from which she would write a paper on this experiment. Miss Hansen did not wish to change any of the family's physical patterns and turned down the offer of a private bedroom for her, which would have meant shifting the children's sleeping arrangement. Instead she took a sleeping bag and slept on the living-room floor.

Originally it had been intended that the family therapist would meet with the family for only a specified period each night, and the remainder of the time would be spent in observation. As it worked out, Miss Hansen soon became caught up in the family life and would make on-the-spot observations and comments that proved useful. However, in being drawn into the family, she became less objective. The multiple family problems seemed overwhelming. In addition to the acting-out son, there was a retarded daughter, the father had a drinking problem, and there was very little income for a family of eight. Although she was frequently frustrated and emotionally spent, by the end of the week the therapist had succeeded in making some changes and also had acquired a tremendous learning experience.

Conclusion

What I have given you here is intended to be only a brief backdrop for the following chapters, which detail the drama of conjoint family therapy as it is practiced today, and in which you may find the role you can play. Those of you knowledgeable in the area of family organization and dynamics will have had additional and equally salient concepts regarding the family and related research come to mind while I sketched this broad background. Certainly many other historical aspects are deserving of mention and consideration if time permitted. For the present, however, we must turn our attention to the "here and now" of helping families to change.

NOTES

1. Edward Westermarck, *The History of Human Marriage*, 5th ed. (London: Macmillan, 1921), pp. 26 ff.

2. Pitirim Sorokin, *Social and Cultural Dynamics* (New York: American Book Co., 1941), IV, 776.

3. Carle C. Zimmerman, *The Family and Civilization* (New York: Harper, 1947).

4. William J. Lederer and Don D. Jackson, *The Mirages of Marriage* (New York: W. W. Norton & Co., 1968).

5. Rustum Roy and Della Roy, "Is Monogamy Outdated?" *Humanist*, 1970, 19-26.

6. Herbert Otto, "Has Monogamy Failed?" *Saturday Review*, April 25, 1970, pp. 23-25, 62.

7. Alvin Toffler, *Future Shock* (New York: Random House, 1970), p. 212.

8. Aldous Huxley, *Brave New World* (New York: Harper, 1939).

9. Crisis in Child Mental Health, *Report of the Joint Commission on Mental Health of Children* (New York: Harper & Row, 1969), p. 2.

10. Toffler, *Future Shock*, pp. 215-216.

11. L. C. Wynne, I. M. Rycoff, J. Day, and S. I. Hirsch, "Pseudomutuality in Family Relationships of Schizophrenia," *Psychiatry*, 21, (1958), 205-220.

12. Nathan W. Ackerman, "Interlocking Pathology in Family Relationships," in *Changing Concepts of Psychoanalytic Medicine*, ed. S. Rado and G. Daniels (New York: Grune, 1956), pp. 135-150.

13. Murray Bowen, "A Family Concept of Schizophrenia," in *The Etiology of Schizophrenia*, ed. Don D. Jackson (New York: Basic Books, 1960), pp. 346-372.

14. Virginia Satir, *Conjoint Family Therapy* (Palo Alto, California: Science and Behavior Books, 1964).

15. John E. Bell, *Family Group Therapy*, U.S. Public Health Monograph, No. 64 (Washington, D.C.: Government Printing Office, 1961).

16. Don D. Jackson, "The Question of Family Homeostasis," *The Psychiatric Quarterly Supplement*, 31, no. 1, (1957), 79-90.

17. Nathan W. Ackerman, "Family Therapy," in *American Handbook of Psychiatry*, ed. Silvano Arieti (New York: Basic Books, Inc., 1966), III, 209.

18. Ibid., p. 201.

19. Bell, "Family Group Therapy," p. 4.

20. Donald G. Langsley and David M. Kaplan, *Treatment of Families in Crisis* (New York: Grune and Stratton, 1968).

21. Robert MacGregor, "Multiple Impact Therapy with Families," *Family Process*, 1, (1962), 15-29.

22. Exall L. Kimbro, Jr., Harvey A. Taschman, Harold W. Wylie, Jr., Beryce W. MacLennan, "A Multiple Family Group Approach to Some Problems of Adolescence," *International Journal of Group Psychotherapy*, 17, (1967), 18-24.

23. Salvador Minuchin, Braulio Montalvo, Bernard G. Guerney, Jr., Bernice L. Rosman, Florence Schumer, *Families of the Slums* (New York: Basic Books, 1967), p. 267.

24. M. P. Andronico, J. Fidler, B. G. Guerney, Jr., and L. F. Guerney, "The Combination of Didactic and Dynamic Elements in Filial Therapy," *International Journal of Group Psychotherapy*, 17, no. 1 (1967), 10-17.

25. Constance Hansen, "An Extended Home Visit with Conjoint Family Therapy," *Family Process*, 7, no. 1 (1968), 67-87.

Introducing Virginia Satir

As consultant, teacher, lecturer, practitioner, and author, Virginia Satir is a widely known authority in the field of family therapy. Since earning her bachelor's degree from Wisconsin State University in 1936 and master's degree from the School of Social Service Administration at the University of Chicago in 1948, she has had experience in a broad spectrum of settings—psychiatric clinics, mental hospitals, residential treatment centers, public welfare programs, probation and parole services, family service agencies, and private practice. Virginia first taught family therapy in the Family Dynamics Residency Training Program of the Illinois State Psychiatric Institute, Chicago, and has been a visiting professor in the Department of Psychiatry, John Hopkins University, and in the School of Social Work, University of Calgary, Canada. She was a member of the initial staff of the Mental Research Institute in Palo Alto, California, and directed the Family Therapy Training Project there. She has also served as director of the residential program at Esalen Institute, Big Sur, California. On both the national and international scene, Virginia has conducted training institutes, as well as didactic and growth workshops, for psychiatric departments of medical schools, social workers groups, government agencies, and legal and religious groups. She is the author of **Conjoint Family Therapy** and **Peoplemaking**, published by Science and Behavior Books, Palo Alto, California, and has written numerous journal articles and contributed chapters to professional books dealing with the psychological dynamics and treatment of families.

Chapter 2

You as a Change Agent

by Virginia Satir

Primary Responsibility of Change Agent

As if it were emblazoned on a neon sign, I see this question before us now: "How can I use me, any me, to make a change in people by working with families?" This is where I want to start —how to use any "me," because I think the difference between whether or not a family grows, a family that comes asking for help, first, foremost, and *primarily*, has to do with the therapist and his input. Now, that puts—not exactly a burden—but a big chunk of responsibility on the therapist.[1]

One of the things I discovered as I traveled all over the country is that the chief reason any family therapeutic endeavor fails is that the therapist does not know how to have the kind of communication that makes it possible for people to get "connected with their guts." This has nothing to do with intelligence, race, color, or anything else except the ability to put people in touch with themselves at the gut level. This places the therapist in a position that could seem scary. If he has a scary feeling in the beginning, I believe that in time he won't feel that way. Making a change requires putting a great deal into the situation. That does not mean you do this alone. The seed you plant has to have a place to grow and has to be nourished; but I consider the therapist the leader of the treatment situation, just as I consider parents the leaders of developing human beings. That does not mean they are totally responsible and do it all by themselves, for what evolves also depends upon the nature of the context that is used.

Early Learnings

First, I would like for you to engage with me in the awareness of something.[2] If you would, at this moment just close your eyes. With your eyes closed, I would like for you to be aware that once you, like all other people in the world, came into this world little —no ability to talk, to walk, to change your own diapers, to eat—you came in little. As a result of your being little, it was a life-and-death matter that people around you made it possible for you to live. Just be aware of that. . . . When you take the next step, you arrive at the fact that people around you, who made it possible for you to live and not die, had a crucial and primary impact on what you learned about how to be you, about what to expect from somebody else, and about how to treat somebody else. . . . Just let yourself be aware of that. You learned about how to be you from the transactions that went on between the people responsible for your life and your reactions to them. If you can, also let yourself become aware that these transactions came from not one person but several. Usually an individual has a mother and father in action around him or, if not, he will have grandparents or other adults in his world. If you can, let yourself be aware that you did not get your ideas and experiences from just one person but from several persons, and that from observing how these persons related to one another you also learned something of how you should be.

With your eyes still closed, let yourself also be in touch with the fact that by the time you were two years old you had engaged in billions of transactions which supported your ideas about what was needed to make it possible for you to live in a given situation. As you become aware of this, can you also be aware that because you were encountering so many "firsts"—because you were like mules with no pride of ancestry or hope of posterity— as far as judging anything was concerned, you had to take the conclusions of what you experienced and make them into something certain. Keeping you eyes closed, let yourself become aware that such basic, impactful learning is extremely difficult to dislodge. Now slowly open your eyes.

In my opinion, most psychologists and other people associated with our mental health discipline have overlooked the fact that we *learned* how to be the way we are—it did not come in our genes. The big problem, therefore, is to find out what it was people learned about how to be people, how they are using those learnings today, and which of the learnings make it possible for them to grow and which make it impossible for them to grow. Essentially what we have to do is discover the learnings people have and help them discard those which at their present time of life are no longer useful.

For instance, as a girl-child I may have learned that men were something to be afraid of. If I am still stuck with that learning at the age of twenty-five, I will not expect much in the way of gratification from males. But I may not know this. I may think it is my personality. So the job of the therapist is to help sort out these learnings people had about how to be people.

That means all of us have learned something. That means, to me, that short of death and having the brain cut out, everybody is capable of learning new ways of feeling and thinking, and of using himself. There are no untreatable people. It is only a matter of calling upon our creative imagination about how to bring out again the thing most people had between the ages of birth and one—a curiosity and willingness to change and to explore. That is the therapeutic challenge!

Let your eyes close again and let yourself be aware that these things are true for all people; no one is excepted. As you let this awareness go through you, just let yourself feel what is happening to you in your insides. If you stopped breathing, let yourself breathe. Gradually let your eyes open and look around as far as your neck will turn without cutting off the oxygen. (I am always careful about oxygen—it's very important!) Within this setting that I just asked you to become aware of is where I begin to work as a change agent.

Over the nineteen years or so that I have been working officially with families (and I have worked with I don't know how many thousands of families), I have found that people have come up with five main kinds of learnings about how to treat themselves in the presence of another person when there is a question of stress and survival—just five, that's all. These were immediately obvious from the way in which people communicated. If I listen to two people in interaction for three interchanges, I can tell where a person stands in terms of what he has learned about how to conduct himself. It is that simple—it's not easy but it's simple.

Communication Beyond Words

At this point I would like to deal with something related to all this. First, I would like to draw your attention to the fact that communication involves more than what comes out of the mouth. Suppose I have a bellyache and you ask how I am. I say, "I'm fine," but have a pained expression on my face and speak with a sarcastic tone of voice. Do you see anything wrong with that? I am, in effect, giving you a double-level message. This is not yet what is referred to as a "double bind." It only becomes a double bind when no one can comment on the discrepancy; that is, when you can't say to me, "Hey, you say that so tight with your mouth and you look so tight, but you are saying, 'I'm fine.' The two things don't go together." Not being able to comment on the discrepancy creates a double bind. We use double-level messages frequently, but people can comment on them. However, a typical kind of thing in a family on the double-bind level is that a parent looks worried and the child asks, "What's the matter, Ma?" The answers are: "Nothing," "It's all right, dear,

never mind," "Ask your father," or something equally unrelated
—all double-level messages, which frequently end in a double
bind.

We speak with our whole bodies. When I speak, words come
out of my mouth. I also have a face that goes with this. My body
makes motions; if you were near me you could feel my muscle
and see it. You could also feel the moisture on my skin. All of
this is part of my speech. Anyone hearing me has to resolve the
double-level message when any part of me expresses something
different from the words coming out of my mouth.

The fact is that very few people know anything at all about
how they give out double-level messages. I know plenty of therapists, for instance, who feel that all they want is to "do good." So
when they get mad in an interview, they try to look happy. Do
you know how to look happy when you are feeling mad? Then
when somebody backs off from them, they wonder why, when
they really have such nice intentions. I suggest that the main
problem (there are lots of them, but I'm talking about the main
one) is in the therapeutic context—the therapist is not aware of
his own double-level messages. He is not aware of how much
what he is trying to keep inside affects what shows on the outside, and what the actual message is the other person receives.

One of the things that follows from what I have just said is
that if you are a child in a family and you cannot find out the
real meaning of the double-level discrepancy, you make up
something to account for it, and *that* will be your basis of fact.
Every person I have ever seen who had any kind of behavior or
coping problem was a member of a family in which all communication that mattered was double-level and nobody could comment on the discrepancies. That is why, for me, the communication approach is the main tool.

Five Modes of Communication

I mentioned above that I saw only five ways in which a person
handles his communication at a point of stress. Let me explain
that. All relationships which have any meaning are based either
on love or trust. Certainly all family relationships have love as
the base, and when any behavior occurs that does not fit the

image of love, *the result is stress*. Friendships, business relationships, and other meaningful relationships are based on
trust. So when you and a partner or friend mistrust, stress is ac-
tivated within yourself. Any piece of behavior which spells out to
you something unloving or something untrusting raises the survival question. All our laws about fair practices are based on
trust; all of our expectations of family relationships are based on
love; but a great deal of what goes on between people presumably hooked together by love and trust does *not* spell out love
and trust. People have developed alternatives to use when that
happens, which are their survival methods.

Placating

One alternative is always to agree, no matter what is going on.
I say, "You are a schlemiel," and you say, "Of course! I didn't
mean to be, but I know I am," whether you believe it or not,
while underneath you want to say, "You son-of-a-bitch!" When
these sweet words come out of the mouth, the body knows better, and so the body looks *placating*.

When I am in the presence of you, you are there, I am there,
and we are in a specific place at a specific time and there is a
specific expectation of what goes on between us. This makes a
complete circle with three segments, Self (S), Other (O), and
Context (C). Context means this time, this place and this situation.

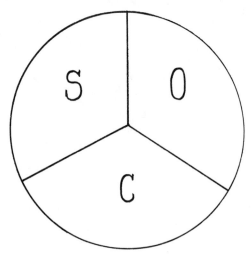

Anytime I am in your presence and something happens to make me question the basic love or trust, something will happen. Every time I handle my communication now, it is a point of stress. This has much more meaning than when the situation is nonstressful. (Have you noticed? Do sixteen things right in a day and the seventeenth one wrong, and you will report, "I did everything wrong today!") So in the *placating* situation, the person undergoes an experience which says, "I'm no good—you are better than I am." Self is crossed out in the circle.

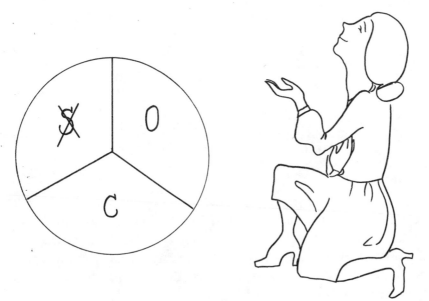

Blaming

This can go another way if I believe that my survival depends on throwing my weight around and showing how much I can criticize you. My words will come out in some form of *blaming*. It doesn't matter whether I agree with what I am saying or whether it actually represents anything, but I have to let you know who is boss. In families they call these people "tyrants," or "dominating husbands," or "domineering wives." However, when I do this, it does not mean I disagree but that I have to let you know I have power, and you have to show me I have that power by obeying me, because that is the only way I can be sure I have it. My body becomes tight and takes on a *blaming* stance.

(Incidentally, do you know the difference between disagreement and blame? Most of the families you will see do not know the difference.) Both Other and Context are crossed out in the circle, and Self dominates the communication.

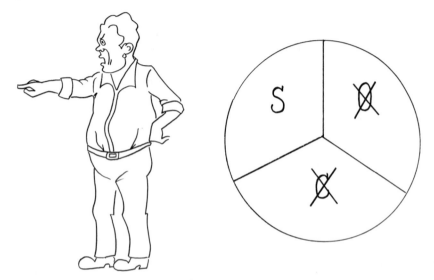

When in a pair of people one is saying, "You are right—I never think," and the other is saying, "You are nothing," how do these two live together? One person feels he is everything and the other feels he is nothing. It creates the greatest bond of dependence you can think of because the one, in effect, is compelled to take care of the other.

Super-reasonable

There is another way of handling communication—a very useful one for school teachers and others who interact with pieces of paper for their livelihood—in which the words come out *super-reasonable*. When this happens, of course, the words bear no relationship to how one feels. So you say in an unemotional way things like, "I know this will kill you, but you will probably have a great time in the next life." With this stance, the body shows no signs of life and takes on a computer aspect. For a long time there has been something in our society which dictates, "Don't reveal your feelings—it is dangerous." Especially if you are a man and your warm feelings come out, it is absolute evidence you are a "fairy." If you are a woman and aggressive feelings come out, it is absolute evidence you are a bitch. Who wants to be a bitch or who wants to be a fairy? In the case of super-reasonable communication, I am not there, you are not there, only the context remains.

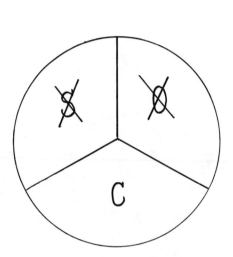

Irrelevant

The fourth way that I noticed was that the words which come out are *irrelevant*, absolutely unrelated to anything that is going on. Of course, since there is no place to hang anything, the body is in constant motion, which amounts to constant distraction. In this case, I am not there, you are not there, and neither is the context!

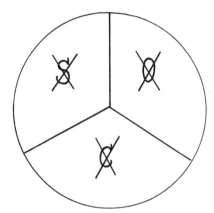

Congruent

There is a fifth way of communicating. No human being is so perfect that he will never indulge or engage in behavior which appears to be either unloving or untrusting. This is not possible for human beings, as you well know. What I am saying is that no human being can have his behavior reflect continual love and continual trust. It does not work that way. In this fifth way nothing is omitted. The words relate to what is real, and the affect is *congruent*. Instead of double-level communication, there is this: I feel angry in my guts—I say I am angry and I look angry. You don't have any trouble getting the message—a nice straight message—I am angry. I have sexy feelings, my voice softens, and I tell you I feel sexy. Nice and straight. I feel helpless, I look helpless, and I say that I am helpless. A nice straight message. Nothing is crossed out. It is all there: Self, Other, and Context. There is total congruence with the situation.

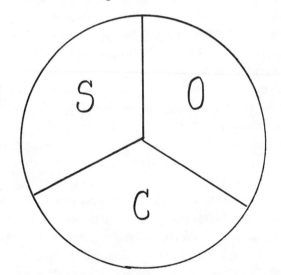

As far as I am concerned, these are all understandable, logical outcomes of how people have learned to manage their survival in the presence of stress—the results of how the early parental situation evolved, how they were brought up. Ninety-nine percent of us were brought up on the authority system which says, "You are okay if you obey me and if you are like me." Maybe that didn't happen to you—if it didn't, you were lucky—but that is the condition under which children are usually reared. I call the first four communication stances "brave attempts to survive when you do not believe you can." I do not see them as anybody's perversions or anybody's deliberate attempts to injure somebody, although they do cause plenty of injury.

Let me mention a few other aspects of these survival stances. If over a period of time a person handles stress by placating, he will soon be a victim of stomach trouble, because it gets you in the guts. All the physiological symptoms connected with the digestive processes become involved in this. That is the price the human pays for that mode of communication.

The blamer gets all the things that have to do with constriction. In the blaming situation, there is a lack of oxygen because most people hold their breath. This tightens the walls of the arteries and the veins. At the same time the adrenalin is pouring into the system, increasing the pressure of the bloodstream. So you have the equivalent of a half-inch tube that grows to one inch to carry three inches of fluid pressure! Something has to give. The physiological reaction extends into the muscles, blood vessels, and all of the tissues.

In handling stress with super-reasonableness, the physiological effect is literally a drying up—saliva stops flowing, tears stop coming, the blood gets thinner—a drying-up thing. With super-reasonableness you find a heavy dose of peculiar physical complaints that defy diagnosis; there is nothing that shows with them.

The irrelevant type, when used over a period of time so that it does not seem any different from your personality (which is true of all of these at some point), affects the central nervous system, and periods of dizziness frequently occur.

You know, we have not been fools over the past years—we have been very fine observers. But just as at the turn of the century we used wagons, because that was the best we had, and then we dropped them and began using cars, so we have learned and discarded ideas in the area of human behavior. The placating stance we could call a simple neurosis; people feel they cannot do what they think they should. With the blaming stance we find all the aggressive, acting-out behaviors. With the super-reasonable we find the things that have to do with people becoming shut off from society, recluses and also those who continually have psychosomatic illnesses. If we were to take the irrelevant stance to its extreme, we would get into the florid psychoses.

There is another facet of these four forms of behavior: they cannot be played alone; they cannot stand by themselves; they must have continual validation. For a person to become a good placator, he must have a good blamer helping him.

Before we go on, I want you to notice again the fifth response, *congruence.* Nothing is crossed out, nothing has to be eliminated. Anything can be talked about; anything can be commented on; any question can be raised; there is nothing to hold you back. So if your penis is hanging out right now, all right, your penis is hanging out. If you have a bloody nose or you think you hate your mother, that's the way it is. You see, I think all therapy is a life-and-death effort, and many of us do not realize that. We are playing for high stakes—for the recovery of another human being. And to piddle around and piddle around, as I have sometimes seen people do with clients, simply does not get the job done. When I was working in a hospital, someone would write on files, "Confidential! Don't tell the kid he is adopted!" What kind of rubbish is that? I don't know how many of you get into this secret business: "I can't tell him because he is too fragile, too young, or too old." So the who *is* the purveyor of the piece of reality that can be talked about? *Family therapy can begin only with reality as its base.*

As an example, there was a four-year-old boy in a family I was once seeing who, apparently out of context, said, "Papa, why do you stagger so at night?" and his mother said, "Sh-h-h!" I said, "What are you shushing him for? Does your guy drink?" She blushed and said, "Well, yes, but we don't want the neighbors to know." In the therapeutic context, people must be able to arrive at the fifth type of response, must be able to be tuned in at that moment in time to what they are feeling and thinking and hearing, without somebody coming along, shushing them, and saying, "Oh, no, you don't."

Exercises in Triadic Communication

If it is convenient now or at some later time, I would like you to form a group of three persons. I use three because that is the unit of identity. Making an individual is a three-person operation, ma, pa, and the kid. You would not be here without the first two. It takes three people for one person to exist. That is one reason the triangle is so interesting and difficult, and until the family solves the problems of the triangle they are not going to make it. I would like for you to be in a triad, and if possible to take the risk of finding two people whom you do not know, so that you will be in a group of three strangers. After you have done this, all anyone knows is that you are together and you are strangers. Actually, this is how people get together in families. Every husband and wife were once strangers and all the kids came into the family as strangers. So the starting of a family is the time when they meet as strangers, and hopefully this evolves to a time when they are known as whole human beings. This does not happen in families that have coping difficulties; the members become stereotypes in their roles. In your triads you are in the situation every family experiences in going from unfamiliarity to familiarity.

The first thing you will do has nothing to do with your intention or lovability, but it does concern your communication. By the way, everything I am asking you to do now is what I do when I work with groups of families. Each of you should choose a new name—and, please, do not use names of relatives, because that fouls up the works. Then decide on a new last name and each of you assume a family role: father, mother, son, daughter, brother sister, husband, or wife. If you have a man and a woman in the group, you start making this a family with a husband and wife, and the natural thing would be for the third person to be the child. I never ask anybody to role-play anything they could not really be, so no woman can take the role of husband-father, and a man cannot play the daughter or wife. You now have a new first name, a new last name, and a family role.

Next I am going to ask you to handle your communication in a very specific way. The adult male is to handle his communication by blaming. To be a good blamer, first of all, you begin each sentence with "You are never" or "You are always." This is very useful for showing how adept and creative you are in finding fault with everything. If someone is standing up, they should be sitting down, and you can find a reason, I am sure. All good blamers have very extensive repertoires for pointing out what is wrong with anything that is going on.

The adult female is to be a placator. Hints for good placators include taking all the blame for everything that goes wrong— even the weather, because if you had been a little better or a little kinder, it wouldn't have rained. It is your job to make sure no one gets hurt or goes without, so you must strain to the utmost to see that everybody is pleased and happy, even if you have to kill them to do it—sweetly, of course! Never, never say anything about what you want.

The person taking the child's role is to be irrelevant. This requires, first, that you are never to get to the point with words. Someone says, "Hello," and you might look up at the ceiling and comment on the lights. Also, you make yourself obvious by moving. Sit on someone's lap, untie their shoes, wiggle their earring, do anything to make it obvious that you are there. Do your utmost to be distracting.

These are the ways you are going to handle your communication in your family triad. The mode of communication has nothing to do with your race, creed, sex, color, intelligence, political affiliation, or religion, as you will find. Armed with these ways of communicating, the next step is to plan something together as a family. Continue this communication for about fifteen minutes.

Some Questions to Examine

After completing this exercise, ask yourselves these questions: Were any of you aware of your own physiological reactions while you were having a particular kind of talk come out of your mouths? Now just for a moment ask yourself what it means in this "play" situation. Were you having this physical response because you were asking your mouth to conform to something that was alien to the rest of you? Ask yourself those questions, and think of what all this means.

Also, I want you to be aware of whether you were going far-

ther away from the others or drawing closer. I wonder how many of you felt that a loving relationship existed. If no one did, I would not be surprised. Now, I want you to be in touch with the probable fate of your planning. How many of your group felt great gratification about what you were planning?

As you "lived" in this family, how many of you were beginning to think of what you would like to do to get out of the situation if you were stuck there? Things like: wouldn't it be great to get drunk; if I could only leave this burden; a hospital bed would look great; a bunch of drugs would be fine; I'm sure every other family is better off than ours; I guess I'll go after that cute chick; I think I'll spend my days off at the office; and on and on. There are numerous ways of getting out.

Exercise

Next, somebody came along and said to this family constellation, "Now look here, Pa, what you need to do is be nicer to your wife." So let's have the husband become a placator. And he says to the wife, "Don't you know you should stand up for yourself?" and the wife becomes a blamer. To the kid, he says, "It's time for you to have some sense, so will you please be reasonable." You already have hints for blaming and placating. As for being super-reasonable, it helps to consider your spine as one continuous lead pipe which keeps the fanny and neck in a straight line. Then it will help if you have the feeling of wearing an iron collar five inches wide around your neck, keep your nose in the air, and have a certain prune-like look on your face. When you do all this, you will find long words tumbling out. You will say "it" instead of "I," and you will find yourself making references to all the research you know about. Research, you know, has many guises: it can be what Mrs. Jones says, what psychologists say, what God says, or what anybody says. "It" is the important thing, and the voice becomes a monotone because you don't have much air and that is all you can manage.

You are now in a new family in which the husband-father is placating, the wife-mother is blaming, and the child is very reasonable. Using these new ways of communicating, once again plan something as a family. Communicate this way for about fifteen minutes.

Increasing Awareness of Self

After completing this exercise I would like you to close your eyes, and with your eyes closed let yourself feel what is happening to your body. . . . Can you get in touch with whether you feel closer to your family members or alienated? Can you also let yourself be in touch with what you perceive the fate of your planning will be? And again, if you are entertaining thoughts about what you would like to do to get out of this situation, let yourself be in touch with that. . . . While doing this, you may find that fatigue sets in quickly. This is a common complaint that I hear from anybody who has any kind of coping difficulties, this constant complaint of fatigue. What I want you to do next is get in touch with your breathing. . . . Just feel your breath in your body. If you have any tightness, just relax. Be in touch with your points of support and, at least for the moment, wash away the pain of your life. . . . Gradually let your eyes open, and experience the feeling that you and the others with you have another chance to make things work out.

The One-Parent Family

Let's take another triad as an example. One typical constellation is a family of all women, which is called a one-parent family. Imagine for a moment one consisting of a mother and two daughters. The mother assumes a placating position on her knees in front of the others with one hand on her heart. This is the "dedicated" mother who says, "I'll do everything I can for you, never mind how it hurts. My life is ended. I have only you to be concerned with." Then we have one blaming daughter and the other one a super-reasonable computer. The super-reasonable daughter stands with feet close together, an iron rod for a backbone, five-inch iron collar around the neck, and hands close to the sides. The eyes always go where they are most comfortable, and in this position they gaze over everyone else's head. The blamer has her arm stiffly outstretched, finger pointing at one of the others. If this were an adolescent situation, the blamer would probably be raising all hell, the mother would be saying she doesn't know what to do with her, and the good daughter would only give bland advice. Which would be the symptom bearer? The mother might be, but more likely it will be the super-reasonable daughter. Everybody in the family is suffering from low self-worth. The question is, what are they paying for it?

This is the situation you may have tried, the blaming, placating, super-reasonable triad. If you looked at the body positions of the people in these exercises or examples, they would have shown something like this model tableau.

If I interviewed the triad, I would get something like the following:

Virginia: Mother, how do you feel?
Mother: I'm tired.
Virginia: You're tired, yes, but you aren't supposed to say that. You are a mother and you work hard all the time. That is your lot in life, isn't it? Are you aware of anything else in your body right now? What if you had to live your life like this?
Mother: I'd be resentful!
Virginia: Yes, very much resentful. You would be thinking, "Nobody sees how hard I work. I can't tell them, because if they loved me, they should know that."
Super-reasonable Daughter: I feel wobbly.
Virginia: Wobbly. Yet she looks straight. So from what shows on the outside, nobody would ever know the pain on the inside, her wobbliness. And after a while she won't have any feeling below the neck, and later not even from there on up.
Blaming Daughter: I am tense. My legs and arms are tense.
Virginia: Do you feel very close to these people?
Blaming Daughter: No.
Virginia: Yes, and you look pretty strong and tough. Nobody would ever know the pain inside; it's not obvious.

Exercise
Now I would like the reader to try another combination. There are many combinations, but these are the ones I see frequently, and you will be running into them. This time I would like for all adults to be blamers and all children to be placators. Try to plan something in your family at this point, given these ways of communicating. Continue this exercise about fifteen minutes.

Increasing Awareness of Self
When finished with the exercise, close your eyes and begin to feel what is happening to you inside. Feel what is going on inside your body. . . . And again, let yourself be in touch with how close

*or far you are in relation to the other family members. Would
you trust them? Would you ask them for some love? . . . Also, try
to perceive the fate of your planning and notice any fantasies
that may have flitted through your mind about how you would
escape from this situation, perhaps even while still being in it
physically. . . . If you can, be in touch with any fatigue . . . and be
aware of your breathing. If you feel tightness in yourself, let it
loosen. . . . Gradually let your eyes open.*

Blaming Parents and Placating Child

Here is how I would sculpture another triad. This time we
have a blaming wife, a blaming husband, and a placating child.
The husband blames the wife; the wife blames the child; the
child is placating to both parents. Now, in an action model, each
of the blamers should move the arm he is pointing with and aim
at someone else. Then they change their target again to where
we have the wife blaming the husband, the husband blaming the
daughter, and the daughter almost not knowing where to look.
. . . In this situation the child is helpless unless she can go to
some kind of extreme. She might have some kind of very "loud"
illness. Those of you who work with families that have battered
children see something else that often occurs. In this process
there is a lot of kicking and clawing, and the child, while trying
to get something, can easily be hit and hurt if she gets in the
midst of this activity. It would not be hard at all for one of those
hands to go down and clout her. Then she starts to cry, and guilt
begins to take over.

The parents have other places to point their blame: "It's the
school. If it did a better job, we wouldn't have this problem."
"It's her friends; if they were better, she wouldn't have the
problem." "It's her mother." "It's his bringing up."

In symphony, I would have the models point to a different
person every minute for about three minutes. This is what I call
the ballet of the "Blame Opera." This keeps going on and on if
the therapist does not know how to get at it.

In interviewing such a group I found the following:

Virginia (to the child): What is happening to you?

Child: I am about to crumble.

Virginia: (to the Father): And how do you feel?

Father: It hurts like hell in my arm and the rest of me.

Virginia: Yes, but just looking at you no one would dream that you were having anything but a marvelous time. (*To the Mother.*) How about you?

Mother: I found it difficult to stare him down.

Virginia: You didn't have to stare him down; all you had to do was keep your finger pointed.

I would now ask the triad members to take a good heavy stance and I would give quick treatment. It doesn't go quite this fast, but almost. I would ask them to close their eyes and do whatever will make them comfortable.

Helping the Individual Take Charge of Himself

I want to point out something in regard to the above exercises which might put some pieces together about how to be individuals in a group. One way some people try to bring about a change is to say, "Look what you are *doing* to each other!" That is not the way I work. What I did in the above example was to get each person to do what fits for him in terms of his own comfort. The father put his arm down because he was uncomfortable, not because he wanted to one-up the mother. The child got up from her kneeling position because it was uncomfortable, not because she thought she was going to get anyone's blessing. It takes a while to bring this about in a family system. Getting down to the matter of each person acting in terms of his own comfort requires that *he take charge of himself*, that he be responsible for himself. The first four types of communication are all forms of saying, "I live because you let me." Therefore, changing the outward behavior is not going to change anything very much until you are able to help each person take charge of himself in terms of his own comfort. In this triad, when the father took charge of his own comfort, he put his arm down, not because he would get a good or bad mark, but because he knew what fit for him.

In this same triad with their original poses (blaming parents and placating child), I would like to describe what could happen. One of the things I could do as a therapist when I see that poor little thing with those two blaming parents is to attempt to rescue her. Without touching the other two, I go behind them and pull her out with me. . . . Now she has been rescued. But you know what she is doing? She is leaning on me—and if I move away, she will fall flat on her face, and I am going to tell people that when I treat somebody I have to be around all the time or they will fall on their faces. Maybe this does not apply to the reader, but I have seen some to whom it does. Next, I will try to get the child safely to a chair and hope I don't break her leg dragging her there without taking my eyes off the other two. Then I can go bluntly in and say to them, "You shouldn't fight!" Then what do we have? *Three* blamers!

As you tried these exercises, you may have been surprised that the dialogue in your triads flowed as easily as it did. I have not worked with any group of people, no matter what their language, who did not know how to blame and placate. You see, I asked you to do in front of yourself what you know you have already done behind your back. These are things you would not do by choice, and neither would anybody else—to blame, to placate, to be super-reasonable, to be irrelevant. They are prevalent behaviors, which also bring about a *distorted* use of Christianity. In my book Christ and Christianity are not at all the same in most cases. The way in which you interact with one another came about because this is how you felt you had to carry out the "authority thing." The "authority thing" is rampant. We all have it built in, but it does not teach us how to take charge of ourselves.

When I do this kind of work with pre-kindergartners, they are very perceptive about the forms of communication in their families. Anyone who works with three- and four-year-olds knows this. Four-year-olds always know what is going on. In a strange way these communication phenomena are almost universal, but they also constitute something that will kill us if we persist in these crippling forms of interaction.

Exercise

Now I want you to do two more exercises. This time we will pretend that somebody came along and said, "Look, you two warring people, be reasonable." So both of you who have adult roles decided you would do the reasonable thing. And I would like the children to take the blamer role. Soon you will find out what a stone wall is all about. Those who are being reasonable, begin by sitting up straight in your chairs. To give yourself a real experience, sit very straight and try not to move anything about you except your mouth while you all plan something together. . . . Carry this out for about ten minutes.

Now just let this experience fade. Just let it fade. . . . Let your eyes close. . . . This time when you open your eyes, I would like all of the members of your triad to be irrelevant. See what happens. Let your eyes open and be irrelevant. . . .

Now please let this experience fade, and again let your eyes close. . . . You may have felt a certain sense of relief, and maybe if you did this exercise long enough you would find out that what you experienced as relief would soon translate itself into terrible feelings of isolation. But right now what you could be feeling is relief. Your triad immediately became crazy when you all became irrelevant. I don't know whether or not you noticed that.

Let me describe another modeling example. We have the mother who takes the super-reasonable position. The iron collar makes her chin go up, and it helps if her eyes go up, because she doesn't have to look at anybody—it's all written on the ceiling anyway. And the child stands in front of the mother, also being reasonable. She stands tight, with her feet together. The reason you can keep from being off balance with your feet together is that you hold your hands tightly to your sides and your head is looking up, so your balance goes up. The father is a blamer. This blamer will get absolutely no place—he is up against a stone wall—because these other two people are up there on the ceiling concerned with more lofty things. After they hold these stances for ten seconds or so, I ask them to all become irrelevant. . . . It's experienced as great relief.

As you conclude these exercises, I would like you to close your eyes and just let yourself come in touch with your own breathing . . . just your breathing. . . . Then come in touch with your own points of support . . . with the awareness that you *are holding yourself up . . . you are providing for your own breath. . . . Give yourself a message of appreciation. As you do this, take off your role hats and put them aside somewhere, and put on the one you had when you began these exercises. . . . Again, let yourself be in touch with your breathing and your points of support. . . . As you gradually let your eyes open, say mentally to yourself, "I am_____ ," and fill in your name. . . . Just look around, however far your neck carries you without straining. . . . And once more give yourself a message of appreciation.*

NOTES

1. Therapist, as used in this volume, refers to any person acting as a change agent.

2. Experiential exercises are set in italics. After reading these sections, readers may want to secure partners, when needed, and expand their own awareness and understanding by performing the exercises.

Introducing James Stachowiak

While he has had wide experience and success as a clinician and educator, Jim Stachowiak is perhaps best known for his extensive research in family systems and dynamics. He graduated from the University of Wisconsin in 1954, and received his
master's degree in 1959 and the Ph.D. degree in 1961 from the University of Kansas.
He was with the Wyandotte County Guidance Center for several years as staff psychologist and later chief psychologist. During that time he also taught courses at the
University of Kansas. In 1962 he joined the university as assistant professor in the
Department of Psychology and head of the Psychological Clinic. Since then he also
served for a time as acting director of the clinical psychology program and attained
the rank of full professor. He is a consultant to the Veterans Administration training
program in clinical psychology in Kansas City, Topeka, Wadsworth, and Wichita,
Kansas; to the Wyandotte County Mental Health Center; to the Department of Child
Psychiatry, Greater Kansas City Mental Health Foundation; to the Catholic Social
Services of Kansas City, Kansas; and in the area of family therapy to the Department
of Psychiatry, University of Kansas Medical Center. Jim is also on the advisory editor-
ial board of the journal **Family Process**. He has conducted workshops and made many
presentations at professional meetings throughout the country. His scientific investigations represent a sustained effort to study family processes and interactions, and his
results have been published in numerous journals and collections of scholarly works.

Chapter 3

Functional and Dysfunctional Families

by James Stachowiak

As we go through the process of assimilating the preceding material, I want to point out certain aspects of functional and dysfunctional families as we have studied them in our research program at the University of Kansas.

Getting Started in Family Therapy

Often when people first observe or hear about skilled and experienced people who have worked with families over a long period of time, they ask, "How do you become trained to do that?" Here is how I personally became involved in working with families.

About ten years ago I was working at a community mental health center in Kansas City. A teen-age boy had been referred to me by a juvenile officer because he had taken a car with the keys left in it from a supermarket parking lot, driven it around for a while, and then brought it back. Someone was there and caught him. I was seeing him individually and also talking with his parents. What the boy kept saying to me was, "Would you please get them off my back?" And all the parents kept saying was, "Would you make him more responsible?" Just at that time somebody put a monograph in my mail box called "Family Group Therapy—A New Method for Treating Adolescents and Their Families," by John Bell.[1] I read it and thought, "Well, I can't lose anything. I'll just bring these three people together." It was fantastic. To this day I don't know exactly what I did, but in about six sessions they were communicating freely and openly. He was telling them how he felt, and they were telling him how they felt, for example, when he didn't empty the trash. We had something of a miracle happen, I thought at the time. It seemed I had really found the answer to the world's problems. So I went on and saw about four other families, still not really knowing what I was doing except that things were happening there—sometimes even faster than I could keep track of! But it all worked out pretty well, and I began to think that all you have to do is sit down with the whole family together and something good happens. I still believe that is probably true. This is not to say that an intervention has no effect on the family (and certainly there is no guarantee it will always be a positive one!). But I have noticed in the ten years I have been working with marriage and family systems that good things can come simply from the caring and trust which develop when you bring the family together.

That was the beginning of my training in family therapy. There were a lot of things I did not know, so I made a lot of mistakes. Those of you who have not had the experience of working with families should not feel that you have to train for ten years before you can sit down with a family. The only way to work with families is to get in there and get your feet wet.

Discriminating Between Functional and Dysfunctional Families

After working with the first family, I became interested in what characterized families who were functioning effectively and those who were not. So at the University of Kansas we started a research project to study family characteristics.[2] We took families who were bringing one or more of their members to our clinic for help and put them into experimental situations. Essentially what we did was to have them take some issue on which they disagreed, discuss it, and try to resolve the disagreement. We taped the interactions and rated them later, looking at such aspects as who talks, who talks to whom, and, at first, the content. As I will explain later, the content analysis has not worked out too well. We saw people in our clinic, in the laboratories, and in their homes. Not too surprisingly, we found that people behave differently in different settings.

Myths Concerning the Family

At the outset, however, one thing we wanted to do was to examine all the myths that exist about families. Let me mention a few of these: (1) *The one-parent family is necessarily bad for children.* That is a belief we have in our society without much data to back it up. It is an assumption that has not really been tested out very well. (2) We thought from reading the literature that what is termed *a democratic family structure is associated with successful family functioning.* (3) We believed that *clinicians would be able to differentiate easily the functional and dysfunctional families.* And (4) *expressions of overt conflict are bad, they are pathological.* Fifteen years ago (and maybe even today) you could read in various clinical journals that if people express conflict openly it is a very bad thing. With these assumptions we began our first study. Two senior students were trained to rate families in interaction. Each of the families studied consisted of a father, mother, and two children.

Clinicians' Ratings

The first thing we found out is that almost without exception our raters rated the families coming to the clinic for assistance as being the effectively functioning families, and those we had chosen from the community, who had been designated by physicians, teachers, and counselors as being very well adjusted, our raters thought were the "disturbed ones." At first I thought, "Well, they are only seniors in college. I'll go around the state and ask some experienced clinicians to listen to these tapes and see what they say." So I went to some hospitals, clinics, and private practitioners I knew and had them listen to excerpts from the tapes. They gave the same ratings the students had given. I began to wonder what was going on here that caused people to have difficulty rating the families. I started to listen to the tapes differently and to watch the families during the problem-resolving sessions.

Democratic Model

One thing that became obvious was that the so-called "democratic model" was being mistaken for effective functioning. For example, people in the dysfunctional family sat there and paid much attention to the actual relationship of what was going on without giving any attention to the task before them to resolve the discussion. Nobody in that group would take the leadership. No leader emerged. It sounded like everybody was having a happy time. The problem was they didn't accomplish anything. When they were asked later how satisfied they were, these families were very dissatisfied.

Open Conflict

Another thing was that the well-adjusted or adaptive families more frequently expressed direct, overt conflict and negative as well as positive feelings than did the maladaptive families. For example, in one of the little periods of interaction, a father might give his son a slap on the fanny, set him down in a chair, and say, "Now, look, we have this task to do and we only have ten minutes to do it." The clinicians, as well as the raters, thought that was indicative of bad parenting. As you have just read in Chapter 2 and may have discovered for yourself in performing the communications exercises, often it is just this kind of direct expression that keeps people from having to act crazy.

Pathology in the Eye of the Observer

A few years ago I had the opportunity to interview a volunteer family in front of about 300 welfare workers. There was a mother, a father, a girl about twelve, and a boy about nine or ten.

This volunteer family had been secured through a church and had agreed to help me demonstrate how to get a picture of a family's life-style, utilizing a modified version of Virginia Satir's technique of the family chronology.[3] As I talked with the family, my impression was that it was probably one of the most open, well-adapted, and functional families I had ever had a chance to see. The father was a professional man, an engineer; the mother had a master's degree and was teaching and doing some counseling; the kids were doing well in school and were active in Scouts and other community organizations, and so on. But over and above all this, the family was able in this tense situation in front of all these people to show disagreement openly. For example, when I asked the father how he felt about his wife's working, he said, "Well, to tell you the truth, I'm not too happy about it, but I know it is very important to her, and therefore to me it is worth the extra effort it takes for her to do it. It helps us get along better, and the kids profit from it." I could go on with this, but what really amazed me were the reactions of much of the audience when this was over—how pathological this family was! What they said were things like: "Did you notice that look on Dad's face when he said this? He really very much resented his wife's working and is taking it out on her in other ways." Well, he had indicated he partly resented it, and it seemed to me that he was quite open about it. Similarly, they thought the daughter was going to turn into a schizophrenic, and so on. What occurred to me then was that people who work in clinical fields have been brought up on the model which focuses on disease, illness, psychopathology, and all kinds of words like that, so that what they get used to looking for are things that are going wrong with the system. They become so highly adept at this that they can see it even if it is not there—it's only in their heads.

Our next step, then, had to be to learn to focus more on people's strengths. What we are really interested in doing is moving in and out and together with systems such as families to help them grow until they can manage their problems in dealing with separateness and togetherness, so that each individual can be an individual in his own right and yet come together with the other members of the family as a group when this is indicated.

Four Major Factors in Family Effectiveness

Some interesting characteristics of the family emerged during this ten-year period of investigation. We finished about ten studies. We observed children in various families at different stages in their developmental cycle (that is, just entering school, in grade school, during adolescence) along with their parents. Four categories have been helpful in trying to understand the differences between families: (1) family productivity or efficiency, (2) leadership patterns, (3) expression of conflict, and (4) clarity of communication. Certain differences were found repeatedly in comparative studies of these families.

Productivity

First, family productivity. What this means is, when the family is put in a disagreement-resolving situation or has the task of planning something together, how does the family as a group marshal its forces and complete the task? The adaptive families in all of our studies reached a significantly greater number of group decisions in the allotted time period than the maladaptive families. Also, the members of adaptive families tended to emit many short speeches over a given period of time, while members of maladaptive families tended to emit fewer but longer speeches over the same period of time. It appears then that effective employment of the family's resources in decision-making or problem-solving requires a balance between work or task efforts and appropriate attention to the social and emotional needs of the members. What we have is a *marked* imbalance in the use of task-oriented and emotional messages in maladaptive families. Either the family members in these groups overemphasize task-oriented activities, almost to the exclusion of attending to emotional needs of the members, or they pay so much attention to emotional needs that they never complete the task.

Here is an example of what I am referring to as an exaggerated emphasis. One family was asked to plan something together that they would do as a group. The father was a very busy man who was gone from home a lot. He spent the whole allotted time period saying something like this to his six-year-old son: "How would you like it if Daddy took time off from one 'til three on Saturday afternoon and we could play a game?" And the kid wouldn't answer. So the father got more anxious and said, "Well, how would you like it on Thursday evenings, when I don't have to go out to my office, if we don't answer the phone for an hour and a half?" The kid wouldn't answer this either, and the father kept getting more and more nervous. Actually, you know, he was asking this boy to tell him how to be a father! This unawareness of one's impact on others in the family is characteristic of the dysfunctional groups.

Leadership Patterns

The second area of difference we found is the leadership pattern. So far in all our studies we find that a moderate tendency toward either matriarchal or patriarchal structure seems to be necessary for effective family functioning. This means that if either "Ma" or "Pa" is able to assume the leader role in the task before them and the other parent has worked out the marital relationship in such a way as to be able to cooperate with the spouse, that family functions more effectively in our studies.

Incidentally, our studies were made mostly of middle-class families. In families with young children, the mother tended most often to be the one designated as the leader in relationships with small children, and as the children became adolescents, the father seemed to take a more active role. In the maladaptive families what we found was either an extremely autocratic position by the mother or father, or an inept attempt to be equalitarian resulting in everybody sitting around not knowing who was going to make a decision or be the leader in the situation.

One intriguing thing is that in the adaptive family different members take on the leadership role at various times. One should not get the idea that either a matriarchy or patriarchy is the most effective system; it is more a matter of some one person taking the leadership and being supported in that role by the other members. For example, in choosing a car, the father might be the leader; in how to furnish the house, the mother might be; and maybe in teaching a game, one of the kids might assume leadership. What really differentiates the families in our studies is the absence of any kind of clear leadership in dysfunctional families.

Expressing Conflict

With respect to conflict, in maladaptive families there is either too much expression of conflict, so that all you get is conflict, or too little expression of conflict. Let me give you an example. I made a speech to a women's group several years ago regarding relationships in marriage and in the family. Apparently I struck a chord with one woman because after the talk was over she came up and asked whether I thought it was bad if people did not fight. I asked what she meant. It turned out that she and her husband had been married about three years. They each had had very stormy first marriages ending in divorces, so when they married they made a pact that they would never argue, never disagree. Three years had passed, and she said they had never had an argument. As she went on talking, it turned out that they also did not talk much together and were finding ways of "hiding" from one another. That would be a most extreme avoidance of conflict. However, I can report to you that they later on presented themselves to work on this, because there was dissatisfaction between them, and they became able to fight very well!

The other extreme is when two or more members of the family are continually at each other's throats and unable to come to any kind of resolution. Those two patterns of dealing with conflict seem to characterize maladaptive families. The amount of conflict and the manner of its expression are not as important as the matter of whether it is possible for differences to be expressed and whether the family has the resources to deal with those differences and resolve them.

Clarity of Communication

The last area is what we call clarity of communication. In the preceding chapter you had an excellent demonstration of the problems involved in trying to achieve this. As you saw, family members can employ many and varied ways to avoid clear and direct communication. They can turn away. They can avoid eye contact. They can engage in other activities while supposedly engaged in conversation. All of these tactics interfere with clear communication.

As I mentioned, in our studies we have been interested in who talks and who talks to whom rather than in looking at the content of the speeches. Research studies which have attempted to examine content have not paid off very well so far. Probably one of the reasons for this is that in the family system there is such a rich history of relating between people that someone coming in for a brief time, like a research investigator, cannot comprehend all the connotations. For example, when we first started our research studies, we tried to break content down into four simple categories—active-positive, active-negative, passive-positive, and passive-negative. We thought this would be relatively easy to do. What happened was that a child would say something like "Shut up" to somebody else. Clearly, in the system that should have gone under the active-negative category. But the rater who was observing the family said, "Yes, but he said it with a smile on his face." You can see the difficulty in getting reliable ratings on content.

So we have looked more at the process and structural things: who is talking, who is listening, and under what circumstances. In all of our studies, and especially in those where we only had tape recordings and no observations, we always had a number of speeches in which it was not clear who was the target or recipient of the speeches. We just attributed this to not having visual cues available, until we did a study in which we also had people watching the conversations. We then added a category called "general speeches" for conversation which did not appear to be directed to a specific family member. The criteria for these speeches were that the speaker did not look at another family member, did not use a member's name, referred to no element in the preceding speech, and generally gave no clue as to which family member was the intended recipient of the speaker's remarks. We found that in every case maladaptive families had a greater number of general speeches than adaptive families. This is especially interesting and noteworthy, I think, in combination with the finding that maladaptive families also have fewer speeches. What you get are long dissertations directed at no one particular member, so the other members can easily tune out.

Importance of Involvement

There is an interesting corollary to this, by the way, in a study done in third-grade classrooms in Lawrence, Kansas. Some of my colleagues were studying the behavior setting of the classroom. Observers were seated in the back of the room and were equipped with dictomasks. A dictomask fits over the nose and mouth and is attached to a tape recorder carried on your back. You can talk into the mask and record your remarks without anyone near you hearing them. So the observers sat in the back of the classroom recording everything the teacher said and did during the day. At the same time, they had a wide-angle-lens camera taking pictures from the front of the room every twenty seconds. The lens could take in about two-thirds of the classroom. What they were interested in was the level of involvement of the kids. Most people know, just through common sense, that a low level of involvement could be expected during unsupervised seatwork; kids are tying their shoelaces, looking out the windows, things like that—and nobody is amazed at such behavior. Nor is it surprising that the highest level of involvement occurs in small group interactions, such as when the teacher is having a reading group. Everybody is involved and getting something out of it. However, one of the lowest levels of involvement for these kids occurred during what is used in every classroom in the country, the show-and-tell period. When one of the kids got up to talk in front of his peers, in about a minute the rest of the kids were completely uninvolved. They were under the seats or looking out the windows. What is important about this finding is not that we should eliminate show and tell, but that we should realize that you pay for what you get. So if you think it is important for a person to stand up and verbalize in front of other people, fine; but you must realize that you are probably going to have a hard time holding the attention of the others very long. After this study came out, by the way, I finally realized why when I offered a seminar, my graduate students would say, "Are you going to offer one of those things where you sit in a corner and we do all the work?" They want the professor to be actively involved. It looks as if this is a pervasive phenomenon.

Cycles in Family Interactions

Something that has impressed me over and over again in these studies is that there is a cycling process, so that rather than thinking in terms of cause and effect, what we need to do is to start thinking in terms of ongoing, chaining systems. Here is an example of what I mean. A family that participated in one of our studies had come to our clinic with the complaint that the ten-year-old daughter stuttered. There was also in this family a twelve-year-old boy and the parents who were in their forties. After listening to tapes of their interviews several times, I began to pick up a cycling process that I wasn't at all aware of at the beginning. It went something like this: the girl would try to say something, the brother would say, "Shut up," the father would say, "Quit picking on her," and the mother would say to him, "Why are you always getting on the boy's back?" Then they would all sit there depressed, of course, and the daughter never did get to finish what she had started to say. So she had a well-reinforced stuttering system going on. The investigators were not aware of this and certainly the family was not, even though we played this back to them again and again and again. Looking at this as a cycle, I don't really know what causes what; all I know is that a cycling process is operating. I do not necessarily even need to know when it started. What I can know is that there are various points in that cycle where interventions can be made which will change the nature of the overall interaction. If one can make interventions without trying to identify who is the bad guy and who caused what, there is a better chance the interventions will free all the family members for growth.

Effective vs. "Normal" Families

Out of our research over the last ten years we have reached a point now where the real question is not "What is a normal family?" but rather "In how many ways is it possible to be an effectively functioning family?" Many, many clinicians, even those who have worked with families, have only a limited perception of what goes on in families that do not present themselves for help. I have often had the feeling that it would be helpful to my trainees at the university if I could have them bring their own families in and videotape them, and then see whether they would find there what they are calling "pathology" in other families. It is not so much a matter of needing to know the perfect way to be a family, but to understand that there are many ways in which people can be a family, as long as they can work out some of the problems in their interacting system.

On the question of what is a family, I recall a conference I attended a few years ago with marriage and family therapists. Somebody there made the statement that we don't even know what a family is. One esteemed colleague said, "Of course, we know what a family is. Parsons has told us.[4] A family is a father, who is the instrumental leader and the task leader, and a mother, who stays home and keeps the home fires burning, and a boy-child, and a girl-child. That's a family." It occurred to me that if we hold onto views like that, we are really going to be lost when we try to help the different kinds of family configurations which we seem to be headed toward in the future. What we really have to look for are the distinguishable limits for functioning in such families so that it is possible to determine the level of deviation at which one or more members of the family are likely to be labeled as "disturbed" by the broader community.

Summary

Thus far various exercises illustrating dysfunctional communication patterns in triads have been presented. Our research findings seem to me to fit very nicely with Virginia Satir's theoretical concepts.

If you examine the four areas of family functioning discussed in this chapter, I think you will see how our research constitutes a validation of the rich, clinically derived ideas Virginia presents in connection with her work in family therapy. We have approached the four areas in this way: (1) The family's productivity, with the family achieving a balance between work and emotionality—that is, getting the job done and having some fun while they are doing it. (2) The control problem and the ability to establish effective patterns of leadership; there should be no one certain pattern of leadership for families, but families should be able to evolve the one that is best for them. (3) Family effectiveness in developing ways and means for establishing and maintaining clear communication channels. This is related to (4) developing the means for minimizing avoidance of disagreements and conflict, and learning to deal openly and constructively with differences to promote the growth of individuals and of the family as a group.

NOTES

1. John E. Bell, *Family Group Therapy*, U.S. Public Health Monograph, No. 64 (Washington, D.C.: Government Printing Office, 1961).

2. S. A. Murrell and J. G. Stachowiak, "The Family Group: Development, Structure and Therapy," *Journal of Marriage and the Family* (1965), 12-18; S. A. Murrell and J. G. Stachowiak, "Consistency, Rigidity, and Power in the Interaction Patterns of Clinic and Nonclinic Families," *Journal of Abnormal Psychology* (1967), 265-272; J. G. Stachowiak, "Psychological Disturbances in Children as Related to Disturbances in Family Interaction," *Journal of Marriage and the Family* (1968), 123-127; J. G. Stachowiak, "Decision-making and Conflict Resolution in the Family Group," in *Perspectives on Communication*, ed. C. E. Larson and F. E. X. Dance (Milwaukee: University of Wisconsin Press, 1968), pp. 113-124; W. A. O'Connor and J. G. Stachowiak, "Patterns of Interaction in Families with Low-Adjusted, High-Adjusted, and Mentally Retarded Members," *Family Process*, 10, no. 2 (1971), 229-242.

3. Virginia Satir, *Conjoint Family Therapy*, rev. ed. (Palo Alto, California: Science and Behavior Books, 1967), pp. 112 ff.

4. T. Parsons and R. F. Bales, *Family, Socialization, and Interaction Process* (New York: Free Press, 1955).

Chapter 4

Intervention for Congruence

by Virginia Satir

Acknowledging Feelings

All feelings are honorable. The problem is how we use those feelings. If I am angry, I have many ways to manifest that feeling. I can slug you; I can cry; I can read you a lecture; I can spit; I can faint; I can do all kinds of things as a result of that feeling. In a peculiar way, I believe we are at the crossroads of a new evolution of man, if we can survive long enough to make it—and I am not at all sure we can. Particularly at this moment it is essential that people be able to be in contact with themselves on the human basis. I am sure you are well aware that in all the families you deal with, and maybe in your own lives, pain comes from the feeling of being alienated, of feeling not loved, of feeling doubtful about your lovability. Isolation, loneliness, distrust —these are the kinds of words people use. I think that these feelings arise because we ascribe to and allow ourselves to be dominated by some kind of idea of "what is right" that actually is *not* right.

This is what I mean: How long do you think it takes a child who is told every day not to display his anger, or is slapped every day for showing his anger, to have that feeling go inside and come out some other way? It doesn't take very long. I am not trying to set myself up as the supreme authority, but in my experiences I have studied and dealt with people who have committed all types of monstrous crimes and been involved in every kind of human pain, and underneath every one of these people was a little, lonely child who did not know how to acknowledge and communicate his feelings openly and still survive. This is true of the majority of people in their communication. As a result, there is no chance for a person to feel good about himself because he is too busy trying to keep himself afloat. There is no way for a person to feel the genuineness and the love between himself and another person. There is no way one can fully use his resources on the problem at hand. The world today is full of many problems; but the one big problem as I see it is that while people try to deal with real problems, they end up dealing not with these problems but with their own feelings of self-worth in an unacknowledged way.

Most of you have served on committees. The committee makeup is no different from the family makeup. If you were to sculpture a committee, you would have your share of placators, blamers, super-reasonable ones, and irrelevant ones. After a meeting is over, somebody writes the minutes, and when you read them you say, "I can't tell whether I was even at that meeting." Did that ever happen to you? You go to meeting after meeting, and after a certain point you think, "I put my time into this, I put my energy into it, and nothing ever happens." The reason nothing happens, in my opinion, is that people are not able to be "straight" in the full meaning of the word.

Foundations of Congruency

Universality of People

I would like to deal with the fifth communication stance, the congruent response, and give you my picture of what it is all about. Whether you consider this a revelation of my immodesty or not, I feel that I can go anywhere in the world, with people of any language, or any race, and make contact with them. It has happened. This is not because I am so special, but because I believe in certain things. I believe all people are more alike than they are different, that all people have red blood, breathe to keep themselves alive, and are the center of their own support. Also, I believe there are no duplicate human beings; if there were no other evidence to support this, there is the fact that anyone's fingerprints, out of the billions of people in the world, can be traced to him. So that means every human being is unique and he will have differences from every other human being.

Should you and I meet, we would have samenesses we could count on. Just as the surgeon who learned his surgery in "Podunk" can count on the fact that he can operate on anyone anywhere in the world without having to learn anything more, because parts of the body are always in relatively the same places, so I know when we meet that we have guaranteed samenesses we can count on. We also have guaranteed differences. For me, the important thing is that I have this belief in my bones, and I start exploring our differences and how we can use them to build a bridge between us rather than a wall. The process of the exploration of differences and how they are being used is a very important part of therapy.

When communication is handled in the four ways discussed earlier, there is no opportunity to use differences creatively. No one gets any smarter and no one ever gets fuller information about the other person. Furthermore, I do not believe that people who handle their communications in those ways do it on purpose—it is the only way they know how to communicate at that moment in time.

Utilization of Senses

Another of my firm beliefs is that a human being is a great, complicated, magnificent working organism that can get out of kilter very easily because of the way most of us are taught, as children, to use our senses. Most children are taught to see only what they should see. So when they see something they are not supposed to, it cannot be acknowledged. For instance, a little child sees the parents fighting and asks, "Why are you fighting? Are you mad?" And the parent says, "Never mind," or "How could you say such a thing about your mother and father?" You are to see only what you are supposed to see, hear only what you should hear. When you were four or five years old, if you came into your house and used the dirty language the boy next door used, you were not even supposed to have heard those words. One mother tried to teach her child to cover his ears with his hands to avoid the naughty language.

When we consider the next sense, the biggest taking-in sense we have, our skin sense, all of us are taught, with very few exceptions, not to allow our skin to be a part of our perceptual equipment. To show you the importance of the skin sense, if your eyes and ears are gone and you have only 30 percent of your skin surface left, you can still make it in the world with only that much sensory perception of your surroundings. Yet most of us act as though we have no nerve endings in the skin. It is buried under taboos. Don't look at your skin. Don't feel your skin. This is all tied up with the masturbation business. The skin has been heavily contaminated by attitudes that put it in the sexual basket, and therefore we have not been able to get the kind of use out of our skin that we should.

We must restore what people had as small children—full sensory perceptions. Children look easily, touch easily, and hear easily up to about a year and a half (maybe not even that long), and after that their senses have to go underground. Many adults behave as though they are blind, deaf, and frozen. They take nothing in through their skins, their eyes see only what they should, and their ears hear only what they should. This is the biggest way to get a hallucination that I know of! This is the situation the therapist is confronted with. Making it possible for people again to see freely and comment openly on what they see, to be able to hear freely and comment on what they hear, and to be able to touch freely and be able to comment openly on that experience—these comprise the restorative task. If you were to see me interview families, you would find that I put more attention on looking, hearing, and touching, and their meanings than I do on the talk about the problem. Somehow there must be restored in the human being the use of all his resources out of which he can create his own wholeness. This is where "illness" comes from, I think—the person's inability to use all his parts.

There is another factor involved here. If I have parts about me that I don't think are all right, I have to act as though they don't exist. Do you know what happens to the body when you have that kind of feeling? You see people with their shoulders hunched and chests pulled in so the breasts do not protrude. You see people walk with their buttocks tucked under and hips shoved forward. You might think there is some physiological reason. It is physiological only in a very small sense. What it really shows to the world is the fact that you have parts of yourself you cannot acknowledge. Women who have big hips, for instance, try to push them in, and the moment they do that the belly goes up. Or women who have big breasts cave their chests in. When they do that enough times there is a secondary reaction in all the muscles, and pretty soon the body does behave as though it has physiological constrictions.

Self-worth

I could go much further into this, but the main points are that to help a human being change and grow, the reconstruction of that person takes place (1) in the area of communication, (2) in the area of belief about being able to grow, and (3) in the area of restoring the use of the senses. Here is one way of looking at it: If the faucet is running, I don't put my finger under the water tap to stop it; I look for the handle to turn it off. It is quite possible that the handle can be ten feet away from where the water is running out and I may have to run to find where to turn it off; but there *are* people who try to keep the water from running by putting their hand under the water tap. The evidence of what is happening is not the same as the thing that makes it happen. The causes of most things that happen in human beings are unseen. When I hit you with my fist, you see my fist; but what determines why my fist bops you on your head is not my fist but something in me. Anybody who strikes out like this feels he has nothing in himself, and he is trying bravely to live. So where do I begin, where do I go? To the self-worth.

When I was small, I lived on a farm in northern Wisconsin. On that farm was a great big black pot about three feet high which stood on three legs. It was a very handsome pot, big enough to hold a 300-pound pig for scraping. In the spring my mother made her own *soap* in the pot from wood ashes and the other ingredients it takes to make soap. My father had a lot of land, and in the summer, when a large crew of men came to help thresh and harvest, my mother would make stew or *soup* in that pot. Then in the fall my father would gather his favorite *fertilizer* in the pot so it could mature over the winter for my mother's bedding plants, before it was time once more to use the pot for making soap. Over time our family came to call it the "3-S Pot." These were the chief regularly scheduled things the pot was used for. Of course, there was time between one and the next for other uses, but there were always two questions you had to ask about that pot to find out if you could use it or whether you wanted to put your energy into cleaning it out: "What is it full of?" and "How full is it?" The dialogue in our house about that pot was very colorful, and word combinations with "empty" and "full" were quite common. Soap was "high pot" and fertilizer was "low pot."

Later on I was working with a family, and they talked about their feelings about themselves, their insides, the feelings of emptiness, or of being full of things they did not like. This experience from the past popped into my head. When I told them the story about the pot, it seemed to say something to them. Thus, the pot concept was born. The pot concept refers to how you feel about yourself, your self-worth. In France when there is trouble they say, *"Cherchez la femme,"* "Look for the woman." I say when there is trouble, *"Cherchez le pot,"* because that is where you are going to find the problems.

It is a common thing for people, as they go from morning till night through the vicissitudes of the day, to feel tired, to feel hungry, to feel disgusted, to feel frustrated. These are common human experiences. At some point you might say your pot feels kind of empty, or it feels full of frustration or want. However, suppose you have a rule to the effect that if your pot is full of something negative, you cannot say so. This is where the trouble begins. You believe it is bad to have that feeling and you have a rule against it, so you have to act as though what you feel is something else. Let us say I am feeling angry, but I have a rule that I should never be angry. My pot is full of fury. My rule in my head says, "Don't be angry," and now I have the worst type of pot you can imagine. Here I am, full, and it doesn't matter what I am full of except that whatever it is, it is something that I tell myself is bad, and I want to get it out of me. At this point I have "low pot," and I am in no condition to make reality decisions, in no condition to love or to be loved.

One of the things which is most important to me about the congruent response is that people are freed of any rule decreeing that some feeling they may have is not a human feeling. They are freed so that the organism can function fully and they can go on to make all kinds of choices about what to do.

Sometimes people double-rule themselves. They have a rule against being angry, we shall say, and then they have a rule against having that kind of rule. The situation looks like this: I should not have the rule, so there is something wrong with me because I have the rule. People like that feel angry and say, "I shouldn't feel angry," and then they say, "I ought not to feel that I shouldn't feel angry!" This puts them in the position of tightening a rope around their waist and another rope around their throat. Just let them try to breathe! This is a very "low pot" condition.

Multiple Options

What makes it possible to be freed of these ropes, the rules that say I shouldn't feel this way and I shouldn't have a rule that says I shouldn't feel this way? This involves the capability of human beings to select the behavior that fits. The biggest obstacle you will ever find in a family system is when they are stuck with a single answer; there is only one right way. So when you come to them with some other way, they say, "Yuh-uh, nope! That's the way it was in my time and that's the way it is." They have the single answer and they are wed to it. Maybe you think you have the single answer, too, so you say, "No, this is the way it is," and then the fight comes. Or they are equipped with two alternatives, which puts them on the horns of a dilemma. It can be either this way or that, just two strings to the bow. You are in a dilemma with either of these alternatives, so you need to go beyond two. If there are not at least three things that a person can say or do about something, they have not yet utilized their creativity, because it is only then that they actually have a choice. There must be three alternatives. The fact remains that it is possible to go beyond the bind of the dilemma, which we call ambivalence, and to go beyond the one answer referred to as "the right way." Neither of those situations permits the human being to function freely. The opportunity and ability really to make choices is most important. Handling communication in the four ways I showed you earlier precludes any possibility of making choices.

Implications of Congruent Responses

So far I have said three things about the congruent response: First, it holds to the conviction of the universality of human beings—always there is something the same and always something different; the question is what? Second, it involves the restoration of the senses to full use. Third, it opens the possibility of having options, real choices, which does not exist when there is a single "right" answer or an either/or situation.

My therapy and my training, whichever I am involved in, feature what I have just said. This is because I see the problems people have in their destructiveness, in their internal pain, in psychosomatic illnesses, in their interpersonal relationships, in their productivity as being the result of (1) not feeling the universality of the person, (2) not being able to use their senses, and (3) not being able to feel that they have options. All of this is accompanied by the fact that whatever they admit to feeling is only part of the things felt, because the rest are so bad they have to try to deny them. That is the equivalent of living with a garbage can stuffed to the brim, and all your effort goes into keeping the lid on the garbage as you carry it with you on your way. You can't even see where you are going and you fall in the nearest open manhole.

Relating this to my schema of the five modes of responding, how can you help a person who uses the placating response so that he can be on his way to making a congruent response? How can you help a blaming responder on his way to congruence? How can you take a computer, super-reasonable responder and put him on the way to being congruent? How can you take an irrelevant responder and do that? This is the challenge for the therapist, and every word that comes out of his mouth either offers the other person an opportunity to be more of what he already is or helps him in a nonthreatening way to begin to see that perhaps there is something different for him. That is why the role of the therapist is so important.

Seeing Ourselves as Others See Us

As for myself, I have the absolute conviction that what is going on with another person in relation to me—how they are talking, how they are looking—is at that moment in time the best that they can do, and furthermore that they are ignorant of what they are sending out to me. I do a little experiment in which I ask people to speak only two sentences to each other. Then one second later I ask them to repeat the two sentences. Most people cannot remember what they said. We talk without listening—we don't hear it at all. People are out of touch with how they look and sound. They are only in touch with their internal intention and not with the way it comes out. Therefore, one job is to help people be in touch with their whole speech, with what they look and sound like when they speak.

A young woman in my training program in Palo Alto was very well trained as a psychotherapist. She was working with a family that had suffered numerous tragedies. Three children were burned in a fire, they lost their house in another fire, and all manner of tragic things had happened to them. I was watching her through a one-way mirror as the people told her all this, and the people were backing off until by the time the interview was over they were literally against the wall. When she came out of the room she said, "My, those people were resistant!" I said, "What were you feeling when the people told you about their tragedies?" She said, "I felt terrible inside." I said, "Do you have any idea what you looked like?" And we told her about the sick smile on her face during the interview. These people were getting a clue from her facial expression that did not fit her feelings and, acting in response to that clue, they drew farther and farther away from her.

Whenever I am in an interview, or, for that matter, with anybody anywhere, and they start backing away from me, I don't think first about them—I think first about the message I may be giving out. For instance, if I am feeling bad for any reason and I am telling myself I should not talk about it or let people know about it, I can be sure I am giving out a double-level message. I can do this with awareness. I don't know what I do when I am not aware, and the risk is there all the time. By accepting the fact that the intention you have may not be registered the way you feel it, it becomes possible for you to begin to help people, first of all, to get in touch with their intentions and then get in touch with how they look when they have those intentions.

Videotape is excellent for this purpose. I have had people videotaped for a short session, and before showing them the film I ask them what they thought was going on. Then they look at the tape, and I don't have to say anything. It is very easy for a quarreling wife and a placating husband to see themselves on the videotape and realize what it is they are doing. I remember one woman who was yelling to high heaven at her husband while I was taping the session. She was telling him that he yelled too much, and he was saying, "Yes, dear," and telling her how hard it was for him. I just turned the tape on, and she said, "My God, the woman is doing the yelling." I said, "Yes, and that woman is you."

Try this experiment. Put your fingers in your ears and whisper. You will hear yourself clearly. Try it. You can hear yourself perfectly, right? Almost everyone has to learn to hear how they actually sound. This is a second kind of learning. People who yell are completely unaware, for the most part, that they are yelling. The next time you have a person yelling in your office, do not immediately jump to the conclusion that he is aware he is yelling and that it is an assault on you. This is not true at all. There is a great big space between your concept of how you appear and the validation of that concept.

I saw a therapist once who in a deadpan manner spoke of our need to have more joy, and the people in front of him showed no reaction. The therapist later said, "You know, they don't respond to anything!" After a while you can become quite aware of not coming across as you intended. When somebody out there gives you an unexpected response or look, you can say, "How did you see me? How did you hear me? What did I look like to you?" Learning this is of utmost importance: you can be perceived in a way you are not aware of.

Do you know how you got your ideas about how you look and sound? When you were little, people said: "My, you are growing tall." "Get that look off your face." "Oh, you look *so* nice." "Gosh, your ear looks just like Uncle Emil's, and he had one big one!" And various other statements like that. You have very little opportunity to observe yourself firsthand. Do you know what you can see firsthand of yourself? Right now of myself I can see the points of my shoulders and the points of my bosom, I can see my arms, and if I put a foot out I can see that. I can't see the back of me. What I can see firsthand of myself is very little—I improvise the rest. If I look in the mirror, I am backward. Photographs are always still. If you have never seen yourself in action on videotape, you do not know what you really look like. The majority of people have absolutely no true concept of how they look and sound. Furthermore, most of us have been brainwashed to believe that what we are thinking inside shows on the outside. Nothing could be farther from the truth. That only happens accidentally.

Symptoms and Systems

There are these three important aspects about congruent responses, and I find as I put my attention to them that I am able to give people much more help. I am giving them some tools to talk, to look, and to be congruent with. That is what I concern myself with. Now you have my view. I do not know whether or not you accept it. You will only do that if you have the experience for it. I count on the fact that any family which has any kind of *symptom bearer* manages its communication in such a way that everybody is in the condition of being "low pot"—everybody, not just the symptom bearer.

Perhaps you are a schoolteacher and you notice this kid is not learning well, or that kid is troublesome to everybody. Perhaps one child is in kindergarten, and another in a different grade, so two teachers get different parts of one family's difficulties. It could be that someone from the family goes to the doctor and he sees that person's problem. Perhaps the mother goes to the Ladies Aid and confides to someone there what a weak husband she has and they tell her about a place where she can get help with her problem. Many people see pieces of the dysfunctioning of families but not the wholes. If you were to retain only one piece of information from all this, I hope it would be that *whatever you see in a person is only a piece of the whole*. It is all right for you to look at the piece, but never mistake it for the whole. Few schoolteachers are going to be able to engage in seeing families conjointly. Some schools, where they have an unusual orientation about bringing parents in for teacher-parent sessions, might present the opportunity to do that. Whatever caregiving role you may have in the community, look at the piece in terms of the whole. Only then can you begin to make the kind of shortcuts that you need to make in order to help.

Not everyone will have access to the families of the people they work with, but they can have a *family systems* point of view, which is not based on "blame" but upon people struggling to get together. The communications exercises clearly show that when a family is composed of a guy who has to say, "Yes, dear," and a woman who says, "You are right, it *is* 'yes, dear,' " and one kid has to be as though he is unfeeling and the other one is irrelevant, the result is a most painful situation. And there is nothing to blame for it except the process, the way people handle their own feelings of self-worth.

Process and Content

What kind of interventions are going to give the kind of feedback to a placating person that will make it possible for him to shift to another mode of communication? First of all, you have to help people know what they are doing. You cannot do it by pointing out, "You know what you are doing? You are placating all the time!" When you do that you are using a blaming process to tell them they should not placate. You talk about placation but you are using a blaming process. The content is not the same as the communication about the content, if you follow me. Like the woman in my office, yelling at her husband, "YOU CAN'T YELL HERE!"

Think about it: the content is not the same as the process around the content. Content can be talked about in any manner. I made some references earlier to sexual organs, to anger, and to a lot of taboo subjects people have. They can be talked about in a variety of ways. I can talk about the genitals in such a way as to be pornographic. I can talk about them in such a clinical way that it is as dry as tissue paper, I can talk about them so that there is a realness, and so can you. The content is not the same as the process around the content.

How do you make it possible for people to be able to understand, to be aware, and then how do you take the steps to make a change?

At this point you might like to try some exercises relating to the congruent response.

Exercises in Perception, Awareness, and Relationships

If you can, find someone to act as your partner whom you do not know. Arrange your chairs so that you face each other. After reading the instructions which follow, start with the initial stage of letting your eyes close and follow through the sequence of experiences.

Perhaps I should first explain why I ask you to close your eyes. When you close your eyes, you can focus internally; you will not receive demands from external things that they be taken in. Some of you may have discovered this lovely little device to use when circumstances are very pressuring, when you are feeling a little panic. Just let your eyes close for a moment, be attentive to your breathing and to your support. It is like a flood of new energy; as though you centered yourself. When I ask you to close your eyes, I am asking you to give yourself the maximum opportunity to let yourself flourish inwardly. For a few moments allow your eyes to close and attend only to your inner being.

Universality

You know that you are now sitting in front of another human being. In a few seconds this will only be a memory, but you still can say for sure that someone is in front of you—a person—and you are a person sitting in front of them. . . . As you let yourself get in touch with this, also come in touch with the fact that before you speak to each other, because you are both human beings, you have samenesses with this person and you have differences from this person. If this person were on public welfare, labeled schizophrenic or paranoid, the store clerk, the pawnbroker, four years old, black, male, President of the United States, you would come to the same conclusion that you have likenesses and differences. Think for a moment about these things you can absolutely depend upon. It is the basic security from which you operate, the fundamental knowledge to build on.

Gradually, after you have let that come into your awareness, let your eyes open and look at the person in front of you without talking. Just look. Then gradually let your eyes close again, and examine what the experience of looking at another person was like. Did it remind you of staring when you were a child? Did you feel you were invading someone? Did you feel that your partner looked at you in a negative way? What is experienced by letting your eyes look fully?

As you go beyond that worry, if it did cause worry, let yourself be in touch with what you saw. Your brain is a lively thing and it operates immediately. What did your brain tell you about what you saw? In other words, how did you interpret what you saw? If you had any kind of body response, let yourself be aware of that too. Your eyes beheld, your brain responded, and perhaps your body did too.

Prejudices

Gradually open your eyes again, look in a focused way for anything about the other person that happens to hit your prejudice—sex, age, hair color, whatever. Let yourself focus on whatever triggers your prejudice. Chances are that if you are more than two years old there are things that hook your prejudice. The question is not whether you have them. The question is what they are and how you are using them. Then gradually let your eyes close again, and let yourself be in touch with what your brain told you about what you picked up and how you felt about it.

Keeping your eyes closed and with the input you now have, think of what possibility there is of the two of you bridging the gap between two human beings. What is puzzling in this situation? Put that efficient brain to work. Take a minute or two for this.

Associations

Next, as your eyes open, look for any evidences in the person before you which remind you of people you know or have known —relatives, friends, work connections, perhaps those you only know about such as movie stars or literary characters, anyone who has meaning to you. Focus on that part of your associations at this moment. After a few seconds let your eyes close and let yourself be in touch with the fact that at least fifty percent of the people you meet remind you of someone you have known before. This is very rampant in families. Husbands are always getting their wives mixed up with their mothers. Wives are always getting their husbands mixed up with their fathers. If you found that the person in front of you reminded you of someone, let the full picture of that other someone come to your mind's eye, and let yourself experience what you feel about that person. It would be very easy to transfer those feelings to the person in front of you. Then let the picture of the person in front of you come into your mind also, and notice the difference between the two. When you have done that, gradually open your eyes and let your imagination flow freely about what you think the other person thought and felt about you. It is not a question of whether they thought or not, because the brain is always working, but precisely what they may have thought and felt about you. Let yourself be in touch with whatever these fantasies are, let them flow for a minute. Then gradually close your eyes and let yourself be in touch with how you feel about the fantasies you had, such as, "My gosh, I wonder if he saw I didn't brush my teeth this morning." Whatever it was, let it be.

Shared Perceptions

With your eyes still closed let yourself be aware that you have a tremendous amount of information about your partner that you have taken in with your eyes and processed with your brain. This is how it is with everyone, but I am going to ask you to do what most people do not do. Take this material, which is your construction, and share it with the person in front of you. Let yourself be aware that when you do not share it (and many people do not) you treat what is inside as fact about the other person and proceed as though it were. Could you just anticipate with your eyes closed what it will be like to share all this with the person in front of you. If you think, "Oh, my gosh, I couldn't say that!" share that too, because this is your own construction. It actually has nothing to do with the other person, and it could be the means by which you build a connection to the other person. Gradually open your eyes and share with one another as much as you can about what your inside experience was like as you literally beheld the other person. See what happens as you swap your impressions of each other.

Face to Face and Back to Back

Then take a few minutes to tell each other something about yourself, who you are, what you do, and anything you might want to share. After five minutes of that type of conversation, turn your chairs back to back, about twelve inches apart, and continue getting acquainted from this new position for another five minutes.

You will soon find how difficult, if not impossible, it is to communicate with each other in this position. If you were to do so successfully, you would have craned, stiff necks and loud voices, and no doubt some frustration would set in.

Here is something I discovered early in my career. When I first started working with families I could not understand how they could continue interacting in such painful ways as they had been doing for so long. After being in many homes, it became clearer. The back-to-back position is the way in which many people carry on their communications. Pa is behind the paper in one room, Ma is stirring something on the stove in the kitchen, and she says, "Did you pay the mortgage?" and he says, "Hmmm." Two weeks later there is an eviction notice and she says, "I told you!"

When you try the above exercise, you become aware that your whole view about the other person can change very quickly. Suppose that you were to continue like this for an even longer period of time. All the things that were beginning to be established when you were face to face are beset by numerous traps. You have to rely on your memory. I have people who come in and say, "Twenty years ago he told me," or "She told me once," but it's not happening now. The big point I want to make here is that unless there is continuing face-to-face validation, the fantasies, the feelings of insecurity begin to take over. One of the hardest things you have to do when working with a family is to get them into the position where they can really look and see each other. If you do not believe this, the next time you interview a family note how they avoid looking at one another. Were you aware of this? And do you know what a person "sees" when he does not see? He fills in the scene with his imaginings.

Reestablishing Contact

Continue the experiential exercise back to back with your partner. This can lead to negative feelings, not because anyone did anything bad but because there is no way to validate your impressions. Try putting your chairs together so that at least your backs touch. This probably would not give you the specifications for building a bridge, but at least in this position you know *there is someone behind you and you have some kind of feeling that you are really making a connection. If any of you work with blind people, you know that one of the most important things in working with the blind is to have them be in touch, literally in touch. This is one of the ways in which they can begin to make connections. The point I wish to make is that just getting the affirmation of your backs touching reduces the feeling of being cut off from one another.*

Parent-Child Communication

Here are some other ways to illustrate how people fail to connect realistically with each other that you might experiment with. Have one person stand up and the other sit at his feet right on the floor. Those of you sitting on the floor are on approximately the same level you were on for eight or ten years from the beginning of your life. You are approximately in the same proportion as any young child to your "parent" who is standing up. Next make eye contact from the positions you are in and hold it for ten seconds. . . . Then if the "child's" neck wants to relax and his head goes down, let it fall down.

Supermarket Tantrum

The parent's neck is probably not hurting as much as the child's. Quite often the parent regards this action on the part of the child as indicating, "I don't want to have anything to do with you," without any awareness that the child is dropping his or her head because it is uncomfortable. Let us suppose you are that kind of a parent. You think your child is not paying attention to you. What do you want to do with this kid who is not paying attention? Do it and see what happens. The "child" next can show how he feels about what the "parent" did, respond to whatever it was, and then the parent respond in turn to that.

What most people find themselves doing when the action on the part of the child is seen as a negative response to them is to jerk the child's head up, give a shove to his shoulder, or shake a finger at him. Then the child responds by grabbing the parent by the leg, making noises, and even crying. This is the supermarket tantrum, all caused in this case by the child's being uncomfortable. Do you know in our society how much we stand discomfort in order not to provoke the attention of someone else? I think these are the beginnings.

Pats and Slaps

The parent probably noticed that his arms are closest to the head of the child. If he were to swing an arm, he would not have to bend very far to clout the child right in the face. Swing your arm but don't hit the other person, just to see how easy this would be. One of the things that I became very aware of as I worked with people is that in their thirties, forties, and fifties they were still remembering the humiliating treatment of being slapped around the face and having their ears boxed. It is almost a natural thing for the adult to use his arms that way unless he knows better. Perhaps you do not know what these thumps to the head feel like. You have a lot more power swinging your arm when you stand up than you may realize. Many of the battered children I have had contact with were battered by parents who had no awareness of the heftiness of their swing. When you are standing up, the swing you intend to be only a little tap can knock your child senseless.

I would like you to try something else. There are some parents who give their children pats on the head when they start to act up. Give your "child" a vigorous pat on the head. Now the child should respond to the "parent" to indicate what that pat felt like. Again some of you could misunderstand. The parent who patted could be saying, "There, there, dear." The child could feel like he had a cranial explosion. The child's response to the pat would not fit the intention of the parent. You who were patted may have started to beat back at your "parent," or you may have started to cry. So here is the parent: "I wanted to give a love message, I wanted to comfort him, and look at this damn kid!" When that happens, the parent feels even more anxious and wants to give a message to the child to the effect that "You should like me." Try doing that. Often people start to tell the child, "You know Mommy loves you" or "Daddy loves you," but I wonder if the kid below thinks this is really sincere.

Another thing I have frequently encountered with adults is the terrible aversion they have to being patted. Many people react against it, and I think this generalizes to other kinds of touching. The touching you have been involved with right now (slapping, jerking, pushing, and patting) in this kind of context puts a negative feeling on touch. I think we can see where it begins.

Child's Eye of the Adult
Next the child who is sitting on the floor should look straight

ahead at the adult and notice the scenery. Remember that you see this scenery for eight or ten years. When you look straight ahead you get a heavy dose of knees, or big feet, if you look down a little, and if you look up just a little you are aimed at the genital area. If your eyes are in their most comfortable position, you are concentrated on your adult from the waist down. Suppose you imagine your adult nude. One thing I get a lot of from the people I work with is this sexual emphasis. From your vantage point for looking, imagine the adult nude in front of you. The natural thing for you to do as children is to explore, to put your hands out, because children explore with their hands. As you start to put your hands out, watch what the adult does. The adult responds almost automatically. As the child rubs on your legs or picks at your legs, or whatever he does, and gets close to the genital area, you want to withdraw. I know people who interpret this as their child's sexual mania instead of the natural kind of exploration that comes about because of where the hands and the visual range are. Here is something else. Many adults keep their children physically close to them. Then you get into the business not only of sexual organs but of sexual odors. It does not take many transactions like this, of the child exploring and being pushed off by the parent, before he begins to feel there is something wrong [1] in wanting to explore, [2] in this whole business of the genitals, and [3] what is more he had better keep all this stuff to himself. Not very many at all. Furthermore, in all families who have coping difficulties, there are always sexual problems and a lack of healthy attitudes about sex.

If the person acting as the child looks up at the parent now, he will experience something else. As he looks up at his parent, which we all do for eight or ten years, he should notice all the protuberances: first of all the belly (if the parent were nude, he would first see the genitals), the breasts, the chin, the nose. Look up and notice the distorted view of the other person. One thing I have encountered many times is that when people tell me about their parents they describe them like no human I ever saw! These early perceptions become fixed unless something happens to change them. Think of how adults look to the child—the big chins, the big noses, and those holes under the noses—and you will begin to get some idea of the terror some children could have about their adults, a terror which they retain.

Next the one in the adult role should look down at the child and notice that he bears little resemblance to a grown-up. One constant problem is that after people have grown to adulthood they do not leave these attitudes behind them. The parent still looks on his child as little and not very much like him, and the child still looks at his parent as belonging to a different world and as not being anyone at all like him. This is one factor in the development of the generation gap: the idea that I-as-a-person am not the same you-as-a-person because of this early experience. Have you noticed how families divide people into two categories? Parents divide them into children and people, and children divide them into parents and people.

Your dyad now can switch positions, the child becoming the parent and the parent becoming the child. Both of you again take the most comfortable pose you can. The adult will be looking straight ahead and the child will be looking ahead, because that is the most comfortable position. At this point, if you are both to maintain your comfort, you cannot make a connection. You can have a connection by the adult dropping his head (which is relatively easy) and the child raising his. Hold that for ten seconds. That is not very long but it may seem like a lifetime. You are a good child and you are doing what your mama wants or your papa wants. Just look without talking. The child must have a tired head, his neck must hurt, so he can let himself be comfortable and drop his head. The adult is the kind who perceives this as the child not wanting to pay attention to him, and he responds. Then the child responds to the adult.

The Security Tackle

When the child feels too insecure, and a lot of kids know about this, one of the best ways to restore equilibrium is to grasp the parent around both legs. Do this and see what happens. . . . The parent will feel he is going to fall over if he does not do something, so do something. This situation is simulated in a sense, but it would be very easy for an adult, not because he hates the child but because he wants to get back his own bal-

ance, to hurt the child somehow in the process. This has nothing to do with wanting to give a negative message to the child, but simply a way of regaining balance. When you push on the child or have to lean heavily on him, this can only be perceived by him in a negative way. I have even known of children who had shoulder blades broken because of this kind of thing. For the adult, there is some humiliation felt when he can't get his balance—the kid puts him off balance but he doesn't realize the child is grasping the parent because he feels scared. Many people interpret this as orneriness on the part of the child. What we have is the beginning of an enemy operation without its ever having been intended that way at all in the minds of people. These early learnings are very powerful.

Holding a Child

The next step is for the child to look ahead at the scenery, at his parent. Remember this is what children see firsthand in comfort. If parents understand this, they will make it possible for the child to have eye-level contact with them either by getting down on the floor eye to eye or lifting the child up to their eye level, at the same time supporting their feet. A lot of people handle children without supporting their feet. I don't know how recently you have been held up with your feet unsupported, but it is a very peculiar feeling. When a child's feet are not supported, and he starts to wriggle in a parent's arms, this is often interpreted by the parent as a wish on the child's part to get away, which in turn means the parent is not lovable. Instead, the way in which the parent holds the child makes him uncomfortable, and he, consequently, struggles for comfort. This is also true in the nursing situation. Many mothers who are not aware of their children's discomfort nearly suffocate them with their breasts by not holding them properly.

The person on the floor taking the child's position is a nice, obedient child except when his comfort is involved, and then everything gets misunderstood. Raise one arm up to the parent and hold onto his hand, just as children are led by parents when they walk along the street. For ten seconds hold your arm up like that. At a certain point when the arm begins to feel numb, the child will try to pull his hand away. Now try to get away. . . . The adult's arm hanging down does not get numb, but the arm held up from the child does. When numbness sets in, you want to do something about it. The natural thing is to pull it down out of the parent's hand. For the parent this means the child wants to get away, and the response is, "You ornery kid," or "My God, you're going to run away from me." The parent hangs on tighter, the numbness increases, the pain in the child increases, the pressure on the part of the parent grows, and before long we have another supermarket tantrum.

Inadvertent Early Childhood Education

So children learn after a while that they must endure all kinds of pain and not comment about it. We have thousands of people in our society who have stopped being in touch with their own pain and are behaving like robots. They will absorb any amount of pain without even recognizing it. The minute you are out of touch with your own pain you become insensitive to the pain of others, because pain does not even register anymore. *Our world is full of people like that.*

One should not underestimate the importance of what the child learns from these misunderstandings. Every parent wants his child to be all right. Every child would like to feel he can depend upon his parent. Inadvertent learnings, like what you have just experienced, become more powerful than any words that can be uttered.

The person sitting on the floor next looks up at the adult and notices the protuberances. Note the view from down there, and particularly notice the belly, the chin, the bosom, the nose, and (if these people were nude) their genitals. Scary, isn't it? Out of this comes a distortion of reality. The adult at the same time looks down on the child. For many people these are images retained through life. The next step is to see what happens as you get on eye level with each other, however you want to do it, on the floor or on chairs. Bring yourselves to eye level.

At this point it would be well to become aware of something else. It may seem eons ago when you first sat down with this person with whom you have "been through the wars." Now you are in a position to really come back to this person and be able to comment eye to eye. Take a few moments to communicate to each other whatever you might like to talk about at present and see what the feeling is within you as you do it.

In doing the previous exercises, you make the complete circle. The meaning I put to this may be very useful to you. You started out with good intentions with your partner. I asked you to let yourself do what people are always doing—to look and to make something of what is seen. This always happens. You shared your perceptions, which is different from what other people do —they treat their first observation as fact. You gained some kind of relationship with each other. Then I asked you to do things which would put kinks in this relationship. I asked you to go back to back. Then I asked you to do the up-down exercises. Doing these things placed various handicaps on the relationship you once had. Now you are back in a position from which you could go on with the important job of clearly communicating with one another. Some of the trust you had at the beginning may now be returning. Look at this in relation to the family. I offer this to you from my experience. When I can make it possible for people to regain the trust they may have once had, perhaps at the age of one or two, they are then open for dealing with the real problems.

Physics of Relationship

One thing that may have occurred to you during the exercises above was how easily looking, touching, and listening can get contaminated through nobody's fault. You saw very quickly and easily that the effect of something was not the same as what was intended. I call this the physics of relationship. Many of you deal with young families and you are in a position to help the adults behave in such a way as not to send these inadvertent, contaminating messages. I repeat, inadvertent. For those of you who work with families who have children older than one or two, be prepared for the fact that the mechanics that really make it possible for people to connect with one another are already contaminated, but they are not contaminated forever. To reawaken the freedom to look, the freedom to touch, and the freedom to listen is a vital part of what restores the human being's ability to function. When you placed yourselves in a position where you could make contact and talk freely, those two things began to restore something that was being destroyed. If you did nothing more when you have a family together than make it possible for them to really look at each other, touch each other, and listen to each other, you would have already swung the pendulum in the direction of a new start.

The meaning behind this may not be as profound to you as it is to me, but it seems basic. You can talk about all the great theories you like, but if you are not able to free people to contact each other, what good are theories? I am sure many of you who are therapists have been distressed and saddened by the fact that something which was quite obvious to you, and which you tried very hard to get across, was not heard at all. That has something to do with you, but it has more to do with what pieces of the whole pie you are working with. This is why I say the problem is merely the ticket of admission, and the ticket only tells you that here are people who are living but who cannot look, who cannot touch, who cannot listen, not because they are unable to, but because it does not even occur to them that they are *not* doing it. Your efforts to make it possible for people to be able to do what you have been doing here—discover how to be in contact with each other—are going to establish the fertile context within which the help you have to offer can be comprehended. And it means *you* also have to be in that condition.

When you work with families, unless there are chairs in which everyone can be comfortable, the floor is the best place to sit; there everyone can feel supported. For people who work in offices, one of the recommendations I make is that all furniture be such that everybody's feet can be supported by something. In regard to homes, much of the furniture in homes is not fit for people. Have you noticed those long sofas? Everybody has to communicate linearly—you get it somehow through your appendix! These are the present physics of relationships.

Enduring Perceptions of Childhood Relationships

The early physics of relationships and the profound learnings that result escape people. "I'm always little—the person in front of me is always big." Have you ever had people six feet tall talk about how little they felt in relation to their mothers, who turned out to be five foot two? "She is bigger than I am," they say. This doesn't come from any present reality, it comes from these early learnings. Think of how many different reinforcement messages you get in the eight or ten years while you are small in relation to your parents. By comprehending that you can go a long way toward understanding also the fears people have of feeling equal in the sense of *being able to comment openly and to use themselves.*

Conclusion

Later I will explain other parts of what I consider the guts of my work with the family. Perhaps we have already gone far enough for you to begin to feel how quickly things can change. This change has nothing to do with anything happening per se, but rather with where one person is in relation to the other person, with establishing the context to put them within touching distance of each other. Of course, actually touching each other all the time is not the solution. However, when one is within touching, hearing, and seeing distance, it becomes very difficult to placate, to blame, to be super-reasonable or irrelevant; but these are easy responses when people do not look at each other, or are ten feet apart, or one is on a chair and the other on the floor.

Chapter 5

Family Structure and Intervention Techniques

by James Stachowiak

It might be well to take a more in-depth look at the nature of family structures and some methods for constructive intervention in family systems.

As you will recall from previous discussions of the question what is a family, sociologists and other social science professionals have for a long time focused on a family pattern consisting of the father, who is the task leader, the mother, who is the social-emotional leader, a boy-child, and a girl-child. Not only are there few families around like that, but the forms which families have been taking recently are many and diverse.

Working with a Communal Family System

I would like to describe a case which came to me just a short time ago. I offer it as an example because the family arrangement was something totally new to me even though I have some familiarity with communal forms of living. Here is what happened.

A fellow telephoned and said he wanted to talk to someone about getting hypnotic treatment for his problem. His problem was sexual inadequacy. He agreed to come in for an interview so we could talk about it more fully. After he entered my office, he said, "There are two things you ought to know about my situation. One is that I live in a communal family." I said, "What is that—what do you mean by 'communal'?" He replied, "Well, there are me and my wife, and this other fellow and his wife." These two couples were legally married but they had gotten together, apparently out of strong feelings for one another. The second thing he told me was that he had no money, which was an interesting way to start. Since I was quite intrigued with the novel family system and was in the midst of doing some research on various kinds of systems, we pursued the possibility of an intervention in what they were calling their "family system." There were no offspring, only the two couples. We worked it out that in exchange for our staff helping them they would allow us to record our interviews with them and make observations of them in various settings.

What the situation involved was that shortly after these couples began living together they developed a set of rules, as everybody living together does. However, one thing which I found most interesting was that their rules seemed even *more* explicit than most rules in two-person marriages. For instance (and this may sound a little chauvinistic to the women, but I am only relaying what he told me), the women each had a bedroom, and on three nights of the week this fellow slept with one woman and on the other three nights with the second woman, and vice versa for the other fellow. Then they reversed it for the next week, alternating the seventh night. But it seemed as though all their rules were set up in such a way as to leave no possibility for freedom. The interesting point is that while they enlarged their family group in hope of getting *more* freedom, they actually built themselves into an unbelievably restrictive system. What his sexual inadequacy problem consisted of was that after the two couples began living together, this man's wife discovered what she had been missing during the earlier years of their marriage. That is to say, the other husband was described as being very "potent," and her own husband experienced premature ejaculation and did not satisfy her very well.

To show you some of the difficulties you can get into if you don't appreciate the interaction of systems when trying to make interventions, here is another interesting thing that occurred. Because of the husband's alleged inadequacy, that couple consulted a marriage counseling pair who were well versed in the Masters and Johnson work in St. Louis with sexuality. So the counselors (who were a married couple also) met with this man and his wife, leaving the other couple out of it. To begin with, the counselors separated the two couples so that they lived away from each other for a while. Then the clients were instructed in the techniques for dealing with impotency or premature ejaculation. This continued for about two weeks, and the fellow said, "And I managed to outlast her twice in that time." They then went back to live with the other couple, and after the first night that the wife slept again with the other guy, she said to her husband the next day, "If you think I am going to be like a machine for you, you're crazy. You couldn't even go out on the street, pick up a girl, bring her home, and ask her to do these things for you." So immediately he could not outlast her anymore, and they were into big problems.

This is where we are with the situation at this point. I mention it because it seems to me that if they are going to structure their system with two couples in it, then that is the only way the system can be understood if one is to intervene effectively and give them some real help with their problems. Therefore, that was our approach. Similar to what you might find in any family, by the way, the husband's first reaction was that he did not want to include the others. After I explained to them the ways in which I would work on it and how I would look at the situation, they all agreed to go ahead.

There is another part to this which should be brought out. As the client reported it, what happened when they consulted the marriage counseling couple was that after a short time the marriage counselor husband got mad at the client's wife and re-

moved himself from the situation. This left the female component of the marriage counseling couple and the client couple,
which soon became a nice three-person group in which the two
females began to disagree, and the client's wife left; and what
remained out of a system of four was female marriage counselor
and male client. I want to stress that this is hearsay for which
there is no validation, but it is interesting to consider. So much
for the interaction processes in this marriage counseling.

Importance of Process over Content

In attempting to bring about changes in family functioning,
analyzing interaction processes between people and in family
systems is much more important than trying to analyze the actual content of communications. Any marital pair or family
group can make life pretty miserable for a therapist if he allows
himself to get caught in the content and makes judgments about
which family member is "right." This is the danger inherent in
the triangle. You probably have noticed that anytime three people get together, there is only a shifting, two-person interaction,
with the third person behaving as an audience. While the interaction shifts around momentarily, at any given instant it occurs
only between two people, with the third as an observer. What
this means, then, is if a therapist intervenes with a married couple, he can expect at the outset that each one will be talking
through him (the therapist) to the other, and also attempting to
get the therapist into a coalition against the other. This is one
problem that must be dealt with.

Before telling you of some of the ways therapists have tried to
avoid becoming involved in the family system, let me mention
that when we talk about family therapy or family counseling
what we are really talking about is not so much getting every
member of a family group together in a room at the same time
as an entirely different approach to understanding or conceptu-
alizing problem behaviors or interpersonal conflict. In contrast
to the early notions that problems and conflict arise only within
the individual and need to be dealt with at that level, the tendency over the past decade or more has been to look at what we
are calling "the problem" as being outside in the relationships

between people. It is this interactional relationship between people that we are referring to when we talk about the family system. Now we can give up talking about a disease, talking about an illness, talking about an emotional disturbance—all of which are concepts extremely difficult to define. Mainly these concepts have been used as a means of managing people's behavior by labeling them, and perhaps the labeling process makes it easier on the group. When you talk about a communication problem existing between a pair or a family group, you could say (and it has been done) that these are psychoneurotic families or psychotic families, but that only compounds the problem by putting it on more people at one time. What we are really concerned with is trying to get a toehold on what is going on between those people and helping them change their interactions in such a way that they have opportunities for growth and further development.

The task for a family systems therapist or counselor who tries to help by intervening in a system of this sort becomes one of fostering accommodation. We can assume that all people living within a group setting are always engaged in the process of juggling their aims and desires against those of the others. Anytime two people get together, they are going to have differences; they are going to have some similarities, but they will also have differences. The problem becomes one of discovering how they can accommodate the continually changing inputs coming into that system in such a way as to maximize the satisfaction for each individual member and to minimize the splitting off or the need to avoid dealing with problems in an open way.

Intervention Without Involvement

How is this done? There are perhaps as many ways to conduct family therapy as there are family therapists. Each person who seeks to assist families by promoting change and growth brings with him his unique background, his experiences, and whatever repertoire of behaviors may be available to him. This is not to say that a person cannot learn new behaviors, enlarge his repertoire, but to a certain extent people do have favorite behaviors—behaviors that are more comfortable, more automatic—and different behaviors would have to be developed and practiced before they could be incorporated in their repertoire.

Even though people approach intervention in their unique ways, the one common thread that runs through all approaches is that the therapist must find a way to avoid being sucked into the system. The therapist has to figure out how to direct the family group so that change becomes possible for them. The difficulty is that any direct attempt to reform or guide the family only heightens resistance to change. For example, suppose a mother asks the therapist what she should do to keep her children from fighting? If the therapist responds, "Leave them alone and stay out of it," she is likely to say, "Oh, but I can't! They would kill each other!" Similarly, you could try to tell a father to "spend more time with your son." You often hear this kind of counseling. His response may very likely be, "I can't because of the time demands of my job," or, perhaps even worse, he may actually take you up on it and proceed to behave in such a way that he proves to you that it didn't help his son at all. The point is that direct attempts to change a system and resolve its conflicts are very difficult for the system to incorporate, and usually they have all been tried before the family ever got to a therapist. Therefore, therapists have had to look for ways to interact with the system and the members in it and, at the same time, avoid getting sucked into the system.

Family Social System Network

I want to describe some of these techniques. The first has to do with the size of the group seen. A psychiatrist in Philadelphia named Ross Speck[1] has developed a procedure called the "family social system network." Most of the families worked with in this way consist of a father, mother, and a child who is an older adolescent or young adult still tied in with the parents and living with them. When the family comes in, according to Speck's method, they are told, "I can only work with you if you will go out and get forty other people, a minimum of forty others, cohorts, relatives, friends, whomever you know, and we will all meet at your house." You can imagine what the family says. They say that they do not even know that many people. Since by the time they get to Speck the families have been through the mill of seeking help from many other therapists and are really at their wit's end, they tend to go along with the suggestion even though they expect dire consequences. What happens is they meet at the appointed time, and indeed there are forty people present—some relatives, some friends, some neighbors.

His reason for doing this is what is important. As he sees it, this is an opportunity to loosen up the rigid triad which has developed between these three people and to enlarge the possibilities of new coalitions being formed. In one case he told me about, a young, adult, unmarried female living with her parents had made several suicidal gestures. The family, in effect, had little or no outside relationships. They were trying to be self-sufficient as a triad and they had worked themselves into such a tight system that they could see few possibilities for making any change. By bringing in the other people, he enlarged the possibilities for creating new coalitions, as I said, so that now the girl, instead of making a suicidal attempt when things got too tight around the house, was able to go to stay with an aunt and uncle who were very happy to have her come to them. This is the kind of structural change which can be accomplished simply by providing the opportunity for other things to happen.

Another interesting thing about this method is that it harkens back to the practice in precivilized societies of the clan gathering to support the family in time of crisis. There are reports in anthropological literature of family systems who live apart, extended families, kinship systems, and so on, who upon hearing that any member of their family is in a state of need or crisis all come together. They meet for the purpose of working out the problem and then they have a celebration at the end of their council or conference before returning to their own respective homes. Enlarging the family system has real possibilities for effecting a change.

I would like to recount to you one experience I had with this method, because usually when people are told about it they respond that this could not work. Although I have had limited experience with this technique, perhaps this will give you some idea of what can be done. I was seeing a thirty-year-old, unmarried, unemployed female who lived with her aged parents in their seventies in a small farm community. It soon became clear that there were some problems of rigid relationships that had been set up over a long period of time which I could not see any other way of working with at the time. So I tried the idea of getting the family together. We set up a meeting with this young woman, her father and mother, her brother and his wife from another city, one sister and her husband from another state, and another sister and her husband from still another state. You might think, "Well, they are not going to travel that great distance," some of them having to drive as much as three or four hundred miles, but interestingly enough they all arrived at the set time. We had about three hours for the meeting. What happened was that for the first time the daughter, the identified client, was able to stand up to her brother in an argument and gain support from other members of the family. A brother-in-law was *very* sympathetic to her and told her about his own experience in having undergone psychotherapy. All in all, although it was an anxious time for everyone, particularly the seventy-two-year-old father, they experienced this as enabling them to loosen up the tightness of the system they were in. It was stimulating and gratifying enough to me that I would like to experiment more with that method.

Working with Subsystems

At the other extreme, limiting the number of members seen is also a way of making a structural intervention. One example of this would be to see only the marital pair and exclude the children in order to strengthen the marital coalition. You can think of the marriage as being a system in and of itself within the larger family system. If the two marriage partners cannot maintain their strong relationship so that each can also have a relationship with the children without upsetting the other one and disturbing the relationship between themselves, you can predict that there will be some kind of disturbance or blocked growth in that family. Let me say that another way: if the marriage partners are unable to work out their own relationship problems in such a way that the child does not intervene within their marriage system and so that they can be free enough for each parent to relate to the child on his own, then they are likely to have a disturbed system. In such cases, limiting the therapy to the husband and wife can help strengthen their coalition and provide the necessary separation and distance from the children so that the children are not constantly between them.

Use of One-way Mirror

There is a therapist on the West Coast, Fulweiler,[2] whose attempts to avoid being sucked into the system include his not even being in the room with the family. He has the family interact and talk with one another about their problems while he sits behind a one-way mirror with earphones and a tape recorder. At any point where he thinks he can make a useful intervention, he goes into the room with them, gets them reorganized around what he wants them to do, and then leaves the room to watch them again. When I first heard about this I was amazed, and I asked him how he happened upon this method. He told me that he had a problem, and that was that he talked a lot. When he was working with a family, he felt he was talking all the time. Then it occurred to me that I have that same kind of problem, so I thought I would try his method, and I can report to you that in some cases it is a way of getting the proper distance. If you need to back off, this is one way you can get out of the room and observe the family interaction without becoming embroiled in the system.

Co-therapist

Carl Whitaker,[3] a psychiatrist in Madison, Wisconsin, likes to work primarily with a co-therapist. Having another person with him, he feels, gives him strength to withstand the pressures of the system that generate outwardly. This also provides two points of view about what is going on in the system, as well as the means for verifying observations.

Groups of Families

Another method which has already been referred to, and which Virginia Satir and several others are using, is that of seeing several families together at the same time. One of the advantages in this, at least as I have seen it used, would be the opportunities afforded for expanding relationships, and different kinds of relationships, similar to what occurs in the social system network I described. In other words, parents meet with somebody else's kids, and kids with someone else's parents. People are often able to relate much more easily and effectively to somebody else's child than to their own, particularly at a time of considerable stress. At our own clinic we have tried this to a limited extent with adolescents and their parents who do not even want to talk to each other. They have been willing to meet as groups, the adolescents meeting with other parents and vice versa, and in this way they at least begin to talk to the other generation.

Videotape and Self-Portraits

Another thing which I like to use, and this also has been referred to previously, is the closed-circuit videotape and self-ratings. I try to relate to the family as their agent who will assist them in making the changes that they want. One way I have found videotaping useful is to record the family's interaction, have them watch themselves on the screen, and then rate what they liked best and what they liked least about themselves and every other member in the scene they observed. Also I ask them to choose what they want to start trying to change. The family members share their ratings, and later we again videotape their interaction to see what kinds of changes are occurring. I got this idea from Sartre. What he said was something like this: In life each man paints his own portrait, and there is nothing else but the portrait. It is not what you would have done, could have done, or should have done—just what you did. That is where you're at. So I decided to ask people, knowing how threatening it is for people to observe themselves, to consider the possibility of painting their picture which would appear on the television screen. If they don't like what they see, the nice thing is that they can erase it and put another picture there. If they don't like that one, they can erase it too, and they can continue to put pictures up there on the screen until they find one that everybody likes.

At first it is almost as if they are afraid the image will be preserved forever, like a still camera shot. But the families I try this with really become caught up with the idea, especially when I stress that the picture can be erased.

Observation of Family Subgroups

There is another thing I have tried along the same line. I was meeting with a family of five one day and had planned to use the videotape. As is sometimes the nature of these machines, it was not working and the technician was not available, so I took in an audio tape recorder as a compromise, and that would not work (I'm very bad with machines). The family was all prepared for something to happen, so I decided to try a feedback system within the family. I had the father, mother, and oldest daughter sit around a table discussing a disagreement they had in order to arrive at some resolution, and the other two children and I watched them with the idea that we were going to be critics. By "critics" I mean that we would provide feedback to those who were having the discussion. When they finished, they found another place to sit, and we, the observers, took their positions at the table to talk about what we had seen. We also role-played how it looked to us. It seemed to me as though the two children observers were better able to discuss clearly the things they had seen and what had bothered them about those three members who were interacting than they would have been had we all been sitting facing one another. At times some distance is useful. After this the whole family again came together to discuss feelings about the kids' reactions to what had gone on.

Switching Roles

Another useful method of dealing with structural changes is to switch roles. This came to my attention as the result of a research study[4] aimed at studying the effect of switching roles; that is, the father took the mother's role, the mother the child's role, and the child took the father's role, both in families with children rated as "low-adjusted" and in families with children who were considered well-adjusted or well-adapted. The first thing we found out in the study was that all families had a terrible time trying to assume another person's role. However, as we measured it, the maladaptive families had tremendous difficulty doing this; some of them even refused to try. The procedure was, first, for the family triads to go through a discussion procedure in their own roles trying to reach resolutions of disagreements; the next phase was for them to do this again later but this time taking somebody else's role, and then do it once again in a different person's role, so that each person had a chance to play the other two roles; finally they again assumed their own roles.

The interesting thing to me about this was that the power ratings or influence ratings of family members changed drastically during role-playing; that is, the members' positions and how they interacted changed significantly, and the maladaptive families maintained these changes after they reverted to their own roles. What I am trying to say is that the adaptive families went into the role-play, did as good a job as they could at it, and when they reverted to their own roles they were once again pretty much the way they had been at the beginning. The maladaptive families changed a lot during the role-playing procedure and maintained the change for some time afterward. The implication, though it has not been checked out thoroughly, would be that if the system is unstable or unsatisfying, an intervention at that point may prove expedient and a change is more likely to occur. On the other hand, adaptive families are perhaps functioning in a satisfactory enough way that they do not need to consider or grasp at a drastic change in the system. This shifting of roles in role-playing is another thing we have been using to some extent in working with families.

Behavior Modification Method

One other approach which I think is rather unusual is used by Jerry Patterson, a psychologist in Oregon. He has been working from a behavioral modification basis and is interested in finding ways of diagnosing disruptions in family systems. He makes observations in both laboratory and home settings of all possible dyads within the family and obtains ratios of the positive and negative reinforcers for each dyad, in other words, how many times each member of the dyad talks to the other in positive and negative terms. What his early results tend to show is that if any one dyad in the family has a ratio which varies a great deal from the rough average of all other dyads, you can predict that one member of the dyad will be labeled a symptom bearer. Let me go over that once again, because the terms sometimes get confusing. What he does is look at all possible pairs in the family to check on the number of positive and negative statements and interactions that take place between them; if any pair in the system has either too many or too few interactions, deviating from the average of all dyads, one member of the pair is likely to be the symptom bearer in this structure.

His approach to changing this is intriguing. Unlike some behavior modification approaches, what he does is to go into the family's home. He deals with lower socioeconomic, poorly educated parents, with families who are not likely to present themselves to clinics or other centers, and so he starts out with the premise that he has to sell these people in some way on making changes. The first kind of intervention that he might want to make is to encourage a greater degree of interaction between a pair who interact very little.

I will share with you the general details of a case I heard Patterson describe at an informal meeting with a group of psychologists. There was a seven-year-old boy in a large family whose problem was that he liked to burn up cars. He would go to a local used-car lot, make his way into a car, set it on fire, and then go home. His father sat in front of the TV a lot and seldom noticed the boy; the mother was always busy in the kitchen; so they never knew when he was coming or going. He had set fire to several cars, and the police were getting kind of upset about it.

Patterson had been working with the family for some time, trying to get them to pay a little more attention to the child, but to no avail. The father would never leave the TV set, and Patterson could not think of a way to get him away from it. He worked out a plan for the mother. She was very interested in learning how to drive a car—it would free her, make her a little more independent than she had been. She could earn points for driving lessons by increasing her interaction with the boy. This she did, and their relationship improved. He could find nothing, however, that the father wanted more than the TV, and he could not use that as the incentive because the father wouldn't let him turn it off. Patterson felt that he had to find some way to get the father interested.

Just at this point, after the boy had burned another car, some law-enforcement official called Patterson and told him that while they were not sure what should be done with this child, something had to be done, so they were thinking of holding him at the jail. Patterson said, "Why don't you do that until I tell you it's all right for him to go home." Then he went to the home and talked to the family, especially the father, about what had happened, and said he did not know exactly when the child would be released because it depended on the father. The father left the TV set, became really angry (no cops were going to do that to his kid!), ran down to the jail, and made all kinds of promises about what he would do when he took the boy home. Unfortunately, when they got back home what he did after a day or two was to return to the TV set.

While I am not sure of the eventual outcome of this case, it illustrates how incentives may be incorporated in family therapy. The use of some kind of incentive for people to make them more open to change has a lot of possibilities, particularly for families below middle class who are not easily engaged in traditional "talking" therapy.

A similar method to institute change was used in a project dealing with the problem of school dropouts. Those working on the project began by paying these high-school kids who had quit school for going back to school and attending regularly. They got money if they just went to school. After that behavior was established, they began to pay them only if they earned higher grades. And the third step was that the parents were paid if the kids received higher grades. Here you see the attempt to build in a value system which would encourage the parents to be interested in what the kids were doing. We may have some concern about whether or not this is the right way to handle dropouts; I only mention it because it is one way of getting some kind of movement and change.

I have just gone through a number of different approaches to structural interventions, and the list is certainly not exhausted. I offer these only as some examples of what is being done. It remains for us to employ our creativity to develop the approach which seems to work most effectively with the families we see.

Triads and Power

One thing I want to emphasize—and I touched on this earlier—is the triangle of social interaction. Theodore Caplow has written a clever little book called *Two Against One: Coalitions in Triads*[5] in which he develops a theory about the coalitions that take place in three-person groups. Ever since the time of Georg Simmel, the sociologist, people have looked upon the basic social process occurring between people as being triangular or triadic; but in reality there cannot be a three-person interaction, only a shifting two-person interaction, with the third member serving as an audience. This means that the three-person group is inherently unstable because of its natural tendency to shift and to divide into a coalition of two partners facing one opponent. In his early writings Simmel stated that ranging from a conversation among three people that lasts only an hour to a permanent family of three, there is no triad in which a dissent between any two elements does not occur from time to time and in which the third member does not play a mediating role. This has a lot of significance for us as we think about family systems.

Consider now a hypothetical natural history of a family triad. In a family of three with a young child, typically the father, as the wage earner, holds the greatest amount of power, the mother has the next greatest amount, and the child the least. In this situation the father has more power than the mother and child together. Generally, in the earlier years of the family, this is the pattern you find.

However, as the child grows in age and strength, his power also is likely to increase, so that the time arrives when the father still has greater power than the mother, but the child approaches equality of power with the mother. Then we have the situation in which the mother and child are equal in power as the child grows up, and the father is approximately equal to their coalition. This would be about the time the child is going into the teen-age years.

What we often see is that as the child grows even larger and stronger, his power increases to the point where it appears to exceed the mother's. Now she has a real problem. If she has used a coalition of herself with her son (and this is more typical with a son than a daughter) to balance off the husband's power, when that son leaves the family home in the normal course of events, the mother is left alone with the father and is on the light side of the power scale. What you would hope to see happen in this hy-

pothetical history of a family would be that as the child's power grows, the mother and father form a conservative coalition, not only to stand off the increasing power of the child but to strengthen their union, since they must continue to live together after the child leaves the home. Unfortunately, and especially in families who are experiencing some kind of difficulty in their relationships, this does not always occur. What happens is that the mother-child coalition is maintained so that either the kid cannot leave home or he does leave and the mother experiences some kind of disturbance.

I remember one family I saw in a veterans hospital not too long ago. The hospitalized male patient was the youngest of a family of seven, the son of a first-generation Italian couple. The parents came with the son for a conjoint interview. The other children had grown up, gotten married, and gone as far away from home as they could. The patient was twenty-nine-years-old and was described as being the nicest boy you could ever know. He would lend you money. If you ever needed anything, just ask and he was there. He was very solicitous and concerned about his parents. During the interview the mother asked him, "What can I do for you? You know we would do anything for you." He said, "Well, you might start by getting married." At this point the mother said, "What are you saying? You see, Doctor, how he talks! Ask him a simple, clear question, and he talks crazy! That's his illness!" The son got the message and started backing down.

In subsequent sessions, however, it became easier to understand what he meant. In the early days of the marriage the father was a laborer who worked very hard and played very hard. He drank. He made the rounds of the taverns, really had a high old time, and stayed away from his wife much of the time. But that was the system—he worked and played, and she was devoted to the home and kids. About the age of fifty the father started to burn out and slow down. He did not drink so much, did not run around. But he and his wife did not even know how to talk to each other; he did not know how to touch her. We have been finding out how important that is. Then we began translating the son's comment about their getting married into action and helped them have a symbolic marriage (with the father courting the mother again), until we were finally able to get them functioning as an interactive pair to the point where the son could leave the family home and live by himself. I bring this up because this is an example of something which happens a lot of times, and people really have little awareness or understanding of the kinds of coalitions they are getting into and for what purposes.

Changing to the Unknown

Let's turn our attention now to the problem of inducing change in systems. I remember attending a psychology convention in San Francisco a couple of years ago, and Eric Hoffer, the longshoreman, was there talking to a group of community psychologists. The chairman, interviewing Mr. Hoffer, said, "Mr. Hoffer, how do you go about getting people to change?" and Hoffer said, in his inimitable way, "Can't be done, can't be done. You know about Moses and what it took for him to change those slaves into free men? He had to take them into the desert for thirty years. What we need here in this country is more deserts." About fifteen minutes later he directly contradicted himself, because he actually has a deep belief in change. This caused the interviewer to ask, "Mr. Hoffer, how come you're not consistent?" and he said, "Why should I be consistent? I'm just here throwing out ideas. You be consistent!"

What I believe he was talking about, which you can all recognize, is the ambivalence in many of us, the tremendous mixed feelings about change even when we are greatly dissatisfied. This may be one of the reasons why dealing with families at a time of crisis often can produce quick, dramatic changes. They are unsettled. They have a real problem confronting them. Let's say one of the members has made a suicidal attempt, or one of them is in danger of being hospitalized, or there has been a bad experience with drugs. If it is possible to intervene at that moment or as quickly as possible, the system probably is so unsteady and has so much dissatisfaction within it that something can be accomplished rather quickly. Perhaps this has some bearing on the work that is being done by the crisis intervention team at Denver, which Dr. Taschman discussed earlier, in which hospitalization was found to be unnecessary for 84 percent of the patients seeking admission. The crisis team works with families at the precise time when those families are desperately needing and wanting to change.

Obviously most of the families you will see will not be in such desperate straits. Usually what we are confronted with are systems in which there is some degree of dissatisfaction but also tremendous fear and concern about changing to the unknown. At least you know what you've got, but you don't know what you are going to get.

This reminds me of all the talk about needing to have insight or understanding before change can take place. I once heard an analyst at a convention say, "Insight [by which he meant understanding] never cured anybody, anytime, of anything except ignorance." What I think he was getting at was not that understanding or insights are not useful and important, but rather that understanding usually will follow when a person has experienced a change in his relationships with the significant others in his life situation. After working out the change, then understanding can come.

Preparing People to Change

What would be closest to home for you right now, as an example, would be the new understandings you have about yourself and your relationship with others after engaging in the exercises Virginia Satir suggested earlier. I cannot imagine how anybody would have been able to tell you anything before you had the actual experiences that would have helped you understand what would happen.

One of the toughest jobs facing all of us is to prepare people to participate in the change processes. Here you are participating in some good examples of ways to get people to enter into situations which are potentially fearful. You did not know what was going to happen ahead of time, but having undergone the experiences you are aware that you have grown a little and that you know a little more—and that frees you a little more. This is the job we have to face with families, to help them risk changing to the unknown.

A basic problem, which we have continually stressed, is how to make people aware of how they are behaving. From what I have discovered using videotapes with families I can only reiterate what Virginia Satir has already said: seeing themselves on film is overwhelmingly amazing to people who have never observed themselves in action, and "seeing yourself as others see you" is a tremendous impetus in itself for helping people change. I remember one family in which the mother was complaining about *her* mother. After we taped the family interaction and she watched the replay, she said, "My God! I'm just like my mother! Exactly like her!" She had never been aware of this before.

Before we demonstrate yet another technique for intervention, I want you to think about the implications of this little story, which came to my mind in regard to the necessity for at least three alternatives in a decision-making situation instead of "the one and only way" or the two-pronged dilemma. The Zen master was teaching his pupils gathered around him, and he said, "If somebody doesn't say something very profound, I am going to kill this cat I am holding. On the other hand, if somebody does say something very profound, I shall kill the cat." The students were baffled—they didn't know what to do—so they did nothing. The Zen master killed the cat. The next day he talked with another group of students about this, and as he spoke one of the students took his shoes off, put them on top of his head, and walked out of the room. The Zen master said, "If that man had been here yesterday, the cat would still be alive."

Revealed Differences Method

Let me introduce to you now a simulated family. This is the Smith family: Mr. Smith, who is a farmer; Mrs. Smith, a housewife; and Mary, their fifteen-year-old daughter. We are going to illustrate a technique which I have used in research and clinical work and which has been utilized by many other researchers and therapists. This is the Revealed Differences Method and it is one of the best ways I know of to engage people in interactions when they are self-conscious or have stage fright or some feelings which make them reluctant to have their interactions observed at the outset. [6]

Each member of the family receives a questionnaire dealing with hypothetical family situations, and they fill out the questionnaire independently, without talking to the others, giving what they individually consider to be the best answers to the questions. When they finish, you look the papers over to find the questions on which their answers disagree. Then the members of the family discuss each disagreement and resolve the differences between them. This is useful for recording and replaying to the family so they can see how they interact.

The Smith family had completed the questionnaire forms. After the description of each controversial issue, the family's responses, designed to resolve any differences, are given.

Controversial Issue #1

An executive must decide which of two supervisors to promote. One of the supervisors, Bill, keeps his group running very smoothly. He has a real talent for attending to all the details necessary to prevent crises from occurring. The other supervisor, Harry, is sometimes short with people and is less careful about details. When swift action on an important decision is required, however, you can count on him to meet the challenge. Which would you promote?

Father and daughter said they would promote Bill; Mother said she would promote Harry.

Father: Well, it seems we have a difference of opinion. Should we just discuss this together? I'll share my feelings first and then let the wife and daughter get in here. I guess my only concern there was that the fellow who could get along day by day, week after week, keep things running smooth, get along with his employees and get the most out of them would be the fellow that would wear the longest maybe. What about you, Daughter?

Daughter: I think I would get impatient with someone who was short with me. I want people to respect me all the time and not make cutting remarks to me, and I would select a supervisor who would keep things running smoothly all the time.

Mother: I was thinking of the executive who must make the decision, and although Bill kept things running smoothly, I felt that there might be things in this company about which they really had to make quick decisions. And although the other man was short with people, he might be able to come through in really crisis situations much better than the first person.

Father: Now part of our job here is to kind of work out our difference. Anybody have any suggestions?

Daughter: I think Mother should come over to our side because it's two against one.

Mother: Well, Mother comes over to your side quite often, but I might just come over this time. There might be something else that I want you to come over on my side for.

Father: There's the resolution.

Controversial Issue #2

Fifteen-year-old Judy is spending an evening with a friend who lives in an apartment two floors below her. Her parents are out for the evening and have told her they will not be back until midnight, but they want her to be home no later than ten o'clock because it is a school night. Judy and her friend finish work shortly after ten and her friend suggests that they fix themselves a snack. Judy agrees, but since she probably won't get home un-

til ten-thirty or so, she is a little worried. Should she be?

Father says yes, she should. Mother and daughter say no, she shouldn't.

Father: Well, Sis, you feel like you need a little more time or something? Is that it? Or . . .

Daughter: I feel that thirty minutes isn't all that much time, that I shouldn't have to worry about it at fifteen. I should be able to choose when it's all right to stay out thirty minutes later.

Father: Well, I can see your point there. I just kind of wondered about whether, you know, eating a baloney sandwich at ten-thirty at night was really that important? More important than our pre-agreed—maybe we didn't agree on it—more important than my edict? What do you think about this, Mom?

Mother: Can I make an offhand comment? In first answering this I think I really felt that she should not have stayed over, that she should have gone, say, at ten, but I was trying to get this done hurriedly, so I wrote no. I think she should have been a little bit worried, but it probably would have been all right if she stayed over until ten-thirty.

Father: As long as we trust each other and can depend on each other as keeping our commitments, why I think that's the most important thing. I would not be that worried and I trust you, but there is some security for all of us, I think, in being where we are supposed to be. We won't banish you if you don't make it.

Daughter: And I feel you should trust me enough to trust my judgment.

Father: That's a good point, Sis, a good point.

Daughter: Does that mean the next time I'm invited over there to study and want to stay thirty minutes later that I won't have to go through all this mess again?

Father: It means if we can't be reached on the phone, you don't need to be so scared.

Controversial Issue #3

The most important things that happen to people are (a) the result of circumstances beyond their control, or (b) more the result of their own efforts.

The daughter agrees with (b), and both father and mother agree with (a).

Father: That's kind of a hard one. I guess I was just kind of being personal there. I think I was just kind of sharing. Many of the really important things that have happened to me have gone this way. Maybe that was not the way the world was created but just kind of my experience.

Daughter: Well, what were some of the things you were thinking of? I was thinking about grades and getting dates with the right fellows, and getting elected cheerleader, and things like that. I think those are the result of your own efforts.

Father: Well, for one thing, you know, getting born was kind of important, and I had little to do with that, kind of an innocent party, and (*laughing*) your mother chased me for so long I really had no . . . (*more laughter*). You know, seriously, some of the big growth times in my life haven't been things I sought after but they've been things I've kinda been forced into, and the struggle through them has turned out to be the most important times of my life. I don't really want to put down your efforts. Maybe you'll be more successful in controlling your life than I was in controlling mine.

Mother: I guess I was thinking, although I might be working on one thing, that really the most important thing was a circumstance that I wasn't even expecting. This is what I was thinking of.

Father: I think this has a good side too. Maybe this is a part of the generation gap that's kind of good. Maybe you will be able to really make plans and have both the gumption and determination to see them through. I think this is fine.

Mother: So, Mary wants to be the cheerleader and that's what she is working on now.

Daughter: Well, I guess that could be if you consider that when you are working on one thing something else wonderful may happen, and perhaps we could all accept each one partially. I could accept each one partially.

You will notice that one of the nice things about this technique is that the given situations often become very personalized. You can choose the kinds of coalitions you want to observe by selecting items for discussion that the family disagreed on in certain combinations. For example, ordinarily in a typical full procedure you would choose three items where the father is the isolate and the mother and child form a coalition, three where the mother is the isolate, three where the child is the isolate, and then two items of disagreement for each dyad.

What I want to impress upon you is that you do not pay so much attention to the content (and a lot of people make the mistake of getting caught up with the subject matter) as to the process the family goes through in arriving at resolutions. Maladaptive families have a terrible time reaching any decision, and so they choose to "agree to disagree" rather than arriving at a new or creative resolution of the disagreement. All you are asking them to do is to reach a resolution of the problem, but the way they go about it is what is of primary interest.

Another point I want to make is that if you keep score on their decisions, then you begin to get a picture of who wins, who has the power. In this particular demonstration, one of the rules, it seems (although we really did not try to check this out), was that the coalition always wins or has more weight, or gets the isolate to change or modify his position. This would be a typical conservative, family-coalition pattern. If this kind of pattern continued as you were working with a real family, you might wonder if any one individual, regardless of content, was ever able to break the pattern and get the others to agree with the isolate. This would be an instance of power. In one family we tried this with, the mother won every decision whether she was aligned with the father or child or was an isolate.

One thing which I found interesting in this "made-up" family was that it looked like the coalition was between daughter and father, with mother the possible power behind the throne, a kind of cross-generational coalition.

This technique can be used for many purposes. One could be simply to provide some materials for the family to deal with while the therapist intervenes. Another would be for evaluation, that is to use it at the outset when people first come seeking assistance, to see how they are functioning at that stage, and then have them repeat it at various stages or after therapy is completed. Or it can be videotaped for the family to watch, rate what they like and dislike, and decide what they want to change. As has been said before, people really do not have much awareness of their patterns of interaction until you provide them with feedback.

One word of caution: after giving the family the inventory to complete, you should say as little as possible, so that people will not try to structure things for themselves ahead of time. You could inadvertently influence how they respond to the items.

Summary

We have looked at some of the characteristics of family structures and interactions and considered various methods of intervening in family systems without becoming sucked into them. I have stressed the importance of the processes rather than the actual subject matter of the interaction. The methods discussed were convening the family social system network to expand the size of the family and open up possibilities for the formation of new coalitions; focusing on the marital couple as the vital subsystem of the family; Fulweiler's method of observing the family with a one-way mirror and earphones; use of a co-therapist; working with groups of families; using videotapes to paint self-portraits which can be erased and repainted; critical observation of one subgroup of the family by another subgroup; switching roles in role-playing; a behavior modification approach using tangible incentives for changing behavior; and the Revealed Differences Method. In discussing the family triad, I have attempted to convey some idea of the strength and insidious nature of power coalitions which are formed over the years. And finally I gave some examples to illustrate how the Revealed Differences Method can be utilized.

NOTES

1. Ross V. Speck, "Psychotherapy of the Social Network of a Schizophrenic Family," *Family Process*, 6, no. 2 (1967), 208-214.

2. "No-Man's Land," an interview with Charles R. Fulweiler, in *Techniques of Family Therapy*, ed. Jay Haley and Lynn Hoffman (New York: Basic Books, 1967), pp. 3-96.

3. "The Growing Edge," an interview with Carl A. Whitaker, in *Techniques of Family Therapy*, pp. 265-360.

4. Thomas Reilly, "Role Enactment in Family Triads." Doctoral dissertation, University of Kansas, 1966.

5. Theodore Caplow, *Two Against One: Coalitions in Triads* (Englewood Cliffs, N.J.: Prentice-Hall, 1969).

6. The instrument used is the Revealed Difference Inventory, which is available from Dr. Fred Strodtbeck of the Department of Psychology, University of Chicago.

Chapter 6

Problems and Pitfalls in
Working with Families

An Interview with Virginia Satir

Question: How do you go about getting the family to take part in instructive role-playing and other awareness and communication experiences? What are the difficulties usually encountered?

Let me answer in this way. People who come to me for help arrive by various routes. Sometimes a judge orders them to obtain therapy. How well I remember the first time a family came to me because of a court order. They came in, sat down, and stared at me. When I asked them why they were there, they said, "Don't you know?" And I said, "No!" "Well," they said, "the judge sentenced us." And I said, "What judge?!" Eventually we got everything straightened out. The point I want to make is that no matter what the reason is for those bodies to be in front of me —whether they were compelled to be there by a judge's sentence, whether somebody they believed told them they could get help by coming to me, or whether they came completely of their own choosing—whatever the reason, initially there are certain common factors. One, they are not aware of how they could do anything differently from the way they have been doing things; two, they are strangers to me and I am a stranger to them; three, they expect from me what they have been getting from all the other people in their lives before; and four, in addition to those expectations, they will expect me to perform miracles.

Foundation of Trust

Before people can be asked to take risks, the first item on the agenda has to be the development of trust. Whatever it takes to engender trust within everyone in the group is what you must do before you can say to them, "Hey, I've got something I think might work. Would you be willing to try it?" With the Revealed Differences Inventory method, which helps people look at their differences without dying, one of the first things the therapist would do would be to arrive at the point of trust, when there is a willingness to take a risk. Then he would say, "I wonder if you would try something," or "I have something that might be useful," and proceed to explain what to do.

Any method—whether it is helping people to participate in the dyadic and triadic games, role-playing, sculpturing stances, or taking any kind of risk—rests on a cushion of trust. Trust is relatively easily engendered if you are congruent. It usually takes a minimum of three interchanges for a person to have trust in someone else. But however long it may take, the building of trust precedes everything else. Once trust is established, you then can explain what it is you want people to try, and ask, "Will you have this experience?"

Steps in the Therapeutic Process

I have been thinking about the actual steps which make it possible for people to change. The first step is the experience of trust. The second is the development of awareness. That means knowing more about what you are doing, and it must be experiential. You find out by something that you do, whether it is looking at a videotape, doing the exercises and games· like the ones presented earlier here, or whatever the new experience may be which the therapeutic situation can produce. Through the development of new awareness comes new understanding. The next step is the application of that new understanding within the framework of having multiple options available when making decisions. At that point all that remains is the opportunity to practice these new behaviors.

These are the steps: developing trust, developing awareness through experience, making new understandings possible, the expression and application of those understandings, and the experience of putting them into use or practicing what has been learned. This is the typical progression. Everything rests on the first step, the foundation of trust. Only after establishing that can you bring into play the creativity needed to help people to see more of what is going on in their interactions experientially through role-playing and the communications exercises. Trust is the life's blood of what makes it possible to see new horizons and reach new understandings.

You see, I do not believe I have ever had a family or group of families which, in terms of my experiences with them, was duplicated. Just as the alphabet has only twenty-six letters but by rearranging those letters we have thousands of words, so we have myriad combinations giving diversity to family therapy. However, there is an underlying theme always present, and my theme is the development of the sense of self-worth and the freedom to comment. Those are the keys which make it possible for people to grow.

Strong Invitation vs. Demand

Part of the therapist's job, in my opinion, is teaching; but those who are being taught must take part voluntarily. When a group and I work together, I give very strong support for taking a risk, but I never make a demand. What this means is that if they say no to something I ask them to do, it is more important for me to let them know that I hear their refusal than it is for them to obey me. This is the difference between a demand and a strong invitation. No one will ever suffer at my hands because they say no. What often happens is that the therapist does not know how to make strong invitations which are accompanied by trust and the willingness to take a risk. What if I ask you to try something and you refuse, and then ten minutes later I say, "Well, if you didn't want to try what I suggested, what the hell are you doing here?" Immediately I have undone everything that has gone before—I've been incongruent. Developing trust and being a strong inviter means being a congruent inviter, not a steamroller. Only then will the opportunities for growth and change open up. What I have found is that it is all a matter of congruency.

Techniques in Proper Context

I have rarely had difficulty getting people to take risks, but I do not begin by asking them to do so. You see, just learning a technique can be dangerous and disappointing. A very sad thing happened one time along this line. I was conducting a ten-session training program with the rehabilitation service at the University of Washington. We were in our ninth session and were doing some communication work with our hands; sometimes when people are unable to talk they can communicate through their hands. We had been working all day, and a nurse came into the group for the first time about three o'clock that afternoon. She saw what we were doing and concluded that what was helpful was to get people to hold hands. She sensed the atmosphere that had developed in the room, but she had not observed what led up to it. She went back to her ward, immediately said, "Okay, kids, everybody hold hands," and the place blew apart. It was almost like asking everybody to have intercourse—no real basis for the experience had been provided.

To be useful any technique must emanate from what is going on at that moment in time because it seems to fit, and it is effective only within a context of trust. I cannot overemphasize that point. This is why I cannot teach people techniques; I can only teach them some ways in which they can use themselves when certain things happen. So I could never teach you or anybody "how to do family therapy." As the leader, I teach people by helping them to come to their own awareness and to become familiar with the kinds of interaction phenomena that people are involved in.

One phenomenon, for instance, relates to the triangle. Do you know what really makes trouble in the triangle? It is when the observer feels that because he is not part of the interaction he is not any good—he is left out. What people become aware of is that there is no way in the world when you are in the presence of two or more other people that you can be continually, manifestly involved. It is not possible. Nature took care of that for us because we can only look at one point at a time. But a lot of people see this as "I am left out if you're not turned to me."

Once you begin to see that the biggest job you have is to help people to take risks on their own behalf, and that you *can* do it, various ways of helping them will occur to you. But if they occur to you when you are thinking, "Well, what did Virginia Satir do?" or "What did Jim Stachowiak do?" that will not get the job done. You must be in touch with the phenomenon of what you are trying to highlight, and then have it come to you, "Ah! It might be useful if I did this." Only when the idea evolves from that immediate situation will you be headed in the right direction. Also you have to keep in mind that what you do might not hit the mark. Remember there is nothing that says you must always be right, must always succeed. Many times I have said to families, "Let's try something," tentatively offering something that may or may not be helpful.

If you feel that any of the things you have learned here seem to fit in with what is going on with a group you are working with, you can say something like this: "You know, I heard about something the other day that might be useful to us here. I don't know if it will work, but would you take a chance?" What you do is let the process flow instead of being the "fancy-schmancy" therapist talking like a "fancy-schmancy" parent, "*I* know the right answer and *I'm* going to do the right thing." Instead you say, "Let's take a chance and see what happens—something may happen that will be useful." You let yourself off the omnipotent hook and let the other people off the obedience hook.

Role-Playing
I don't know what your experiences were if you participated in the exercises and interactions described in previous chapters,

but I am sure some of them had pain connected with them. As you look back you may see that you actually were in a threat situation. You lived through it, and you got some kind of awareness from it. Whether it was "Damn that woman for having me do this" or "I can't do things like that," you did have an experience. This is true of any of these experiential situations, including role-playing.

All that role-playing requires is that you portray or express what you already know about someone else. You know how someone else would feel because you know about yourself and how you would feel. You may not have committed all the acts. You may not have killed anybody, may not have raped anybody, may not have strangled anybody, may not have cheated anybody; but you know what it feels like to be afraid, to feel jealous, to feel hurt, to feel alive. You know all those things. You know what human feeling is, although you have not had exactly the same activities. Therefore, in role-playing you can consider yourself knowledgeable about human feeling. What you are able to do, then, is too let yourself play with a different form of behavior than what you are used to, which helps you ally with it. Everyone is capable (and I know this without ever asking anyone anything) of experiencing the feelings of somebody else and portraying them.

Role-playing has two very important aspects. Through role-playing a person is, in effect, demonstrating that he knows more than he thought he did. That is Number One. It is fascinating, for instance, when you ask the son, in a family where there has been trouble between a father and son, to role-play his idea of how his father feels. I have had some fantastic things happen when I said, "It looks like at this point in time you don't really know what it is like to be in each other's shoes, so let's reverse things for a moment. You, John, be your father, and you, Father, be John. Now how would you two deal with the son asking to use the car?" The results can be incredible. Role-playing is a very good means for tuning in on what the person already knows. How many parents feel so lonely and so ineffective with their children, but cannot express that. When they play the role of the children, they can let that feeling out.

Role-playing provides us with a rich variety of opportunities to help people do another thing, and that is to discover that they have more facets than they thought they had. Most people get stuck with "This is *the way* I am," twenty-four hours a day, three hundred and sixty-five days a year, and they are completely unaware of all the magnificent facets they possess for being many different ways. Role-play helps them achieve this awareness.

Many families that I have treated in the past use role-playing as a censoring device when they feel they are getting out of balance. Most of them recognize the danger signs—they begin to feel afraid and they begin to feel unloved. These are indications that the system is out of balance and they need to do some centering. One thing they do is to sculpture the body positions illustrating how they are feeling at that moment about their ways of communicating. This brings them to a new awareness, and they can go on from there.

I worked with a family not long ago in which there was a six-year-old boy. One of the stress patterns between his parents was that the mother would blame and the father would placate. This had come out in our work together. The mother wrote to me later and said, "You know, we really have a great time, because every time Charley and I get into our old pattern, Paul says, 'Hey, Mom, hey, Pa! You know you are blaming and placating again!' " That was all he had to say. He didn't have to say, "How terrible you are in the way you treat each other," or anything about the content of what was going on. All he mentioned was his awareness of the process. This from a six-year-old. The mother was joyfully saying that when they lost their center, somebody else there could bring them back into balance. Many creative things can happen.

Role-playing takes many forms. One is the psychodrama; another is exchanging roles. All the forms of role-playing make it possible for the person to use his own self-knowledge on the feeling level to be able to understand what it is like to walk in somebody else's shoes. For example, if you were to role-play your mother right now, you would bring a lot more to the role than you would have before you started thinking of her as a person.

Perhaps the biggest problem is removing the apprehension that "If I open myself to role-playing, I will stand revealed to everybody." Everyone expects that when there is a revelation all the dirt falls out. Actually there is a lot more there than dirt; while there is a certain amount of that, there also is a lot of realness and a lot of creativity, and that comes out too.

Question: Virginia, is there a place for honest bargaining? When someone is working with people and is not sure of himself and feels he needs a little time to think things through, can he simply say he doesn't know what to do?

I think that is a marvelous question. Is there anyplace for saying that you don't know? There surely is, and do you know where that place is? Wherever you don't know! I can't pretend to know when I don't. Can you? Did you ever try to carry on as though you knew when you didn't? This makes an interesting spectacle on the videotape. Anybody seeing you in that circumstance will immediately recognize what is going on. There is a lot of pain and burden in trying to behave as though you know when you don't.

Once in Palo Alto I had a group of eight people who trained intensively with me. For them, one of the most unnerving things that could happen when they were working with a family was to come to a point where they didn't know what to do. At first they felt they had been poor students if they didn't know everything. We had to work that out, because the fact is that when you meet something new the chances are that you will not know what to do. That's all right. When these people were able to be honest and say to the family, "Well, right now I don't know; I wonder if anybody knows more about it than I do," the chances were pretty good that someone had something to contribute, and sometimes it was a four-year-old. Of course, this was a very revealing thing. However, quite often no one had any suggestions. By the way, these student therapists were Ph.D.s, M.D.s, and M.S.W.s for the most part, all with experience, so when I talk about students I am not talking about complete novices. Sometimes they would say, "Well, I don't know, but I think there is somebody behind the screen watching us, so let's ask them for help." It is honorable to get help. It is honorable to say you don't know when you don't, and you can proceed from there with honesty, and search together with the family.

Question: If each person is to be congruent with himself, what happens when "A" wants to do "X" and "B" wants to do "Y"?

That is a very interesting, basic question. You know, no one ever "promised you a rose garden." The problems of management that arise with people who have attained what I call the "integrated state" are different from the problems of those who have not. The possibility always exists with human beings that two people will not be in the same state in terms of time or place. Sometimes with a married couple, for instance, the husband wants to go to the movie at seven o'clock and the wife doesn't want to go to a movie at seven o'clock. This is not an unusual kind of thing. The question is how do people deal with that if they are really integrated.

First of all, hubbie says, "I want to go to a movie." He doesn't say, "Wouldn't you like to go to a movie, dear?" He makes a direct statement: "I want to go to a movie." Whereupon wife says, "Well, as for me, I don't want to go to a movie right now," instead of, "How dare you ask me when you know I'm dead tired." The husband has choices at that point. He can say, "Okay, I respect that. I'll go by myself," or "Gee, would you consider again? I don't mind if you're too tired to be a great companion; just hold my hand once in a while." What has happened is that the negotiation has changed. The wife does not now have to go to the movie because she should enjoy it; she can go because she would like to be there for her husband at that particular time.

Not everybody has the same investment all the time. The difficulty lies within the nature of the contract. Do you know what I mean by that? Somebody wants you to go somewhere with them and you don't want to go. The contract is that you should enjoy it as much as the other person and if you don't something is wrong with you.

In the congruent, integrated state, when there is a difference you negotiate. Some people try to behave as though there is some kind of negotiation in a situation of differentness which is joyful for everybody. I think this has some of the shades of what you absorbed when you were growing up from your mother telling you that if you were good, nothing bad would happen to you, you would never have any pain. She forgot that "no" always brings pain. What we can get rid of is the secondary pain, that there is something wrong with *you* because there is "no" in the world.

If you are congruent, you are solving a new kind of problem; you are into the problem of negotiation. There is no easy, fairy-tale ending. The point is that when you are dealing with the reality and the literalness of the situation, you really can negotiate. What authority has decreed that because you love me or I love you that means I always do what you want me to or you always do what I want you to; or if you don't like spinach just as much as I do that means you don't love me?

Love Contracts

This brings up the whole question of what are the contracts about love? One contract is "If you love me, you will never be angry with me." Another contract surrounding love with some people is "If you love me, you will always know what I want and give it to me without my asking." Another, which people join in and call love, is "I will always see to it that you are happy and you will see to it that I am happy." This one is basically dishonest, because you know such a thing can never happen. You can become unhappy all on your own—did you ever have a boil? To come to grips with what a love contract should be about, it imposes no ties; and unless it provides freedom for people to be real within it, it is going to be a hamstringing, ball-and-chain experience.

Many women tell me how guilty they feel when they want to do something on their own because it would take them away from their mothering duties, or their husbands would be mad at them. What people try to do is get rid of the bind of such contracts. After a while, when the bind begins to strangle them, they get sick or go crazy or run away. We have done terrible things under the guise of love. You remember how it went when you were a child. "If you love Mother and Father, you will do what we tell you." That was a way of control, and our parents did not use it to hurt us. They were desperate to find a way to control us, and they saw the situation as being an emergency calling for the strongest control. As children we could not be aware of all this. Many times adults are unaware of their own contracts of love.

Maintaining Contact with Feelings

You may remember my analogy of the pot and feelings of self-worth. I can only maintain the composure of the integrated posture if one does not hook my pot. If someone calls me an aggressive bitch, if he had hooked my pot, I would likely tell him, Who the hell are *you* to tell *me* what kind of person I am!" The point is your pot is either hooked or it isn't. You cannot pretend. What makes for congruency is to say that it is, instead of trying to make believe that it isn't. Whatever, wherever I am at a moment in time, that is where I am. I can't be different. If something happens to make me feel angry or dizzy or off-center to the point where I recognize what is going on, then I say so.

When you have people really blasting back and forth at each other, they are not in touch with what they are doing. One of the things that needs to happen is for them to get in touch with it, but that comes later. What makes for congruency is that you can let yourself know where and how you are. Many people, probably 95 percent of the world, have had no training in how to be in touch with their feelings. Most of what you are taught when you are growing up has to do with how to be good and how to do things right.

I'll tell you the difference. You know how it goes about taking out the garbage. You will have noticed that every home has garbage. And you are aware that garbage is essential. Yet we regard it as bad. Because we have garbage and not many plans for reusing it, we usually throw it out. Somebody has to carry out the garbage, usually an eight-year-old boy—and if you don't have an eight-year-old boy, an eight-year-old girl will do. (Incidentally, many people feel like the garbage that is being thrown away.) Nobody arranges garbage aesthetically, so it is not pleasant to see, and nobody sprinkles it with Chanel No. 5 to make it smell

good. So when it stinks and looks bad, if you were being congruent you would hold it at arm's length, wrinkle your nose, and
turn your head away to avoid the sight and smell as much as
possible. That would be congruent, and it has nothing to do with
grumbling all the way to the garbage can. But what do we say to
the young garbage "thrower-outer"? We say, "Look happy
while you carry it to the garbage can—it's character building."
That is the difference. People have a funny idea that if you look
happy you are going to do whatever you are supposed to do, and
I think nothing is farther from the truth.

Sometimes people get the idea that we are substituting another "should": that you should always be congruent. You cannot
always be congruent if you have to always be congruent. Congruency is a state of awareness, clearly stated, openly acknowledged. But you don't always understand. You are not always
able to be in the position of being aware. But you can be aware
that sometimes you are not aware. This may sound like double-
talk. It isn't. Just as in teaching people always to be polite, they
can try to do it but carried to its extreme it becomes phony and
stifling. I sometimes go to formal dinners, and the politeness is
nauseating. Everyone is like a fence post, a bunch of sticks, and
I can't wait to get away with some of them so we can really talk
and have some fun together. I have never found fence posts very
interesting, and neither have you. Have any of you ever gone to
some of these big gatherings where you might as well be there
without anybody else in the world? You look around and everybody is like a stick, and what better reason to get drunk! That is
why I think cocktail parties are bad; nobody feels that he is actually "with" the others. Perhaps that is only my personal reaction and no one else feels that way.

*Question: Could we discuss congruency a little more? Are you
saying that if a person is congruent within himself, he will be
able to respond in that manner to others? I was thinking of this
in terms of how the therapist responds. The way I looked at it
was that I would have trouble trying to deal with clients or families when I found myself caught up in not being congruent with
them. Is it a matter of being congruent with them or with yourself?*

With yourself. Let me ask you something. What happens when somebody you are interviewing stinks, literally stinks? What do you do? Whatever is going on in the situation, you have a reaction to it. Isn't that true? I use the example of stinking because I encounter it a lot.

If I am in an interview and somebody smells, I have a hard time trying to keep my attention off my nose. Because there is a great big taboo about telling people they smell (you know the soap routine about slipping a note under the door suggesting they use a certain kind of soap), I have learned to say, "I smell something that smells bad to me here, and while this is going on I am having a hard time thinking. I wonder if anybody else smells the same thing?" One of the things I discovered is that people do not smell their own smells; only other people smell them. This is another piece of awareness that people need to come in touch with. We don't hear our own voices, we don't smell our own smells, and we don't see ourselves unless we have worked on becoming aware of these things.

I have done some of my most effective work when I was able to comment openly on what was going on. Sometimes I see terrible behavior. One day I saw a father clout his little boy so forcefully that the boy flipped across the room and his face started to bleed. I felt all churned up inside and I felt outraged. That is what I told the father. I said, "I just wanted you to know what I am aware of feeling right now." My face reflected what I was feeling and saying. The man looked at me in absolute amazement. You see, I didn't tell him that he made me mad; I was dealing with what I was experiencing. He looked at me, greatly puzzled. I asked him, "What are you aware of feeling right now as I tell you how I feel?" He had never thought about this aspect; it opened up a whole new conception for him. Do you realize that as all of us grew up we had little access to what was going on inside of other people?

One time I was working with a woman who burned up her two children in a furnace. I could not do anything with that woman until I was able to admit the rage and the fear that I had. I did not say, "You made me feel this way." I said, "This is how it is with me." You know very well that you get involved with all kinds of the ugly things of life. People do not come into your office wearing Chanel No. 5; they come as they are. What I am talking about is your being real with yourself at that time. It is not easy, believe me, because all our training has been to behave as though we do not see what we see or smell what we smell.

I remember another time when a family came to me. This was the family: the woman came in on crutches, having lost a leg because of diabetes; one child had a "duck arm," an arm abnormally attached to the body; the next child had one ear missing; the third child had a wry face; and the father was the only one who was physically whole. This group came trooping in, and I began by saying, "I notice you don't have a leg; what happened?" Very soon tears were flooding the place, and do you know what they were about? Relief. People could talk about what they had not been able to talk about before with an outsider. Some of you must have had this same experience. You ask with genuine care about what you see, and then it can be talked about openly and straight. A whole different sort of communication might go like this: "Oh, I am so sorry. Something terrible must have happened to you." Or what would be even worse would be to pretend not to notice.

So the smells are there and the sights are there. I suppose if there is any real bravery in anybody, it consists of the courage and the ability to say straight out what they really see and hear—straight, not crooked. This is what I see; what happened? This is what I smell. This is how I feel about it. This is how I put it together. There is great healing power in that, in being straight.

Question: You have learned different ways of being able to do this with people, based also on your judgment of how they can receive your congruent response at that time. What I find puzzling is that it almost sounds as if you are saying that if you just express what is in you at that time, however you feel, you are being congruent and you should be able to elicit a congruent response in return. But what happens if this does not occur?

Then you go on to another transaction, and then another. It is not the end, you know, not in my experience. I have only had people walk out once in my whole career.

Let me show you what the point is. I am going to tell you in five ways that you stink. This is the hooker. *Placating:* "I hope you won't get mad at me. I had—there is—and maybe it comes from me, I don't know. But there is a funny smell. Oh, well, maybe I shouldn't mention it. . . ." *Blaming:* "For Christ's sake! Don't you ever take a bath? It stinks like hell in here!" *Super-reasonable:* "I understand from my experience that there is a certain potential for ill scents. I have a hunch that we are at that potential. . . ." *Irrelevant:* (gazes at the ceiling and walls in a distracted manner). *Congruent:* "I notice an odor in here. I smell it. Do you?"

Question: Aren't you really trying to get across that everyone must find the way which is real for him in his interactions with people?

Well, sure. But I don't consider any of the first four ways "real." They are avoiding ways of talking. What is difficult about these categories is that while they *are* real in the sense that people do behave that way, they are not the responses you want to make. You want to make the responses that deal with reality, the congruent ones. You can go on forever without knowing the kind of responses you are likely to elicit, but you can only elicit the "game" responses from people who are in the game—you can't elicit them from anybody else.

Question: We have talked a lot about the need for awareness of behavior on the part of our clients or trainees, and I would agree with you that if a person stays in this kind of work and makes any kind of growth and development on his own part, he should become more aware himself. What troubles me is that there are times when I have thought I was behaving congruently, and only later because of feedback from others or observing what had happened on videotape I saw that I had not been congruent. What then?

That is all right. When you find that something was missing that you had thought was there, you acknowledge that. People do the best they can, and there isn't any such thing as total awareness.

Once when I arrived at a conference, I didn't have any luggage. Why do you suppose I left it on my front porch? The awareness problem! It caused all kinds of difficulties to get my things. When I found out I didn't have the luggage, I felt silly inside, and I also started to get a few guilt feelings about what others had to do now because of my negligence. While all these feelings were going on inside me, I could have said, "You know, it was all the work I did that day. It was too much. Somebody should have helped me." I cannot deal with myself that way anymore. I cannot give myself that phony stuff. The fact is, I left it. I had to be willing to let myself experience all the difficulties I had to go through to get the luggage. But I cannot tell myself stories anymore—that it was somebody else's fault or something out there caused the trouble. I am willing to accept what happened and from now on try to help myself remember better. I don't ask myself to be perfect.

Question: Would you describe how you deal with your warm or positive feelings toward the person you are working with? This kind of thing may be difficult for the therapist.

That is right, it is. I deal with warm feelings toward people in the same way as any other feelings. It is probably easier for most people to handle hostility than intimacy. To say "I like you" is one of the most frightening things in the world because people are apprehensive about what the cost will be. But this is a very essential thing. So if I like somebody, I tell them.

This brings up something else, and that is the timing. If I can feel relatively centered with what is going on, there is a flow. I am just flowing with myself. When something comes up that stops the flow, I have to look at myself and the clues I am reacting to from others. I try to teach people the same thing. When in the flow of events the feeling comes, it is important to have the ability to say straight out to someone, "I like you." And it is not that "I like you because you did something for me and I am paying you back for it," but that "I like you without any strings." I believe we suffer more from a lack of intimacy than anything else. The warm feelings are very important, yet they are often feared. But don't you like a lot of the people you work with? You like them very much. Maybe some of you feel that when you like people, you shouldn't, that it will get in the way somehow. I hope you do not have that idea.

There is one rather sticky way in which you can like people, however, and that is when it carries the message "Because I like you, you should like me better than anybody else." This is something that often happens with child-care workers. They see the terrible parents and the lovable little children, and they express their liking to the children with the implication "Don't like anybody else." I am not talking about that kind of thing. What I am referring to is open expression of feelings: "I enjoy this," "I feel upset by this," "I feel puzzled by this." Warm affection is an important part of those human feelings. Many of us are yearning both for genuine, positive validation and genuine, negative response. Sometimes when a wife asks how she looks, she really wants to know. Don't forget that.

Question: Are you saying the way to deal with countertransference is first to acknowledge the feelings to yourself and then express them to the other person?

There is no rule about this. Just have the feelings straight with yourself. It is a pretty sure bet that within the course of a week or so the people you associate with will remind you of somebody you knew in the past, usually your mother or father. Learning for yourself whose hat you are putting on somebody else's head is very important. Often this is where I get a clue about how to proceed. I might say, "You know, when you look like that it reminds me of when I was five and my father was telling me 'don't.' And just at that moment I was suddenly feeling very young and helpless." Sometimes this has helped to clear the air, particularly in a situation where I realized I was not getting any place.

When your therapy does not move, for the most part there is something holding back the flow between the therapist and the family, and it may be the recollection of feelings about someone the therapist has known that one of the family members reminds him of.

Another impediment to the flow may be the feeling that you *must* help the family. I once had the governor of a state ask me to take a case. Though I was much too busy and did not have the time, I took the case against my better judgment. For three interviews nothing happened. Then I got in touch with my narcissism, my feeling of "Oh, boy! The governor wants *me*! And it is someone close to him, and wouldn't that be great!" When I told the client about all that and got past it, then we could get to work.

Question: I would like to know how to go about being straight and open in telling a person exactly how you feel. At times I feel I have a barrier and I just can't tell them, or I can't muster the courage to tell them, or, if I do, I feel that I shouldn't have and I have been too bold. I want to know how a person can feel natural about this kind of thing.

You are asking how you can feel natural about saying what you feel and think. One of the exercises that I ask the people who train with me to do is to practice making the following statements for five minutes: "I am feeling_____(fill in one word describing your feelings at this moment)." "I am thinking____ (fill in one word)." This is to help them become connected with the awareness and acknowledgment of their state. This is all new to most people. To be focused on your condition and to be able to say it without deception or embellishment is usually a new experience. "I am_____." And sometimes I ask people to do for ten minutes whatever they feel like doing and verbalize what they do with one word at the end of "I am_____." This is to sharpen the awareness. One can become aware of how frequently his states change and can also become more comfortable with making direct "I am" statements. This is very important.

For another thing, to strive to be congruent within yourself, to be able to express yourself more openly is a risk. At first it may have sounded as though congruence were being defined in terms of everything working out well. There is no guarantee at all that if you act congruently someone might not reject you. Who said that you were always 100 percent lovable anyway? Some may want to be congruent, but they also would like to have the guarantee that people are going to be very nice to them in return. If anyone wants a guarantee they will never face any unpleasantness, they are asking for the impossible.

All I am saying is that for me and the people that I have worked with, striving for congruency has seemed to be the way in which we can keep on the track of the reality of situations. Maybe some of you girls have had the experience of being pursued by a young man whom you couldn't stand. I don't know what you did, but when this happened to me in my salad days I would hide, I would get my mother to lie for me, and I would do all kinds of evasive things rather than come out and face the fact that he was just not for me. Going through all that amounted to a great deal of pain. What it boils down to is which pain do you want, the pain of being straight and taking your chances with what will happen, or the pain of feeling like you are a "nothing" and constantly calling yourself names? Which pain do you want? I elect the pain which deals honestly with the reality of the situation.

It takes two things, you know, to make a rejection: "no" plus "you are no damned good." That makes a rejection. In addition, somebody has to offer it and somebody has to buy it; it takes two people to make one rejection. The rejection has two parts; not only are you told "no," but you are told "no" because you are bad.

Question: What if the other person or the family says "no" or refuses to recognize what you are telling them? What if the client rejected your congruent statements about something smelling bad that you just illustrated?

The next thing would be to ask how they felt about my saying this, and they could tell me. The difficulty is that you have one foot in the matter of wanting to do something that works and the other foot in trying to find out how things really are. If the stink gets too bad and I have to say, "I'm sorry but I can't stand it here anymore," I have reshaped the contract by saying, in awareness, I cannot go on with this. What I lose, I lose.

This is a very important point: Is there any way you have no loss? I know of no way. When you help people get to the reality of a situation so they can make choices, while there is something gained by the choices made, the options rejected constitute losses. If you work in child-care services, when you take a child out of a bad family situation, it is the same thing. The question is not does losing mean you are no good or does winning mean you are great—it isn't either one. The winning-losing proposition is taken out of the self-worth "pot" and put into the frame of negotiation. I am neither good because I win nor bad because I lose.

Question: If something in a counseling situation makes you very angry, do you say something to the effect that "I am angry now," or do you say, "You make me angry"?

I would never say, "You make me angry." You are not responsible to me. I would say, "I want you to know that I am angry." That is an entirely different thing, a whole different kettle of fish.

Question: What would happen if the client then said, "What made you angry?"

You are ready at that point to give some kind of enlightenment. You can say, "When I heard this, this is what happened inside of me." The fact of the matter is that if you take any four people observing the same incident, one could laugh, another might be angry, somebody else would feel helpless. Nothing guarantees that everyone will have the same reaction; the reaction is always idiosyncratic. Haven't you noticed this when several members of your staff are working together with a family? For example, if there are small children in the family and a father is seen playing roughly with a little one, some women will be horrified, and a man right along with them will look at this as good training for maleness. He finds joy in an incident from which a woman will get terror. The action does not guarantee the reaction. I tell you what my reaction is and then I tell you how it came about.

This difference in reactions is quite common. I am sure you are familiar with it. It is one of the things that "bugs" people in families; the kids get different reactions from different parents from the same incident. Take a child who is sucking his thumb. I have seen fathers come along and slap that thumb. "Get the goddamned thing out of your mouth," they say. Mother comes along when he is sucking his thumb and gives the child a love pat. So what should he do with his thumb?

The importance of the congruent response is that it opens up an opportunity for you and me to get acquainted. It is not a matter of: "You did something that makes me mad, and it would make anybody mad. You are a bad person." This does not work, as you very well know. Rather it is: "When such and such happened, this is how I felt inside."

Exercises in Understanding Messages

Perhaps these questions and discussions will set new wheels turning and produce new ideas about how you might do things differently. We need to devote more attention now to the subject of the fifth mode of communicating, the congruent response, which is a process response.

To summarize, you would discover these important things in the dyadic exercises discussed earlier. If you try to have any effective communication when you are not on an eye-to-eye basis, the traps of misunderstanding become very big; and if you are not able to use your senses and free them to work for you instead of against you, you also will probably fall into traps. In addition you probably were able to get in touch with the fact that your internal intellectual and feeling experiences were always rich, but unless you knew how to share them, no one was any the wiser from your experiences.

Another obviously important aspect of congruent communication should be considered, that is the literal understanding. I would like to show you how to clarify literal understanding. If possible, select a partner and seat yourselves facing each other.

Exercise

Now here you are with another human being. Let your eyes close, and be in touch with the fact that you know there is another person in front of you. . . . Let yourself just be aware of all the samenesses you can be sure of and the unknown differentnesses which also are surely there. . . . Can you also, with your eyes still closed, let yourself know that the person in front of you has lived a significant number of years during which (because he is still living and breathing) he has had trillions of transactions that made it possible for him to exist. You do not know how or what he learned about how he should be. . . . Can you also let yourself be in touch with the fact that this person during every day and every minute of his life has learned something about the world we are in. . . .

What we have are two fountains of rich experience facing each other. Let yourself be aware of this. . . . If you can, let yourself be aware that anyone sitting in front of you would also be a rich fountain of experience. The question would be how many of these personal experiences do you have in common . . . ?

For a moment, would you let yourself imagine that in front of you sits someone from Nicaragua . . . a ninety-year-old person in a geriatric hospital . . . a man who earns his living doing scientific research . . . and you could imagine many others, each containing a rich fountain of experience. You have the awareness now of the reserves of experience each of you has, but you may not have had the particular experience that will help you understand the other person, and he may not have had the experience that would help you understand him. Perhaps some teaching will be called for. . . .

Just let your eyes open and look at this person, feeling your richness of experience and his. Even if this person were a sharecropper from the south, the same things would be true—he would have a rich background of experience, but not necessarily the kind that would insure mutual understanding.

Without talking, decide who is to be A and who B. These are merely identification labels and not grades. . . . What I would like for you to do is for every A to make a statement which he believes to be true, and then B will attempt to tune in on the direction of A's meaning in a stylized way. B is to ask, "Do you mean (such and such)?" until he receives three yesses. If it looks like you (B) are not going to get three yesses and you have done your best to understand what the other person is saying, ask the other person to teach you to understand him.

Let me illustrate that for you with the following dialogue.

Virginia: First, Dick, make a statement to me that you believe to be true at this moment in time.

Dick: I believe that we are all alive.

Virginia: Do you mean that sometimes people are not alive?

Dick: May I answer with something besides yes or no?

Virginia: Try to limit your answer at this point to yes or no. If the question is correct in any way, you can say "partially."

Dick: Partially, yes.

Virginia: Do you mean that you would like all the people in your group to know that you feel the aliveness?

Dick: Yes.

Virginia: Do you mean that you would like me to know that you believe this?

Dick: Yes.

Virginia: Now I would like to ask you something else, Dick. As we did this, were you aware that I was using all of myself that I possibly could in an effort to grasp your full meaning? Did you perceive that?

Dick: I felt that way.

Virginia: How did you feel as you became aware that I was struggling to get your meaning—not correct it, but really understand it? How did you feel?

Dick: I felt that you were concentrating on my meaning to the extent that it was the most important thing you were doing at that moment.

Virginia: How did that make you feel?

Dick: It made me feel very warm.

Virginia: Another thing that also may have happened as I pulled questions out of myself to ask you to get the fuller meaning of what you were telling me was that you discovered your statement contained more meaning than what you had initially thought and said. Is that true?

Dick: True.

Virginia: And as you came to feel that you had much more to offer than what you had originally said, you had a different or a new feeling of worth about yourself.

Dick: Yes, that is absolutely true.

Virginia: Thank you, Dick.

This illustration may have given an indication of the potential in such transactions. So often what happens when one person says something is that the other person gets busy thinking "Is that right?" or "Is that wrong?" The second person then becomes busy mentally correcting the statement instead of really listening. It could happen, also, that I would be in the position of not knowing how to ask more questions. I just wouldn't get it —I wouldn't be on that wavelength. That does not make me stupid; it only means that I do not have the certain piece of experience which is necessary for understanding, and I need to be taught.

Exercise

What I would like for you to do now is for A to make a statement he believes to be true, and then for B to use these words: *"Do you mean . . . ?" Not, "Does that mean . . . ?" but "Do you mean?" The whole intent is to get the direction of meaning by obtaining three yesses. If you cannot obtain three yesses, ask the other person to teach you how to understand. Each person take two turns making two different statements which you believe to be true. See what happens as you do that. . . .*

I wonder if, as you participated in the above exercises, you were surprised to find that you did not always understand the other person. To some that discovery may have seemed like a quirk, in the sense that inability to understand was not a case of stupidity but a matter of your not being together in your orientation or frame of reference for the moment. I wonder if you found yourself in the spot of not being together at first; then after you struggled to understand the direction of the meaning of the statement and finally were headed in the right direction, you discovered that you had a feeling of connectedness with the other person. Also, were you as a listener able to focus all of your attention on capturing the other person's meaning? You probably found yourself very much directed toward the other person with your eyes and the attitude of your body.

If you can, and I think you can, get an awareness of when you are really listening. This is very important. Probably you have been in the presence of somebody who was chattering away, and instead of listening you have something going on inside you like, "Oh, my God! I have to listen to all that stuff again," or "I wonder what they are saying—I couldn't possibly understand it." Frequently, when you are talking with people who speak broken English, or use idioms that you have not heard before, or talk in a kind of shorthand or specialist's jargon, if you ask yourself to construct meaning out of that conversation without checking with the sender, you will misunderstand. But during the time I am truly listening to you, I experience what I find to be a lovely feeling of being totally engaged. All of me is geared to you, and I feel this in my body. It is a lifting feeling.

Some of you also may have experienced in this exercise what it feels like when you start to correct or judge what is said. You were no longer listening. The listening stopped. This is how it goes with everyone.

Understanding the Meaning

The striving for literal understanding is another way of attaining closeness, and it is done without ever touching the other person. What is readily apparent is the creation of the feeling of connectedness and trust through the struggle for understanding of meaning, not the struggle for agreement. Many of us wander way off into left field by getting into the agreement/disagreement negotiations before we really understand the meaning. The search for *meaning* is another process which is healing. It is also a learning process. You are able to tune in and learn what you did not know.

I am going to ask you to do another part of this, and that is to find the meaning of a question. This has even more cracks in it than a statement. Frequently in families I hear things like, "Mom, can I__?" "No!" Many people answer questions without having the vaguest idea of what is being asked, but they say to themselves, "I ought to be able to answer the question."

As an example, when my daughter was sixteen we had an agreement that on Friday nights she could make her own plans for dates. Early one Friday night the telephone rang, and after she answered it I heard her say, "Mom, can I go out tonight?" I said, "Of course." Then two minutes later she asked, "*Mother*, can I go out tonight?" I said, "Of course you can go out tonight," and I was getting a little irritated. A few minutes later she asked again, even more irritatingly, and I said, "No! You absolutely cannot go out tonight!" After she hung up, I asked her what that was all about. She replied, "Well, that was a guy I don't want to say 'no' to, but if I can get you to say 'no' it gets me off the hook." There you have it—what is the meaning of the question?

What I would like for you to do now is to experience getting at the meaning of questions. One of the things you will find when you start asking questions is that you do not have many real questions. Much of our early training in questioning consisted of something like having our hand in the cookie jar and mother and father coming along and asking, "Are you getting a cookie?" Often people make statements in the form of questions. Also, there is the fingering or needling comment in the form of a question, such as "You do always mess up, don't you?" A real question has a categorizing aspect in the form of who, why, how, when, what.

Exercise

I want you now to have the experience of asking a real question. This time the listener responds with the question, "Do you mean you want to know . . . ?" The original question should not be answered at the moment; you may do that later if you like. What you should do is respond with clarifying questions about the initial question until you obtain three yesses.

As an example, one question people frequently ask is, "What time is it?" Many times this is not really a request for the time, but means "Shouldn't we be getting out of here soon?" or "My gosh, hasn't this been going on long enough?" When you begin asking about the meaning of the question by the semantics, "Do you mean you want to know . . . ?" you can uncover the true meaning. Let's see now what your experience is as you ask a question. . . .

In these exercises you had something happen within your pair. Presumably you sat down together not knowing each other completely or even very well. Take a moment now to express to each other what it was like to work as partners in the way that you did and what you felt as you did this. . . . As you shared these experiences you may have felt there was much more that could happen. Many avenues were opened up that you could continue with. Again there may have been that nice feeling of slowly building up some trust which made it possible for you to be more and more open. As you terminate the exercise, in some kind of nonverbal way, make a feeling gesture to your partner and then again take a moment to relax, to become centered, and to find your points of support within yourself.

By this time you have probably discovered the opportunities both for traps which block understanding and for connectedness through genuine understanding. One other thing about striving for a literal understanding of statements and questions is that through the medium of focused conversation you can achieve something else that is needed. You can discover the uniqueness of yourself. As therapists we find that many times our language carries a meaning we never suspected or intended. It is important to be alert to two things: (1) we are always dealing with another human being with rich experiences; but (2) the experiences may not be the kind which enable us to understand what the other is saying and we must teach each other how to understand.

That lovely process of knowing you have made a connection on the understanding level shifts the whole situation of agreement and disagreement into the reality bag from the "pot" bag, the self-worth bag. This may be something of great value to you.

In every family I work with, my awareness of making meaning with another person is uppermost. While this process is going on between me and one person in the family, the others develop trust. Any interaction pair is at the center of the group's attention, and whatever is going on between those two becomes an example for the rest. Only one set of words can be in the airwaves at a moment, but in a silent way the other people in the group benefit and learn. The time you devote to searching out real meanings makes it easier for you to help the family deal with reality as they should. Nothing is guaranteed, but the possibility for dealing with reality becomes greater. At the same time, you are presenting a living example of what is desirable, what works better, to the other people in the family. Always keep in mind that one of the most important things you do in family therapy is to model what you preach.

EDITORS' NOTE: In reading the demonstration interview that follows the reader should attend particularly to the manner in which the interviewer responds to the family's defensive maneuvers. One finds in the demonstration family the patterns of indirect and direct attack, the hurts, the communication breakdowns, the feelings of loneliness, isolation, and of not being understood typical of so many families in trouble. Note how the interviewer avoids reinforcing much of the dysfunctional behavior the family demonstrates, and instead deftly works to clarify messages and achieve congruity and synthesis. By not getting drawn into the family's defensive system, the interviewer keeps the interview flowing and under control. At the same time, in dealing with the issue of names, the interviewer asks the family, by implication, to admit her into their group as an intimate. That families find such intimacy troubling is clearly illustrated. The interviewer during the early part of the interview, however, keeps the intimacy theme clearly in focus and attempts to work it through with each family member. A significant lesson in this interview is the manner in which the interviewer's focus quickly begins to uncover the interactional processes that characterize this family. To the reader familiar with Gestalt Therapy, the focus on the "here and now" will also be striking. Because the interview flows smoothly, it is possible to miss many of its subtleties. Therefore, it deserves a careful rereading after some of the salient issues have been explored.

Chapter 7

A Simulated Family Interview

by *Virginia Satir*

Introduction

What happens when the principles of intervention are implemented in a family interview? I shall try to describe how an interview evolved using a group of people who volunteered to simulate a family before a large audience.

As far as I was concerned, this simulated family was as "real" to me as any family, in the sense that the people role-playing family members were real people doing real things. As you read the interview, you too will very quickly come to perceive them as a family. Recall for a moment what is involved in role-playing. Each person brings with him all of his knowledge and experience of how people feel and act in certain situations. Without coaching or rehearsing, this group of volunteers from the audience became a family system.

The ability of people to assume roles within a simulated group and become very real in the process is one factor which lends support to my conviction that people can change; and it follows that because people can change, I can be a therapist and help them. The actors in the simulated family felt the change, and you, as a reader, will perceive it. Then you will understand what I am talking about. If you can arrive at the firm conviction, incorporated into your very existence, that every human being has the potential for developing more and different ways of behaving than he has shown before, then you will never ask, "Can this person change?" Your questions always will be, "What can I do to help make it possible for this person to develop and grow?"

Family Therapy and the Therapist

One other thing should be said. I do not believe that everybody can or should choose to work with people in this manner. Not everyone wants to take the time, particularly if they feel that it is not going to yield something for them. Further, I believe that it is perfectly all right for you to say, "Yes, I probably could put my time and my energy into this situation and make something happen, but I am not going to do it." People have the right to make choices. But this is quite different from categorizing someone as "untreatable." Possibly none of you has ever worked in a place like Skid Row in Chicago where people for years have been making a living by panhandling or mooching. Certainly this is not the best way to earn a living, but quite a number of people eke out an existence that way. They are referred to as Skid-Row bums, and they are frequently robbed and killed by others who are part of that scene. I do not know how many of you would want to devote your time to helping such people change. But if you do not want to invest your time in the undertaking, I do not think you should say, "Those people are untreatable."

Let me make it abundantly clear that, at least from where I sit, when you work with people you are making choices, and what you choose is related to you and what you want to do. In the past in a peculiar kind of way, and perhaps unintentionally, we have done a very different kind of thing. When we saw some-one whom we did not want to help or could see no way of help-ing, we labeled that person "untreatable." When I say to you that everybody can change if two conditions are met—that they are alive and their brain has not literally been cut off—the chal-lenge is laid down for you to use your creativity and to go as far as you want to in working with people. However, I am not saying that you should always change everybody.

I should mention another thing before we begin the interview. If you had watched me interview a family in 1951, you would have seen something quite different from what you will read here. When I worked with families at that time, the families grew, but some did not grow as much as I hoped they would. In 1955, when I had learned some more things, you would have seen exclusively therapeutic operations. In 1960 you would have seen something still different, and in 1965 something somewhat different yet. This interview with a simulated family represents the stage where I am now. That is not where I shall be in another five years, and it is by no means a model of how things ought to be, but an example of how things can be with me and these peo-ple at this time. Sometimes when I describe a family interview to a group, people say, "Oh, my God! I couldn't do that!" No, no one can ever do what someone else does. The important thing to remember is that what you read here is the result of twenty years of struggling with the task of understanding and growing.

Some Basic Concepts

During all that time I have used some basic ideas which make family therapy possible. One was viewing the family as a whole unit. I worked with a systems approach long before I understood anything about it and before I had ever heard a name for it. Then in about 1957 I read Don Jackson's article "Toward a Theory of Schizophrenia,"[1] and I began to know what was going on. As time had passed, my belief in a family systems approach has grown deeper and stronger.

Until about 1964 I was unaware of how to utilize the senses directly in the service of helping people to grow. I was using the senses, but unwittingly. I have found as I go along that I come in contact with newly voiced concepts about family therapy that I have been using in my work without having ever spelled them out. As a result of these concepts being verbalized by others, I have learned more about what I have been doing.

Another belief basic to my work through the years has been that people function according to their feelings of self-worth or value, and if a person does not value himself, he cannot make it. In the past I have often been deeply hurt and even nauseated as I have gone from one place to another and watched various care agents trying to help people change by using force or discipline. That does not work. I believe people are like flowers, and flowers grow because they have sunshine, fertilizer, and water. I have yet to find a plant that would grow by my issuing the edict, "If you don't bloom, I am going to beat you." As you know, plants do not respond very well to that. In fact, such treatment can be fatal. I also know that a plant sometimes becomes too heavy to bear its own weight, and I then have to put in a stake to help hold it up until it grows strong enough to support itself. This is my model, and everything I do is related to how I can help the human being open up and blossom.

What provides nurture for the human being? It is his own ability to ask for what he needs and to be in touch with himself. Then he can work out gratifying interdependent relationships with all other human beings—not dependent or independent, but interdependent. Interdependent means two parts functioning together, not two parts merged into one. The water for our human "plant" consists of the senses. These are not merely mechanical systems, but dynamic in that they can learn and grow in effectiveness. What is poisonous to the plant within us are the inhuman rules we have about how we should be and how we should act. Getting rid of those poisonous rules will help restore health in the person.

This is the way I look at things. So at this particular time you will see me as I am right now and in transition, as I always am except for these fundamental beliefs.

Organizing a Simulated Family Interview
In the family interview that follows, I began with five people

willing to be a family. As instructed, each person selected a new first name, after which the group decided among themselves what their family roles would be, their ages, and their last name. Also, each member decided privately what his type of communication would be. They were not to let me or anyone else know what they chose—placating, blaming, super-reasonable, or irrelevant. As in a typical first interview with a family, the therapist has no way of knowing the members' main ways of handling stress.

The family was seated clockwise around me in the following order: Marilyn, the wife/mother, thirty-seven years old; Johnny, the nine-year-old son; Jim, the husband/father, forty years old; Mary, the fifteen-year-old daughter; and Susan, the sixteen-year-old daughter. This was the Smith family.

The setting could have been a public welfare office, a mental health clinic, a rector's office in a church, a suicide prevention center, the waiting room of a hospital's emergency room, or any place into which people come who have some kind of crisis or who apparently want something for their family that they are unable to achieve for themselves. This time the setting was a walk-in clinic. With the stage set in this manner, we begin the interview.

Virginia: (approaching Jim to shake his hand): I am Virginia Satir and I have not met you before.

Jim: Jim Smith.

Virginia: Jim Smith. Jim, would you introduce me to the rest of your family, please? (*Jim performs the introductions.*)

Johnny: Can I go to the bathroom?

(*Virginia sits down in the circle of chairs between the mother, Marilyn, and the older daughter, Susan.*)

Virginia: Just a minute while I put my cigarette out (snubs out cigarette). Do you have to go potty, Johnny?

Johnny: I want a drink of water.

Mary: I'll take him. He can't go by himself. Come on Johnny.

Jim: How do you know he needs to go? You're always siding in with John. Just let him take care of his own problems.

Johnny: (sulking): You never let Mary do anything for me.

Virginia: John, we haven't known each other very long, but is your father giving you a message?

Johnny: I don't know. I just want a drink of water.

Virginia: Well, we have a couple of glasses of water right here. Take this one.

Johnny: Thank you.

Virginia: You know, I introduced myself as Virginia Satir. I like to be called by my first name and I like to call people by their first names. (*To Jim.*) I wonder how you feel about that.

Jim: At this point it is not too comfortable. I don't ordinarily call people by their first name, especially a stranger that I've only met, say for a matter of minutes, so I would be uncomfortable with that right now.

Virginia: So what you say is you're uncomfortable using a person's first name until you get to know them better, is that right?

Jim: Well, for now I'd like to just call you by your last name.

Virginia: How about me with you?

Jim: I'd be more comfortable if you called me Mr. Smith at this point.

Virginia: When do I know that you are no longer uncomfortable?

Jim (*laughs softly*): That's a good question.

Virginia: I think I would like to know.

Jim: Are you asking me then to signal you when I want you to call me Jim?

Virginia: Would you do that?

Jim: I guess so.

Virginia: How do you feel about what we were talking about just now? We are relative strangers, that's true. I wonder how you feel about what you and I were talking about.

Jim: Well, I feel kind of (*clears throat*) uncomfortable on the inside because I wondered what—why you were making a point about first names and everything.

Virginia: Do you want me to tell you why? For me, your first name is just you. There could be a thousand Mr. Smiths, and I like to use something that says it's you. Does that change anything?

Jim: I find my feelings here (*points to chest*) begin to disappear. When you're asking questions, you know, I always feel like there's some reason, and I'm really uncomfortable about why you might be asking me these questions.

Virginia: What I hope is that you will do just what you did just now—ask me what the reason is. I told you why I like to call people by their first names. I feel good when you can ask those questions. Would you be willing to do that as long as we work together?

Jim: Do what? I didn't understand.

Virginia: Ask. If I ask you questions and they don't make sense to you and you wonder why I ask them, would you be willing to ask me why I am doing it?

Jim: Oh, I think you'll find me asking questions fairly frequently.

Virginia: I can count on that?

Jim: Oh, I think you can count on that.

Virginia: That's great. I like that. (*To Marilyn.*) How do you feel about me calling you by your first name?

Marilyn: It's okay as long as you are a woman.

Virginia: If I'm a woman, it's okay. It would have some other meaning—and I'm not a man so it's kind of iffy, but I am curious—if I were a man what is the objection?

Jim (*sarcastically to Marilyn*): You think she is going to turn into a man or something?

Marilyn: No, it's just that I am uncomfortable at being called by my first name by a man that I don't know.

Jim (*sarcastic again*): What aren't you uncomfortable about?

Virginia: Would you like to move in a little closer, Marilyn? (*Marilyn moves chair forward a few inches.*) Your husband, I think, was asking something of you.

Jim (*bitterly and sarcastically*): You know, it always seems that you are uncomfortable and I—uncomfortable about this and that—and uncomfortable about the money I make, and more specifically the money I don't make. And I think that is probably what we are doing here—it's some of your uncomfortableness.

Virginia: How are you feeling right now as you are saying this to your wife?

Jim (points to chest): I'm getting some of that old uncomfortable feeling here.

Virginia: I felt some pain in what you were saying, almost like "Gee, I never can do anything to please you," something like that. Was that how it was, Jim?

Jim: Kind of.

Virginia: Well, let's hold this one minute while I get to Sue. *(Turning to Susan.)* And how do you feel about my calling you by your first name and you calling me by mine?

Susan: Well, I feel comfortable having you call me by my first name, but Mom and Dad have always told me to respect my elders, and I feel uncomfortable calling you by your first name.

Virginia: Well, maybe—

Jim (interrupting): You seem to forget that sometimes, though.

Susan (whining): Well, Dad, I'm sorry, I don't know quite what you mean. I don't remember calling any of your friends by their first names.

Jim: Well, maybe—I'll just let you two talk then. We aren't going to make any point here, so we'll just let you two talk.

Virginia: Could I just make this comment, Jim? What I am hearing you say is that sometimes the way Susan comes up for you is disappointing to you. Is that true?

Jim: Disappointing? *(Pauses.)* Oh, I think so, even stronger than that sometimes, even stronger than disappointment sometimes.

Susan (whining): But, Dad, you know I try. I try hard. I try and please you and Mama.

Virginia: And I gather what you are saying, Sue, is that you don't know yet how to guarantee pleasing your Dad—kind of the way in which your Dad was feeling about your mother before.

Susan: Right.

Virginia: Well, you said it's okay for me to call you by your first name, but you don't know how your mother and father would feel about your calling me by my first name. Would you ask them?

Susan (*to Jim*): How do you feel about me calling Mrs. Satir by her first name?

Jim: Sure, call her by her first name. Why did you call her Mrs. Satir?

Susan: Well—

Virginia: Did you get an answer to your question, Sue?

Susan: Well, I guess.

Virginia: Well, what answer do you think you got from your Dad?

Susan: I think my Dad would rather have me call you by your last name.

Virginia: Check with him, because he looked surprised then. Can you see that at this moment? Maybe you had better ask your question again.

Susan: Dad, tell me yes or no. Shall I call her by her first name or her last name?

Jim: Do what you want.

Virginia: (*to Susan*): How did you feel about that?

Susan: Well, I'd like to call you by your first name but I feel kind of uncomfortable. I know my Dad doesn't like that.

Virginia: Do you think your father didn't mean what he said, "Do what you want"? You think he didn't mean that?

Susan: Right. I think he meant that I should respect you and call you by your last name.

Virginia: Gee, that would be funny, because I heard him say, "Do what you want." (*to Jim:* Is that what you said?) But then I guess there was something else that made you think that maybe he didn't mean what he said with his mouth.

Susan: Yes, his actions.

Virginia: What actions made you think that?

Susan: Well, he kind of raised his eyebrows and his eyes, and well (*shrugging*), "Do what you want!" You know, this kind of gave me the message that although he said that, he didn't really mean it.

Virginia: You know, I don't know your father very well, but I have a hunch about something. We'll check it out. I think your father really inside often feels that nobody really listens much to him. Did you ever have that feeling?

Susan: Well—

Virginia (to Jim): Do you ever have that feeling?

Jim: I have the feeling we are getting somewhere now.

Virginia: Do you ever feel that you don't get listened to?

Jim: I come home from work and, you know, I put in a hellish day and I start trying to talk to somebody about it, you know, and here Marilyn is, you know. First thing she hits me with is Johnny. Johnny this, Johnny that, you know, and Lord knows she never could control that kid. I come home tired—

Marilyn (overlapping): As if it's all my job!

Jim: See what I mean? Nobody was listening.

Virginia (to Marilyn): What were you aware of that Jim was saying when he said that? What did it feel like to you, Marilyn?

Marilyn (angrily): That it's all my fault that he acts like that!

Virginia: Hold it one minute, because I think Johnny's got something going here—

Jim (to Johnny): Just sit still.

Virginia: Let's take a minute off, because I'm aware that John is only nine and I've been putting my attention on one and another here and (to Johnny) not to you yet. I wonder how you felt, John, with the action going on over here.

Johnny: Well, I—

Susan (critically to Johnny): You act like you know what was going on but you were playing tic-tac-toe.

Mary: Johnny, if you'll come over here and sit, we'll play in a little while.

Susan: You just stay there now. You're not supposed to play, you're not supposed to play.

Johnny (moves to sit between Susan and Mary): I want to play. (to Mary.) You have a pen?

Mary: No, but I'll—

Marilyn (loudly and angrily to Jim): Why don't you do something with that kid? Don't just let him move over there!

Jim: All right.

Mary (wheedling): Oh, Mom! Let him, let him!

Jim: Six of one and a half-dozen of the other. Here we go again.

Marilyn: (continues loudly and angrily to Jim): Now see! It's all your fault that he acts the way he does.

Virginia (to Jim and Marilyn): There was an interesting thing that happened when Johnny moved over there. You two could sit closer together and I was aware of something. Maybe this sounds strange—I wonder—Mary. Mary, I'm wondering something at this moment about how you felt when your father said to your mother, "You don't do the things I want," and she said, "Well, it's—"

Mary: I didn't hear it.

Virginia: Are you sure?

Jim (sarcastically): That's right. She never hears anything that she's supposed to.

Mary: I was thinking about Johnny. I hate to see him get caught between Mom and Daddy and I wanted him to come over here.

Virginia: Kind of like saying that you can offer him something?

Mary: Yes. I mean, Dad and Mom get mad at one another, and Johnny and I are buddies.

Virginia: I see.

Johnny: They always beat at tic-tac-toe, too.

Virginia: I wonder if at the moment, because there are some things I want to do on the other side of the circle, if for the moment we can let this be. Because already what I am seeing is that it is very easy in this family for people to know how to make other people uncomfortable. I kind of get that feeling. I'd like to check this out a little bit more. *(to Marilyn)*: I was wondering what you were aware of feeling when Jim was saying, "When I come home at night there's this and there's that and there's something else." What were you aware of feeling, Marilyn?

Marilyn: Well, I guess I got mad, because he acts like he's the only one that does anything.

Virginia: So are you in this—

Marilyn (overlapping): I'm hurt because he doesn't know I'm busy and have troubles too.

Virginia: That you are in the same boat, that you feel kind of like he talks?

Marilyn: Yes, but I never get the chance to tell him.

Virginia: I see. How are you feeling right now as you are telling me this, Marilyn?

Marilyn: Relieved, I guess.

Jim (in a snide manner): She's feeling like she's getting somebody to listen to her.

Virginia (to Jim): Kind of like you were feeling before.

Jim: She's trying to win you over to her side, you see.

Virginia: Do you worry about that?

Jim: You know, when I got—four is enough, but pulling you into it too—

Virginia: Is that how it kind of feels right now, that you're standing out there by yourself?

Jim: Well, you are hunkering over there by her close and soaking it all up, and I figure you're going to be number five. You know, I am surrounded by people that, you know, I kind of shut my eyes and feature how they see me coming home as a paycheck. Here comes in Jim, the floating paycheck comes in, and along comes somebody who takes a piece of Jim here, and then a piece there. You know, there's not even a stub left over—

Johnny (overlapping): I still haven't got my bicycle yet.

Jim: —that tells how much the government took out.

Johnny: When do I get my bicycle? She got her ring *(indicates Susan)*, but I don't have my bicycle.

Virginia: John, I wonder what you were aware of feeling as your father was talking about how he feels about himself. I know you're just nine, but I wonder how you felt when your Dad said, "I don't even feel I have a stub left," or something like that.

Johnny: I felt like everybody else gets what they want before I do.

Virginia: Do you feel like this sometimes, that you don't have anything left?

Jim: Yeah, join the club!

Johnny: I don't know. I don't have anything.

Virginia: John, how do you feel about calling me by my first name and having me call you by your first name?

Johnny: You can call me by my first name, but I am not going to call you by your first name.

Virginia: Is there anything that stands in the way?

Johnny: Yesterday a teacher *slapped* me when I called her by her first name. I'm not going to do that again!

Virginia: I see. So it's kind of like I would be the same as the teacher.

Johnny: I won't do that again.

Virginia: I can appreciate that. It won't happen here, but you won't know that for a while.

Jim (to Marilyn): Did he have trouble in school that you didn't tell me about?

Marilyn: Well, you wouldn't have cared anyway.

Jim: Next thing I know the *school* will descend upon me like a bunch of hungry vultures—

Marilyn (overlapping): Maybe it would make you do something.

Virginia: Wait a minute, Jim. John was just saying that yesterday he took the risk of calling his teacher by her first name and she slapped him.

Marilyn: Well, we taught him not to do that.

Virginia: You see we are in kind of a funny situation here, because now I'm asking the children to do something that you've trained them not to do.

Johnny: And that was the teacher I like. She was my favorite teacher, and she *slapped* me. (*Angrily.*) I'm not going to study anymore for her!

Virginia: You feel very hurt about this?

Johnny: Yes, I do!

Jim (laughing sarcastically): You really don't have much to lose the way your grades are anyway.

Virginia: Jim, I wondered something when Johnny was talking. Do you know what it feels like to be disappointed by somebody you really care about? Do you know anything about that feeling?

Jim: Oh, I think I know a lot about that feeling!

Virginia: Could you say that to John, tell him what you know about that, because that is what he is feeling right now?

Jim: I can imagine you kind of counted on this teacher, and the next thing you know she's rapping you upside of the head.

It's just like maybe the whole world caves in.

Virginia: I think that is what you were saying when you first came in, that your world has just kind of caved in, Jim.

Jim: Well, it's not in the best of shape anyway!

Virginia: Yes, I feel that. (*turns to Mary*) Let me find out from you, Mary, how you feel about calling me by my first name, and my calling you by your first name.

Mary (*long pause*): Mrs. Satir, I just couldn't.

Virginia: How do you feel about telling me that, dear?

Mary (*very softly*): I'm afraid.

Virginia: Afraid?

Jim (*gruffly*): Speak up. That's what we are doing here. If you can't tell the whole story then there's no use being here. Speak up!

Johnny: (*loudly*): Don't pick on Mary!

Virginia (*to Mary*): Well, I hear you—

Jim (*overlapping and muttering to Johnny*): Oh, John, you're really aching for one!

Virginia: Mary could you say what you would be afraid of? Does it have something to do with what Sue was saying, that if you say to me that it would be okay, that maybe Dad would get angry with you?

(*Long pause.*)

Jim (*to Mary*): Can't you sit up and talk to the lady? (*Mary begins to sniffle.*) Oh, here comes the waterworks! That's another routine we go through quite frequently—the waterworks!

Virginia: That means people cry a lot?

Jim: People cry a lot around our place. Every time you talk to them, they start crying.

Virginia: What do you think—

Johnny (*interrupting*): I've never seen Mom cry. She always gets mad at *me*.

Virginia (*to Susan*): What do you think is behind Mary's tears, dear?

Susan: Oh, she's just a big baby that's got to grow up!

Virginia: Do you ever feel like crying?

Susan: No.

Virginia: Do you know what it feels like to want to cry?

Susan (*vehemently*): No!

Virginia: You don't know that feeling. (*To Jim.*) Do you know what it is like, Jim?

Jim: I don't really cry on the outside, but I cry on the inside.

Virginia: That's what I wondered. So Mary cries on the outside, but (*turning to Susan*) you don't know what it feels like inside to want to cry?

Susan: No.

Jim: Yeah, I wonder about that sometimes.

Virginia (*to Mary*): Well, the way it stands right now, I gather you're saying it's okay for me to call you "Mary," but you don't know yet whether you can take the risk because you don't know how your Dad will feel if you call me by my first name. Is that right? (*Mary nods.*) Well, how did you feel about what he did with Susan?

Mary: It's okay.

Virginia: What's okay, dear?

Mary: It's okay.

Virginia: I don't understand. What is okay? What could you tell me about that? What's the "it"?

Mary: Well, it's okay that Susan calls you "Virginia." It's okay.

Virginia: But not for you?

Mary: No.

Virginia: Is that something that happens in the family, that it's okay for Susan but not for you?

Mary: It's okay.

Virginia: By the way your eyes are looking right now, I have a hunch it isn't okay.

Mary: Well (*long pause*), I don't want to talk about it. Okay?

Virginia: I hear you. What I hear you saying is "I can't ask for the things I want." Is that true?

Mary: Yes.

Jim: She's just naturally quiet.

Virginia: I don't know about that. I have a feeling that Mary was experiencing some of the same things that you were experiencing.

Jim: There was one spot that I just kind of cried on the inside myself.

Virginia: And I hear Mary saying, "I'd like to do things differently, and I want things for myself, but I can't ask for them." (*To Marilyn.*) Is that anything you know anything about? That you want something but feel you can't ask?

Marilyn (sounding bitter): Of course I can't ask. He doesn't make enough money.

Virginia: Are the things that cost money the only things you want?

Marilyn: No, but I wouldn't *dream* of asking for anything else. He doesn't know anything about that.

Jim: I don't hear about anything else but money.

Marilyn: He should be able to know what I need without me having to tell him.

Virginia: That strikes me as a little curious. I think you believe this, but I would have a hard time knowing what anybody wanted unless they told me. How do you figure this works, Marilyn?

Marilyn: Well, when you get married, people are supposed to tell you they love you and be nice to you, and not just come home with all their gripes and stuff. *Surely* he knows that.

Virginia: I don't know. I don't know what Jim knows, but you might ask him.

(*Johnny and Mary have been talking together and begin to get noisier as Johnny takes off his shoe to play with.*)

Jim: All right, you two are going to have to settle down.

Susan (low, contrite voice): I have a feeling, Dad, that well, gosh darn, I know you couldn't hardly afford this class ring, Dad, but you didn't have to buy it for me. I *told* you I really could get along without it, and I feel bad, Daddy.

Jim: Oh, I remember that routine. You came and said (*mimics a high, wheedling voice*), "Oh, Dad, I could do without this but I sure would like it." Dribble, dribble, dribble. And so what was I supposed to do? (*To Johnny and Mary*) You guys are going to have to settle down or that's it.

Virginia: Jim, let me stop for a minute. Look, you're a very tender man— (*Johnny interrupts with a loud snort.*)

Jim (to Johnny): I think I'm beginning to be interested in what she is saying. Just stay out of it and put your shoe back on.

Virginia: When I said this to you—

Jim: You mean tender—like—

Virginia: No, I think inside, inside you have all the yearnings that Mary's talking about, and I think you know something about how Susan feels. And right now I am feeling that there is a great pain in this family. When you feel your tenderness isn't understood, then I hear you becoming very sharp. (*Turning to Johnny.*) And Johnny, I wondered something. When I said to your father that I could feel his tenderness and you laughed, it sounded like a clown laughing. I wonder what you were feeling.

Johnny: I have never seen him be nice to anybody. It just sounded funny the way you were talking to him.

Jim: You see how he can spit it out when he gets that way?

Virginia (*to Johnny*): I can feel from you, too, that you have put bands on your own tenderness.

Johnny: Put what?

Virginia: Bands on them.

Johnny (*lengthy pause*): You mean stopped myself from being tender? Ho, you think I am going to be tender around here?!

Virginia: If I lived in this family, I would worry about what would happen to me if I showed my tenderness. I sure would.

Johnny: Yeah!

Virginia: I feel your father's worry if he shows his tenderness. I could feel your worry. And I have a hunch in this family that people feel very scared.

Johnny: You better believe it! You've never seen him come home *mad!*

Virginia: I think I can understand how your father would sound, and I think I could understand how you would sound.

Johnny: How I would sound?

Virginia: Everybody in this family has got a way to look and act when they feel tender. But I just feel—

Jim (*interrupting*): I would like to say something. A while ago I was beginning to feel like I halfway wanted to call you by your first name. Then you jump over there and I kind of feel left out.

Virginia: I'm glad you told me that, because in this family I'm

already beginning to get the feeling that everybody feels left
out. You know, when you and I are talking, then I hear—

Johnny (interrupting): Susan shouldn't feel left out. She gets
everything she wants.

Virginia: I hear Johnny really feeling left out, and (*to Marilyn*) I
don't know how you feel when I am talking with Jim.

Jim: I would like to know how she feels, too.

Marilyn (to Jim, rather bitterly): Well, it's okay. You might as
well be nice to somebody.

Virginia: Well, how do you feel about what is going on between
Jim and me? (*Aside to Johnny.*) Would you like to come in a
little closer, Johnny? (*He refuses.*) You wouldn't. Would you,
Mary? Would you come in a little closer, Susan?

 (*The girls move their chairs in closer.*)

Jim: You might as well come in, John. (*Johnny bumps against
Jim as he drags his chair in closer.*)

Jim (loudly): You don't need to knock me down! Just come in
closer!

Marilyn (to Virginia): Maybe I feel jealous, I don't know.

Jim: Jealous?

Marilyn (angrily): Well, you've never been nice to me!

Virginia: Never?

Marilyn: Well, not for the last hundred years.

Jim: Working the kind of hours I work, riding the commuter
bus two hours and a half every damned day, and you don't
think that's nice?

Marilyn: Well, I get up and fix your breakfast, and you've never
told me "thank you"!

Jim: Ho! You set out the cereal and the milk!

Marilyn: (loudly): Well, at least I'm up! I even take my hair out
of rollers, and you never notice!

Virginia: How do you feel when you say that, "No matter what I
do, you don't notice me"? How do you feel, Marilyn, when
you say that to Jim?

Marilyn: Maybe like crying.

Virginia: It almost feels that way even now as I am looking at
you.

Jim (sarcastically): When was the last time you cried about anything?

Johnny: Yeah, you don't cry, Mom.

Virginia: Wait, wait. Let your mother have a chance.

Marilyn: Oh—it won't matter anyway, I guess.

Virginia: What happened just this moment, because I could feel your sadness about nobody noticing you and then something happened and you said, "But it doesn't matter." Were you aware of what you were feeling?

Marilyn: Well, they wouldn't care anyway.

Virginia: Are you aware now of what the song in this family is? "Nobody Cares and Nobody Listens."

Mary: Mom, you know I care.

Susan: We, we all care, Mom, you know that. We care about you and Daddy. We try to make you happy, Mom.

Mary: We always want to please you.

Johnny: But you never pay attention to anything we do to make you happy.

Virginia: It's part of the song.

Mary: We try and get good grades, and we try to do well in other things besides school.

Johnny: I mowed the lawn yesterday, and no one thanked me.

Marilyn: Oh, yeah, I meant to mention that. It did look nice.

Virginia: Could you say it now the way you would feel it? Johnny does the lawn. What could you say to him, now that he's brought it up, about how you felt about his mowing the lawn?

Marilyn: Thanks for mowing the lawn. That looks nice.

Johnny: Thank you. That's the first time you've told me that.

Marilyn: I always just *forget!*

Johnny: And Dad *never* does.

Virginia: Have you noticed the lawn that John did yesterday, Jim?

Jim (offhandedly): Yeah, it wasn't bad—not bad at all.

Marilyn (angrily): It's a lot better than you ever did!

Virginia: Wait a minute now—

Johnny: Thanks, Mom.

Virginia: In a funny kind of way, something that really could make a person feel okay got turned around—something got turned around. (*To Johnny.*) Your mother told you that she liked the fact that you did the lawn and you seemed to feel good about hearing it.

Johnny: I liked that. I liked it.

Virginia: Then you said, "I wish I could have it from Dad." Then I heard your father say, "Well, you did a good job," and I heard you take this as a—what—an accusation, or what?

Jim: Yeah, he's kind of hard to get to, you know. I don't really understand these kids.

Virginia: Jim, I was wondering something. Were you aware of how your words sounded?

Jim: What words?

Virginia: Your words: "Well, it was a good enough job." Did you hear yourself saying that?

Jim: I just told him I liked it.

Johnny (loudly and angrily): No, you didn't!

Virginia: There it is. Wait a minute. *(to Jim)* Could you say that, "I liked it"?

Jim (quietly): I liked it.

Virginia (to Johnny): So when your father speaks in these low, level tones he means maybe something else than what he said before.

Johnny: I never hear him like that, he *never* talks like that!

Virginia: He just now did, he just now did.

Jim: I said I liked it. What do you want?

Johnny (in a low voice): I don't know, Dad.

Virginia (to Johnny): Is there anything that you have to say to your father along that line about something he has done that you appreciated and that you remember, even if it was five years ago?

Johnny: When we went fishing three weeks ago. I really liked that, even though I caught the biggest fish and he didn't like that.

Virginia: Are you sure about how your father felt about your catching the biggest fish? Would you ask him?

Johnny: Ask him?

Virginia: Ask him how he felt about catching a fish smaller than yours.

Johnny: How did you feel about catching the littler fish?

Jim (to Virginia): I'm not sure whether he wanted me to take him fishing or if he just wants me to—

Virginia: Could you ask him?

Jim: I'm not sure whether you enjoyed the fishing or whether you enjoy socking it to me about catching the biggest fish.

Johnny: Both.

Virginia: A very funny thing has just happened. I asked you to find out from your Dad how he felt about your catching a bigger fish than he did. Have you found out? Would you ask him again?

Johnny: How did you feel because I caught the biggest fish?

Jim: Didn't bother me any.

Virginia: True or not true, Jim?

Marilyn: You didn't even bring yours in the house. I found it in the garbage.

Jim: Well, he might have caught the bigger fish, but, I mean, who set up the tackle for him and who told him what kind of lures to use?

Johnny: I picked out my own lure.

Jim: Anybody can fish but it takes somebody special to teach.

Johnny: Why don't we go out more often then? Maybe I can teach you something.

Jim: Do I hear you saying you want to go fishing more often?

Johnny: Yeah.

Jim: I'd like to take you fishing more often, but you're always off—

Virginia (interrupting): Could you just say you would like to take him more often?

Jim: I would like to take you fishing more often, because I enjoy it.

Johnny (to Virginia): That would be good, but he always sleeps on Saturday mornings.

Virginia: Tell him how you feel about that—"On Saturday morning—"

Johnny: I don't believe him. I don't believe him.

Jim: You see, Virginia, this is the way he does.

Virginia: John—

Johnny (interrupting): He's saying that here, but when we get home he won't take me fishing.

Virginia: You won't know this until next Saturday.

Johnny: Well, I know my Dad.

Virginia: I don't know if you do.

Johnny: He won't take me fishing—

Jim (overlapping): Sometimes I wonder if he knows I'm around at all.

Johnny: —once a year. (*loudly, to outtalk Jim.*) Maybe you don't want us to know that you're around.

Jim: I just told him that I would like to take him fishing. First he bitches about not being able to go fishing often enough—

Johnny (interrupting): Because you don't mean it, Dad.

Virginia: John, will you say to your father, "I think you are lying to me"?

Johnny: I think you are lying to me.

Virginia: Now do you believe what you are saying?

Johnny (softly): No.

Virginia: Now you tell him what you really do believe.

Johnny: I believe—

Virginia: Would you look at him while you are doing this?

Johnny: I believe that even though right now you say you want to go fishing, when it gets around to it, you won't go. You'll find something else to do and you'll be tired from a long week's work. We won't go fishing, Dad, and you know it.

Jim: Well, maybe we'll go fishing this—maybe we'll go fishing. Let's just—uh—you know, Saturday's a few days off. I want you to believe me this time. I know sometimes it's been, you know, a little rough to—

Johnny (interrupting): I don't believe it!

Virginia: Let me interrupt. (*To Marilyn.*) What was happening to you when your husband and your son were contacting each other, Marilyn?

Marilyn: Well, I guess I felt kind of left out.

Virginia: Would you like to do something with Jim too?

Marilyn: It would be kind of nice.

Virginia: Do you suppose that is something you could work out with Jim, like what Jim and John are working out with each other right now? Is that a possibility?

Marilyn: He probably wouldn't want to do anything.

Virginia: So we'll have to find out about that.

Jim: What makes you think I wouldn't want to do anything?

Marilyn: The last time you ever went anyplace with me was to the wedding!

Jim: Well, you know, there's—I think that's what's wrong with this family, you know. We—

Marilyn (interrupts loudly and bitterly): Yeah, you've got all the answers.

Jim: We're always splitting off in different directions, you know, and I kind of felt bad when he said I wouldn't go fishing, because there wasn't anything I could say because I've promised him so many times. Then he was kind of, I thought, was giving me a hint that he would give me another try. Then I began to kind of loosen up a little bit. So, you know, so I'm asking you the same thing. If you would just trust me one more time to take you somewhere, just you and I?

Virginia: What were you feeling as Jim was talking to you?

Marilyn: Like Johnny. He won't do it.

Virginia: Okay. I saw your shoulders go like that, like there's no hope. Is that how you feel?

Marilyn: Uh-huh.

Virginia: Would you do something? Would you turn your chair around so that you could really look at Jim.

Marilyn (giggling): He's getting some gray hairs!

Jim: You see what I'm up against, Virginia?

Virginia: Wait a minute, Marilyn. As you look at those gray hairs, would you tell me how you feel when you see them?

Marilyn: Maybe he did kind of work and worry about us.

Virginia: And how do you feel as you let those words come out of your mouth?

Marilyn: Sorry that I didn't tell him "thank you," too, I guess.

Virginia: Could you say that to Jim?

Marilyn: I'm sorry I didn't thank you.

Jim: For what?

Marilyn (to Virginia): For bringing home his paycheck.

Virginia: That's the part you could thank him for, but there are some other parts you don't like very well. Isn't that true?

Marilyn: Yes.

Virginia: Would you be willing to let yourself tell Jim at this point some of the pains that you have, and look at him while you are telling him?

Marilyn: He'd just get mad.

Virginia: Would you take a chance on telling him? Nobody died from getting mad as far as I know. Would you tell him something about your pain?

Marilyn: Well, but then we never could get along if I told him all that.

Virginia: Well, I don't know. Let's take a chance on it. But before you do, instead of taking my word for it, will you ask Jim how he would feel hearing about your pains? Would you ask him?

Marilyn: Would you get mad at me?

Jim: Oh, I'd probably be uncomfortable but I don't think I am going to die. I believe I could take it.

Marilyn: You won't not talk to me, or anything?

Jim: I don't know.

Marilyn (*hesitantly*): Well, I don't know.

Virginia: Could you stand it if there was a time when Jim didn't speak to you?

Marilyn: That would be worse than it is now.

Virginia: So you have to decide if that should happen whether you could still live through it.

Marilyn (*long pause*): Mm, I guess I could always go to mother's.

Jim: Oh, brother! That's what we need.

Virginia: Well, what I'm hearing—

Jim: We need her mother, that's just what we need!

Virginia: How did you feel when Marilyn asked you that question of what will happen, Jim, if she tells you some of the things that hurt her and maybe that she doesn't like about you?

Jim: I felt uncomfortable, but I told her I didn't think I was going to die, you know.

Virginia: That's been one of the problems, I think, in the family is that people were really awfully careful about people's feelings, and you know—

Jim (overlapping): God, you're treating me like glass. It makes me sound like I'm some kind of sissy or something that I can't take just a few negative things.

Johnny: You'd rather take it out on everybody else.

Virginia (to Marilyn): Well, where are you at this point? Do you suppose you could tell him, Jim, some of the things that hurt you? Johnny's been talking about some of the things that hurt him, like when his dad makes a promise and doesn't carry through, but in this family when people are hurt they act mad. And Jim has been talking about feeling hurt when people don't notice him. And I heard Mary say that she feels hurt—

Jim (overlapping): She feels hurt when she should feel mad.

Virginia: I don't know about that, but I feel that hurt. And I even hear Susan feeling hurt when she gets things that she thinks are at the expense of others; remember the talk about the class ring? So I wonder, Marilyn, what you could tell Jim makes you feel hurt?

Marilyn: Well, you didn't buy a Mother's Day present this year either.

Virginia: Could you tell him what you hoped that he would do? What you would have liked?

Marilyn: Well, he knows I like roses.

Virginia: Could you say to him, "I like roses"?

Marilyn: I like roses. Why didn't you get me some?

Virginia: Could you say that you would like to have them from him?

Marilyn: I'd like to get roses for Mother's Day.

Virginia: How did you feel when you were saying that to Jim?

Marilyn: Foolish.

Virginia: It's foolish for you to ask for what you want?

Marilyn: Yeah. I ask for too much anyway, he says.

Virginia: Do you? Well, I don't know about that. But you know what I was feeling this moment? That here you are having all kinds of wishes and feelings that you can't bring into the open, and in a way you are asking Jim to look through your skin.

Marilyn: Well, any husband should know that his wife would like something for Mother's Day. It didn't have to be roses; it could have been anything.

Virginia: But you would like roses. Could you tell him that?

Marilyn (explosively): I did!

Virginia: But you sound kind of angry right now. Are you feeling angry?

Marilyn: Probably guilty.

Virginia: Could you say what that's about?

Marilyn: Well, we don't have enough money to buy roses all the time.

Virginia: So you're kind of like Susan. You'd like the roses but there isn't enough money to go around, you think. So you have a wish and then you say to yourself, "I shouldn't have it." But then a funny thing happens. You say, "Well, why didn't you take care of my wish?" That comes out funny, doesn't it? Do you feel what I am saying to you?

Marilyn: Yeah, but—

Virginia: Marilyn, I don't know about all the wishes we may have that can come true, but maybe it would be useful if you let yourself know what your wishes are, because maybe more can come true than what you realize. Could you say to Jim, "Jim, I would like roses, and would you be able to buy them for me?" and see what happens.

Marilyn (to Jim): I like red roses. Could you buy some?

Jim: I think so.

Virginia: How do you feel about that?

Marilyn: Well, if I insist, he'll get them.

Virginia: Do you feel you are insisting now?

Marilyn: If I mention it again, I will be.

Jim: If I had known that it was that important to you—

Marilyn: But you *know* I like roses! You *always* sent me roses before we got married!

Jim: Yes, but roses were only $8.95; they're $12.50 now.

Marilyn: You don't have to buy a dozen.

Jim: Well, I think if I had known what they meant to you, you know, that I—well, we can manage it.

Virginia: How do you feel right now, Marilyn? What's going on?

Marilyn: Maybe he really didn't know.

Jim: That's what I said.

Marilyn: You say a lot of things.

Virginia (*to Mary*): I wonder what is going on with you right now, Mary? How do you feel about what is going on here?

Mary: I'm glad Mom and Dad are talking to one another instead of yelling at each other. It's a good feeling when they don't yell.

Johnny: Mom never yells. Dad always yells, and Mom listens to Dad.

Mary: I know, but they're—they don't like each other. That's what feels bad. Daddy doesn't like Mama, and Mama doesn't like Daddy, and they are fighting all the time—

Virginia: Is that going on right now?

Mary: No, they're kind of nice to one another right now. It's a good thing.

Virginia: I wonder what you were aware of feeling, John, as this was going on between your mother and dad?

Johnny: I was thinking about catching the biggest fish. I'm going to get him the next time.

Virginia: You know, between two guys when they go fishing, one of the fun parts is who can catch the biggest fish. It might be your father the next time. Could be.

Johnny: He can't fish—he's a bad fisherman.

Jim: Who taught you?

Virginia: I wonder, however, John, what you were also feeling about what you were seeing here.

Johnny: I was thinking that Dad won't do what he says he is going to do. I was thinking that he knew Mom liked roses. He knew this, and he knew it was Mother's Day. And right now here with you he'll say, "Yes, I'll get them," and tomorrow he'll say, "Nope, can't afford it."

Mary: But, Johnny, Daddy really does work hard, and there really isn't enough money to go around. Maybe Daddy could buy Mama one rose. That wouldn't cost much, and he really wants to help. Daddy—Daddy tries. I know he does.

Susan: He bought me this class ring.

Virginia: You know, we have gone a long way and I haven't even asked you why it was you came into this place. (*to Marilyn.*) How did you happen to come here?

Marilyn: Ask him (*indicates Jim*).

Virginia: No, I asked how you happened to come, because I didn't notice any chains around you. How did *you* happen to come in here?

Marilyn (*gives a short laugh*): It would have looked kind of funny if he had come in without me!

Virginia: Well, he could have. People do that. How did *you* happen to come in here?

Marilyn: He just said we should go. So I couldn't lose anything, I guess.

Virginia: Well, what did you hope to have happen for you when you came here?

Marilyn: Maybe that we could all just be happy.

Virginia: So you hoped maybe something could change.

Marilyn: Yes.

Virginia: So in a funny kind of way, since Jim was able to bring his family in here, it was possible for you to come, and you didn't have to ask for it for yourself.

Marilyn: Yes.

Virginia: Okay.

Marilyn: He probably would have thought I was crazy or something.

Virginia: Crazy about what?

Marilyn: If I'd mentioned it.

Virginia: I don't know. Could be, but I don't know. But I do get a feeling from you that you have to wait for somebody else to make things possible for you. Maybe we can change that, because a lot of people won't always be that knowing.

Marilyn: Yes.

Virginia: So, we'll see. What about you, Jim, what brought you in here?

Jim: Oh, I think that madhouse we live in. You know, I was in hopes that some of that would smooth out and, you know, that we would just go about talking to each other civilly for a change.

Virginia: How did you even know that such a place as this existed, Jim?

Jim: Well, I read about it.

Virginia: So you were in search of something better in your home.

Jim: Sounded like what we needed.

Virginia: How about you, Johnny, why did you come?

Johnny: He brought me (*indicates Jim*).

Virginia: Your dad brought you. But again, I didn't see any chains around you. But I hear you wanting to please your father. I wonder what it was you wanted for you?

Johnny: To have my dad take me places.

Virginia: Get closer to him. This is what I feel. How about you, Mary, why did you come in, dear?

Mary: Well, of course, they said, "We are going."

Virginia: And what else?

Mary: I guess I wanted us to go places and have fun as a family. I thought it would be nice. Maybe even Sue and I could go fishing sometime.

Virginia: Why not?

(*Johnny gives a loud snort.*)

Mary: Well, I like to get out and wade even if I don't like the worms!

Virginia: How did you feel about Johnny's reaction at this moment? Could you tell him?

Mary: Well, Johnny, I want you to go and have fun too. I like to see you and Dad have fun together.

Virginia: How did you feel about the snort he made?

Mary: Well, that's Johnny. He's always poking back. It wasn't so bad. Johnny's not bad.

Virginia: Well, he can snort good, and when he's doing that he sounds like Dennis the Menace, as far as I am concerned. Doesn't he to you?

Mary: Yeah, well Johnny's not so bad. Maybe he shouldn't snort at Dad, but, you know—

Virginia: I like his pixie quality, but that doesn't mean he isn't Dennis the Menace sometimes, and when he's Dennis the Menace I think you might want to wring his neck. You ever feel that way toward him?

Mary: Well, yeah, but—

Virginia: Well, tell him about it.

Mary: I mean, you know, Johnny is my buddy. I'm not going to get onto him.

Virginia: Why don't you look at him and tell him that sometimes you would like to wring his neck.

Mary: Well, Johnny, you remember when you went to my pig bank and got that quarter? I was *really hurt* about that!

Johnny: I had to buy a lure. We were going fishing.

Mary (loudly): Well, it was *my money!* I had saved it for a long time.

Johnny: You weren't using it.

Mary: Well, I was saving for something I've wanted a long time, you know.

Johnny: You never use it to get anything for yourself.

Mary: But I was saving it.

Johnny: All your money would just sit there and do nothing.

Mary (yelling angrily): Even so, I was mad because you got my quarter!

Virginia: How do you feel about that, Johnny?

Johnny: Surprised! That's not Sis.

Virginia: This *is*, right now she just showed you. She'd like to wring your neck and is damned mad at you, too!

Johnny: That's not like her.

Virginia: Well, it just now happened.

Mary: It was my quarter, and I saved it and you spent it.

Johnny: I'll have to go out and mow lawns and get you another quarter.

Mary: Would you?

Johnny: If you'd like that.

Mary: We could work together. I could pick up the grass after you cut it.

Johnny: No, I'd want to do it myself. It was your quarter. I would want to do it alone.

Virginia: Mary, how did you feel when you told Johnny about the time when you were mad at him? How do you feel right now about telling him that?

Mary: Well, I don't like to tell anybody that I'm mad.

Virginia: Well, how did you feel telling him that right now?

Mary: Well, it felt PRETTY GOOD, you know, WOW!!

Virginia: So there's also a feeling in this family that if people really are annoyed with one another they shouldn't say so.

Mary: No, because I don't want them mad at me.

Virginia: Well, see this is what your mother was saying: "If I tell my husband, Jim over there, some of the things I don't like, then all kinds of terrible things will happen." I have a funny hunch in this family everybody is keeping this all inside, and they get sarcastic or clown around and all the rest of what goes on when underneath they really have some things to say to each other. By the way, do you have something for your mother?

Mary: I love you, Mama.

Virginia: All the time?

Mary: No.

Virginia: All right, when are those times when you don't love her?

Mary: When don't I love Mama? I'm scared of her when she's sarcastic and fighting.

Virginia: How do you feel when that happens?

Mary: Like I wish I could get in a closet and shut the door.

Virginia: What do you do? What you wish is that you could get in the closet and shut the door, just kind of turn your back. Is that how it is when those things happen?

Mary: Yeah, I want to get out of there, but there's no place to go. I live in that house and there's no place to go. So the best thing to do is just be good.

Virginia: That doesn't work too well.

Mary: You're good, and you're good, and you're good, and the noise goes on.

Virginia: What did you hope would happen here for you, more than what you've said just now?

Mary: Like I said, I wish we could be happy. I wish we could have fun.

Virginia: Your face is looking now as though it has a lot of lights in it. How are you feeling?

Mary: Well, I feel better. I feel better, but I still hurt way down inside.

Virginia: Could you put your hand where you feel the hurt?

Mary (putting hand on stomach): Here.

Virginia: What does it feel like right there, Mary?

Mary: A big lump.

Virginia (to Marilyn): What hurts on you?

Marilyn (long pause): Usually my head.

Virginia: Your head. Where does it hurt in your head?

Marilyn: I don't know, by my eyes.

Virginia: Right by your eyes, you've got a headache. What hurts on you, Johnny?

Johnny: I had a broken toe once, but—

Virginia: What about other times when you don't have broken toes, because you don't have them all the time. (*No response from Johnny.*) You aren't aware of a hurt. How about you, Susan?

Susan: I feel the same way that Mary does, I hurt in there (*puts hand over stomach*).

Virginia: What did you hope would happen for you by coming in here?

Susan: I hoped maybe I could learn how to please Mom and Dad a little more than I do.

Virginia: Do you have any idea how to go about finding out how to?

Susan: I guess I could ask them.

Virginia: And what is it you want from them?

Susan: I just want them to love me.

Virginia: What makes you think they don't love you? Have you ever asked them?

Susan: No.

Virginia: Try it now.

Susan: Do you love me, Daddy?

Jim: Of course I love you.

Susan: How come you never tell me?

Jim: Well, it's kind of hard to say those things sometimes.

Virginia: Could you practice right now?

Jim: I feel kind of embarrassed to tell her here that I love her, but I do love her.

Virginia: Can you say it, from you to her?

Jim: Susan, I love you.

Virginia (to Susan): You have doubts about that sometimes?

Susan: Yes, I don't think I have ever heard Daddy say that before to me.

Virginia: How did you feel hearing it?

Susan: I felt good.

Virginia: Do you believe what your dad said?

Susan: Yes.

Virginia: Could you tell him you believed it?

Susan: Dad, I believed you when you said you loved me.

Jim: I'm glad. I'm glad you believed me, because it's true.

Susan: Mom, what about you?

Marilyn: I love you too, you know that.

Susan: You never tell me, Mom.

Marilyn: I guess that's something I just keep forgetting to do. It never seems to be the right time to tell your kids that. I guess it's easier to tell you to pick your clothes up.

Virginia: How do you feel hearing your mother say this?

Susan: I really don't feel that she's convinced me that she really means it when she says that.

Virginia: Can you tell that to her? "Mother, I have trouble— whatever it is—hearing you or feeling convinced." Maybe if you moved a little closer to her that would help.

Susan (moves chair closer to Marilyn): Mother, I sometimes, or right now I don't get the feeling that you really mean that you love me.

Marilyn: Well, why not?! Every mother loves her children, you know that!

Virginia (overlapping): Not true!

Susan: Yes, but you really don't tell me—

Virginia (to Marilyn): Could you say what you feel about what Susan is telling you?

Marilyn: I guess I feel scared, because I thought they knew I loved them.

Virginia: Could you just talk to Susan about that?

Marilyn: Don't you remember your birthday parties and all the cakes and stuff?

Susan: Yes, Mom, but you know that just doesn't take the place of a simple "I love you" every now and then. I mean, I appreciate what you do for me, Mom, I really do. I appreciate the birthdays and the cakes and presents, and this class ring. But it's just not quite the same as hearing you say, "I love you."

Marilyn: Well, nobody ever tells me.

Susan: Mom, you know I love you.

Virginia: Do you hear what you are just now saying? Your mother said before, "You know I love you." Your mother is now saying that she has the same question that you had, Susan. Are you aware of that?

Susan: Yes. Well, Mom, I love you.

Marilyn: And I love you, too.

Virginia: That feel different to you?

Susan: It feels good.

Virginia: Johnny, what about you right now, dear? I notice there's a little moisture in your eyes. I wonder what you are aware of feeling.

Johnny: I was feeling that I like both of them. This is the first time I've seen Mom and Susan like this, and I was feeling left out.

Virginia: Where would you have liked to be?

Johnny: Right here. I mean, uh—when are we going home?

Virginia: I noticed that as you two really connected with one another that you reached out to each other with your hands. Were you aware of that? I wonder if you could just let yourselves move together as close as you were before. Now, Johnny, I wonder about you in relation to this. Do you want to come in closer?

Johnny: I'd like to, but—

Virginia: Well, could you act on what you want. Johnny, what you were indicating when you wanted to move up closer, by the way you looked at her, was maybe your sister Mary would be left out. Then your father put his hand on your knee as if to say, "It's okay, John." Were you aware of that?

Johnny: Yes.

Virginia: Now what do you think will happen with Mary now that you have moved where you wanted to be?

Johnny: I think she feels left out. I think it hurt her feelings.

Virginia: Would you like her to be closer here with you?

Johnny: Yes, I would.

Virginia: Would you like to ask her if she wants to come in closer with the rest of you?

Johnny: Would you like to come?

Virginia: Mary, how did you feel about Johnny's worry about you?

Mary: I guess I was glad Johnny worried about me. I wanted him to be close to Mama and Sue, but—

Johnny: Somebody has to worry about you. You never worry about yourself.

Mary: But I wanted to be there too.

Johnny: What do you mean?

Mary: I wanted to be there too, but I wanted you to be close to Mama and Sue. I mean it didn't matter if I wasn't real close, I—

Virginia: True or not true?

Mary: Well, it mattered, but I did want Johnny to be in there close to Mama.

Virginia: Is it as though if Johnny were close to her, you could not come closer?

Mary: No, I thought if Johnny got love, well, that would be a good feeling.

Virginia: For whom?

Mary: Johnny.

Virginia: You know, Mary, maybe this can help open a new door for you, because I see you sitting back and waiting for somebody else to ask you in, you know? Maybe that can change. Now you four have drawn closer together in a smaller circle. What are you aware of now?

Johnny: Dad's being left out. Where's Dad going to go?

Virginia: Well, would you ask him?

Johnny: Dad, come on in.

Virginia (to Jim): I wonder how you felt about what Johnny just did?

Jim: Well, I began to wonder whether he was going to ask me, but I kind of knew he would. It made me feel good.

Johnny: I'll let you catch the biggest fish next time.

Mary: Can I go fishing with you?

Jim: Sure you can go.

Johnny: If you don't scare the fish away.

Mary: Maybe we could all go.

Jim: There you are! We'll all go!

Virginia: I think at this point we can stop for now. One thing I would like to suggest is that we get together again soon and spend about four or five hours to see what we can do. I have a hunch now that some ideas have occurred, some new windows have been opened about how things *can* be different. I get that feeling. How would you feel about that?

Susan: I think that would be great.

Jim: I think that's a good idea. (*Laughs.*) I feel good. Seemed at first I was all knotted up, and now there's a glow inside.

Susan: I feel good just seeing Mom and Dad feel good, and Mary and Johnny.

Virginia: I want to tell you something about me too, because my insides are feeling okay at this point, and at times they weren't. Maybe this is what we can learn more about, about how we can be more in touch with our insides and with what is going on.

Comments, Questions, and Discussion Typically Raised by Such an Interview

Comment: You probably noticed that although this was all obviously made up, the feelings became warmer and warmer, and tears came to the eyes of family members. There were even tears in my eyes. This is a beautiful thing. If all this could come out of an "artificial situation," it occurred to me that even more feeling must be generated in a real family situation.

Comment: As some of the members of the family were drawing closer and others were feeling left out, I had a feeling myself that as an observer I was so involved that I had feelings of being left out.

Virginia: At one point when I began to get some feedback indirectly from the family that they wanted to be closer to one another, I helped them by having them move closer physically, rather than leaving them seated in their original positions. This helped to bring them in closer contact. I watch for the clues and for the opportunity. Did you understand how quickly Jim spelled out at the beginning that "No one really sees me"? The typical procedure would be to pick up that complaint and start answering it. That may be faster, but this is not where the real problem lies. Instead, I talk to the self-worth "pot" underneath. That pot has much to tell you if you will only listen. But first you have to realize that it is there, that inside every human being is a delicate little creature, present from the moment of birth, which has been battered and bruised many times, and in the process has learned not to reveal the pain. The pain is there, however, and if you know how to communicate with the pain, you can give people the encouragement they need to let it out.

Question: What is the lower age limit of children for family group therapy?

Virginia: The family includes every member, sometimes even the family pet. Once a family I worked with had a horse for a pet, and I carried on the interviews in the stable.

Question: It was apparent that at the beginning of your session you were interacting with one or two members of the family at a time, and toward the end there was more of a pulling together of the whole group. It is common when you have quite a number of young children that they do a lot of goofing off and they, in essence, form their own group and are not involved. How do you deal with that?

Virginia: What happens with the young children is that when the process begins to unfold and people are really contacting each other, interacting honestly and openly, that provides a context in which the kids stop their monkeyshines. As a matter of fact, I use the activity of the children as a way of detecting when the process begins to emerge.

For example, when I do marathon sessions with groups of families, I always like to have one family with a child under the age of one. Better yet is to have a nursing mother and baby, because that baby will be very sensitive to the crosscurrents that are not meshing. I like to have young children in the group because of their sensitivity to the process, to the flow of events. In demonstrating family therapy, I often have a family with four or five children under the age of six years. It is amazing what happens with those children.

As the therapeutic process evolves, it provides a cushion for many kinds of change and growth. This opens up many possibilites. But until that happens, the kids are going to act out. I give up my ideas about making them behave and treat the family as something to be explored, instead of letting myself become distracted from the main issues and getting into the child-tending business. In Palo Alto I have conducted family therapy in the midst of expensive machinery, with wires strewn around to operate recording equipment and all kinds of delicate gadgets within the reach of children. Often the families included children who were described as hellions, crazy, and uncontrollable. I have never had one serious mishap occur with the children, no matter how bad they were purported to be.

One of the things I do is to give everybody my attention in a very total, genuine manner. The matter of calling people by their first names is quite important, because by getting on a first-name basis we immediately establish one connection, one bridge. They all receive my attention in a very real way. Suppose there were a two-year-old boy in the family and he was sitting on the floor. I would talk to him on the floor. As much as possible, I give up the idea that a therapy session is a behavior session where I have to control people. Instead, I try to regard the family as an organism, and count on the fact that this organism is made up of people who feel little and defenseless on the inside and on the outside will manifest their distress by blaming, placating, and the other communication modes I have talked about.

Try to identify, in our simulated family, the stances they had at the beginning. Visualize the typical poses: Johnny is irrelevant; Father is blaming; Mother is blaming; Mary, the next-to-the-oldest child, is extremely placating; and the oldest child is also placating. By the time the session was finished they had relaxed from these stress stances. At that point they were in a position to deal in terms of reality with the issues troubling them.

One of the things I do is to establish the cushion of openness and trust before I go further, because only then can I get at the real issues. Before that I am always dealing with "pot" issues. Some classical interchanges occurred after Jim began to trust me and he started trying to tell his son and wife that he really wanted to hear them. There was an interesting triad. First Father would make an offering, Johnny would reject that offering with some sarcastic remark, and then Mother would come in and echo Johnny's reaction. If this state of affairs continued without intervention, the father would have become increasingly uncomfortable, begun blaming in return, and probably would have eventually turned his back on the family. The interactions can develop into a veritable ballet as the members of the family shift their blaming and placating from one to another. The whole interview could have been done in terms of these shifting tableaus.

Question: Where would you be as the therapist in this family ballet?

Virginia: I am always moving in the scene, with my words and my hands.

Question: What are your thoughts about Mary, the middle child? It appeared that she was the most hurt.

Virginia: When you think about this family, Mary's hurt showed more than anybody else's at the outset. But each of these people was hurting so much that during the interview my insides were churning with the pain.

Comment: The father and mother were so obviously hurting that they were unreal.

Question: When you were able to see what the communication stances were, did you use that information to bring about more awareness?

Virginia: The way I used that was by helping Mary, who seemed to have the most barriers, be in touch with her angry feelings and make her anger known to Johnny. The whole family saw that they could survive this and, in addition, that they felt good about it. You see, Johnny was a stereotype to begin with.

You could read the stereotypes in this family. Jim was a bastard, Marilyn was the complaining wife, Susan was a nice, good girl, and Mary the quiet girl. Mary and Johnny took care of each other. Recalling that lovely bit at the beginning when Mary got Johnny to sit with her, the message was that Mary was the protector of Johnny. Johnny was the good person, and Papa was always after him. This was part of the myth of the family. Johnny wasn't the good guy. As for Mary, it would have been easy not to see the tremendous loneliness that she had. As far as Mary and John were concerned, while there were lots of good feelings going on, he was also fast getting into the position of being Mary's substitute for a guy for herself, evoking her mothering being instead of allowing her femininity and wholeness to develop as it should at her age.

Comment: I believe that Mary was six years old at the time Johnny was born, so she was the baby for six years. Then her hero, Daddy, got a son, and perhaps she felt a little guilty about not wanting Daddy to have a son and throw her out of the favored spot. Maybe she tried to make up for her resentment by mothering Johnny.

Virginia: The situation is made up of the kinds of learnings Mary might have had that would predispose her to behave this way. I do not know whether or not that was one of the learnings Mary used, but it could have been.

Comment: How much of Mary's concern for Johnny was real and how much of it was trying to get close to Daddy again by being his helper in taking care of Johnny?

Virginia: Even if the latter was true at one time, it would no longer be true unless something right now in the family situation was supporting it. No old learning continues unless there is current support.

I think this is a good point to bring up. How things occurred in the past is relevant to how things are now only if that history plays a part in the now. The past is relevant to the present (1) to explain the present, and (2) if it contaminates the present. Whatever is lived through and integrated from the past does not contaminate the present—it is no longer active. Only when it has not been integrated or assimilated is it still around so that it can become relevant to the current issue.

Question: In order to maximize the opportunities for people to move around and to draw closer physically, do you usually use portable chairs rather than overstuffed chairs?

Virginia: Yes, I do not want to have a situation in which people cannot move easily. Also, I do not use tables. Tables come between people. There should be nothing between any of us in the group.

Question: What is the impact of these people on you and your feelings? Was there any time when you felt irritated or angry with any of them?

Virginia: I talked about all of my feelings that might have gotten in the way. I did have an awful feeling, like something was piercing my guts, when Jim blasted out every time he was hurt. It was like an arrow going through me, but I did not feel that as an angry reaction. In order to experience anger, I have to feel both hurt and helpless. All I felt was pain.

Question: Do you ever feel like crying when you have these moments in an interview, and if so, do you?

Virginia: If tears come, they come. I don't do anything to hold them back.

Question: One time you said "no" to Marilyn when she made the statement "All mothers love their children." Why?

Virginia: I said "no" because I wanted to get her out of the stereotype.

Question: When you are working with families, do you ever, for their benefit, accentuate the roles you see them playing by having them pose?

Virginia: Oh, yes. It didn't flow that way in this interview, but one of the things I would do when the family came in again would be to teach them the various roles. Sometimes if the interview heads in that direction I say, "You know, I have a picture of how you were right now and I would like to sculpture that for you. Would you be willing to do it?"

Question: When there is resistance and nobody wants to communicate, would that be the time to do this?

Virginia: No. Role-playing should not be used to break resistance, but only when trust is high. Here is how I look at resistance. When someone is behaving in a way that tells me he is resistant, I see this as his using a technique for survival. That causes me to wonder what it is about the situation that is threatening or scaring him. For me, what is termed "resistance" is the thing that protects me and keeps me going. It is my most important resource. Although it is a barrier between the therapist and his clients, it is a defense, a way of staying alive. When anyone resorts to resistance to defend or protect himself, what I try to do is determine what his fears are. That must be dealt with first before I can involve a person in any kind of role-playing or sculpturing.

Question: How did you feel after an hour of this interview, and how much of this could you do during the course of a day? The emotional impacts were tremendous. Do you ever get to the point of overload?

Virginia: I have worked forty and fifty hours at a stretch without sleep and I can go right along. It's as though while the flow of the process continues, I can go on almost indefinitely with that flow. But if I start to react internally with "Oh, no! That's not the way it should be done," or "What can I do with these characters? I better give them up—they're going to kill me!" then emotional overload comes on the scene. There is a difference between feeling fatigued and feeling tired. I can go on for hours and end with only a lovely feeling of being tired, but I do not get fatigued anymore. In the past I did get fatigued. That happened mainly because of the image I had of myself. My image was that there were about five hundred bosoms on me with faucets that I could not turn off, and there was a big sign that said "Drink." And, boy, did I get worn out! What I had to do first of all was realize that I only had two and that I could turn off the faucets and take down the sign—I could be in charge of myself. It was not a matter of controlling the outside, but my feelings on the inside.

Question: Isn't there some contradiction between what you just said and what you had stated previously about letting your feelings out?

Virginia: I don't see the contradiction, but maybe there is one.

Question: Are there not multiple feelings generated at any instant in relation to five people, which calls for discretion in choosing one of them to express? One can't pick all of them. For instance, is it not difficult to operate all the time on the congruent level? Some conflicting feelings get in the way. When Johnny snickered as you were becoming close to the father, my response as I projected into the therapist's role was, "Wham! You're blowing it for me, kid!"

Virginia: Yes, but I don't feel that way anymore. In effect, what you are saying is, "Here I did that nice thing, and he threw it in my face." If I think, "That dirty son of a gun! He doesn't take my goodies!" or "My, he must be sicker than I thought," or "I'll never get anywhere with this guy—I feel helpless," then I am going to generate a lot of negative feelings. However, that was not the way I felt at the time you refer to.

Question: But if you do feel that way, what do you do?

Virginia: All right, suppose I thought I was being slapped in the face. If I were in that position, I would say, "You know, I just want to tell you how I feel. I really felt slapped in the face by you." Also I would go on and say, "I don't know how you feel about my telling you this. Could you let me know?" The whole interchange can bring about a new awareness.

Question: But it does call for some direction on the therapist's part to lay aside some of his reactions. Are you saying that the key is to be aware of them?

Virginia: Yes. To go further, let's suppose that something like this happened, as it did to me once, and I came out with "Why, you son of a bitch!" I could feel myself blushing, and I said, "Whee, how did you feel when I said that? Was anyone else feeling like I was?" Even something like this can result in a good thing when it can be plowed into the process.

Along this line of what the therapist feels, every once in a while there are guys I meet that I find to be rather sexy. Not too many of them who come in for treatment seem very sexy to begin with because they hide it, but later on they do. This is a natural kind of human reaction. When it occurs, how can that feeling be used for growth? Let us say a wife is talking about how she wishes the husband would be more romantic, and I say to her, "I want to tell you how I feel about that character right now—I feel kind of warmed up about him. How do you feel about that?" One woman said to me, "Well, teach me how to respond to him that way." Maybe I will get the reaction, "I don't know what you see in him that I don't!" Then I ask the husband, "How do you feel about our discussing you like this?" All feelings can be useful. They enrich the flow and the process which is operating.

Let me be quite explicit. I do not have sexual intercourse with my patients. At the present there is a lot of sexual acting out under the aegis of therapy, mostly between male therapists and their patients. To my way of thinking that is not a therapeutic event, and I do not like or condone it. In addition, there is no violence in my group therapy. No violence and no sex. The emphasis is kept on the level of feelings. And what nicer feeling can one have than that of being attracted to someone of the opposite sex? When I ask the wife, "Have you ever felt toward your husband the way I am feeling right now?" the feelings can be used constructively. If she replied, "Yes," then I can ask what she does when she feels that way, and quite often the wife will say, "Well, I have to wait for him to make the overture." So she somehow has to learn to express her warm feelings, and my modeling of openness of expression may be of help. The inability to be open about feelings is one of the biggest obstacles to effective family functioning. That is what the simulated family was having trouble with, letting out their positive feelings and trying to break the taboo that they should not express their negative feelings.

Question: Do you get into conversations about sex when there are little kids present?

Virginia: Of course, One can take any subject and talk about it placatingly, blamingly, super-reasonably, irrelevantly, and congruently. I wrote a paper once about a family I worked with which had several young children. It was called "The Care and Maintenance of the Genitals." What more lovely thing can you do than take the sexual component of people away from the scum and the mystery and place it in reality, in the life force where it belongs. I am convinced that people who feel whole and acceptable in all their parts are not going to destroy themselves or anybody else. Integrated people are in harmony with their whole being—their teeth, their genitals, everything about them. They can care for and treat well not only themselves but others. We pay a heavy price for eliminating parts of a person's being in an effort to help people be "good." The amount of sexual crime in this world is fantastic. Mainly it is committed by men. Men have more taboos against being sexual than women, although it is a significant part of their whole life force. Arriving at the realization of the beauty of the whole self is, I believe, a great goal. You cannot misuse that which you honor and love.

Question: How does the dimension of religion enter into your family treatment program?

Virginia: Earlier I commented that I see a difference between Christ and Christianity. What I meant is that I see a lot of people who claim to be Christians who are blaming, placating, super-reasonable, and irrelevant. They exemplify the neurotic use of religion, of Christ's teachings. Christ, Buddha, and other religious figures have preached about the holiness of man, the divinity of man. When someone spouts religion to me and does not reflect this attitude toward man, I call that the neurotic use of religion. Religion per se for the individual is subject to however the person himself is organized.

Question: Would the particular stance a person takes also be projected upon God?

Virginia: Sure. Fortunately, I was taught about a loving God as I grew up, and therefore I did not have very much to overcome in this respect. But I see many people who in the name of religion (just as some in the name of therapy) do all kinds of things which I consider harmful and not conducive to the nurture of the human being. So I do not argue about the subject of religion—that is too irrelevant. Some people say that girls should not wear lipstick before the age of fifteen because God said so. I am not going to argue the point—it is irrelevant. What is important is how they feel if they have this belief and what happens to them if this belief does not work out right. I try to bring all those feelings into the process.

The sexual ideas that people have are handled the same way. One thing is certain: if there is any coping problem it will be reflected in the areas of sex, money, work, religion, discipline of children, and food. Those are all things that have a joint outcome for the family. The inability to cope with life will show up in those things. Many times people come in with symptoms of frigidity or impotence, that type of thing. That is only the starting point. From there I look at the communication mode, how they handle stress. Just imagine for a minute the placating vagina and the blaming penis. What kind of intercourse is that going to be? Or the placating vagina and the placating penis?

Apply the ineffective communication patterns to meal preparation and what results is a lot of food that nobody wants to eat. "I always have to cook spinach in this house," the housewife thinks. Spinach has a lot of meaning for me. I happen to like it. But I had a family in therapy once and in the process of the husband and wife becoming able to speak about what they really felt and how things were, the man said, "I can't stand spinach, and you feed it to me all the time." The wife said, 'What?! I thought you loved spinach." This was after thirty years of marriage. My curiosity was aroused and I asked her where she got the idea he liked spinach. She replied, "I had a terrible homelife. My mother never did anything to please my father, so I made up my mind that I was going to please my husband." How did she go about doing that? She said, "I watch to see what pleases him." Did she ever ask him? No, she had not. Why not? "I want it to be a surprise," she said. This is why they had spinach so often. Before they were married they visited the husband's sister, and the sister served spinach. The man ate two helpings. That meant he liked spinach. The wife cooked spinach two or three times a week. Sometimes he ate it, sometimes he didn't. When he didn't, she interpreted that as his not being very hungry or that some other food in the meal was even better and he ate too much of it to eat the spinach.

When the story came out, he said, "My sister was extremely proud of her cooking, and I just couldn't tell her when something didn't taste good. I always ate two helpings to let her know I thought the food was okay, but I destested eating that spinach!" At no time in all those thirty years did the wife ever say, "How do you like spinach?" and at no time did he ever say, "Stop with the spinach—I can't stand it." This sounds like a fabrication, but it is true. I could relate many similar examples.

One couple had been married for forty-five years, and when they came in for help they were still carrying around the scars from the honeymoon. At the time they were married the man was working in a firm owned by his father, and as they were about ready to go to bed on their wedding night the phone rang. His father was calling about some kind of crisis in the business. The husband said to the wife, "Goodbye, I'll be back in the morning." She never forgave him for that, but what she said to him as he went out was, "All right, dear, I'll be waiting." He thought she was understanding; she thought he was the cruelest monster ever, but she could not comment on it. Forty-five years later she still remembered. His leaving her on their wedding night was evidence that he did not really love her; and he thought she was very understanding, but he was the silent type and had not said anything about it. This is what comes out when communication is opened up and people are free to comment.

Question: You mentioned at the end of the interview that you would like to see the family for four or five hours. Do you usually use the marathon situation with a group that is as intricately related as the family, or do you ordinarily see them for the regular amount of time, like an hour or so?

Virginia: Some of the things I do I can't take full credit for. They have come about almost accidentally. I grew up on the 50-minute hour. While I did have social work training, I also had psychoanalytic training and was a lay analyst. Now, everybody knows about the sacred 50-minute hour, and the meeting always takes place in an office. I have operated that way. However, when I started to work with families, it seemed we could not get much done in fifty minutes, so I stretched it to a 90-minute hour. Then I found after a while that the 90-minute hour every week did not work out. I traveled a lot and was doing many things other than therapy, but I still wanted to work with people and they still wanted me to help them. So I told them, "The only way I can do this is if we get together during whatever time I can scrounge and the time is agreeable with you." On one occasion in San Francisco, all I had was four or five hours between planes, and the family and I met in a lounge at the airport to see what we could do with the amount of time we had. Gradually it got through to me that the process of treatment never follows the clock. It does not happen that today you work on personal growth for one hour and you take it up again next week at five o'clock. It doesn't work out that way. You may have noticed that sometimes interview sessions become tedious. They will not be tedious if they are following the course of growth, and the course of growth is not governed by the clock.

Concurrent with this new use of time, I came upon the fact that a different contract was in effect. *The contract was not to heal people, but to do whatever could be done with all of us together to shed light on what was going on.* This gave me a different viewpoint about what I was trying to do, and what I do now is to work until an enlightenment occurs for the group.

For instance, the first time I meet with a family, we work until they experience a new cushion of nurture, however long it takes. This usually requires three hours when therapists are just learning. Now it does not take me that long. The purpose is to help a new experience happen, and you are the one who brings about that new experience. For me, the amount of time spent with a family is determined by the time I have available to do whatever has to be done, the time people coming to me have, and how we can arrange to get together.

Also, I have been impressed by the fact that no longer is it a matter of working together and being bound to each other forever or indefinitely long. Instead, we get together to do what we can and I have practically nobody hanging on my coattails, because there is nothing in what I do that says to them that they cannot get along without me. Not anymore. This is the way therapy is evolving for me.

You develop what might be called a rhythm for this kind of work. Very shortly your people come to know and trust you, and they realize that you give them whatever time is necessary. When you work with people, you can pretty well gauge how much time you will need. Usually a three-hour session is sufficient.

Something else that I went on to do was more or less born of expediency. I began to work with groups of families. The first family group started with a family that flew to Palo Alto one weekend from Utah. As we worked together, I told them about a family in San Francisco that I was going to meet with for a couple of weeks, and I asked them to join us. They did, and this led to my having groups of families get together. The results have been quite good because of all the new dimensions and possibilities that are afforded by that kind of setting. Now I am working with designed groups, and we go to the wilderness for a couple of weeks. Some of the public welfare departments I worked with in Minnesota are taking groups of families out in the country on weekends instead of having regular office interviews every week or something of that sort. Every month the staff rotates in working with the weekend retreat, and they have learned how to deal with large groups. They have found that they can help a great many more families that way.

Question: What is different about working with several families? Do you mix them all up together, or still work with the family unit, or what?

Virginia: There are several ways I work with groups of families. The largest group I have had was ninety persons, representing eighteen families, that met together for one week. However many there are or whatever their problems may be, at the beginning each family sits together. Then I ask that they have a consultation within their family constellation or cluster, and prepare one statement defining the problem they want to work on as a family. When they have done this, I ask them to present their statement to the whole gathering and explain how they decided upon it. Then I touch slightly on the differences in the decision-making processes, just enough to introduce the fact that decision-making is not the easiest thing in the world and to hold it up for their consideration.

Suppose Family A says, "We want to be happier in our family." When I ask them to give me some specific ways in which they want to be happy, they say, "In our family we have one son, John, and it seems like he runs the house." Then I go on to the other families. It may be that another family has a similar situation, one boy in the family causes them a lot of concern. So I say, "You're kind of like the A's over there. The two of you are looking at pretty much the same problem." What I do is determine what the most important problems are, the process behind devising statements about them, and then tie it all together. You never find more than five problems in a group. That is not to say that the content is restricted to five specific things, such as someone is using drugs or somebody is an alcoholic, but the systemic process within the family results in about five different problem areas. At that point I have some other tasks. For one thing, I say to them, "You know, my experience has been that people in families do not look at each other very much, and though you may think this is strange, I want you just to look at each other accurately and deeply without turning away." There will be some who cannot do this, and I will say, "I notice you are looking away from your husband. What is going on?" "Everytime I look at him, I remember." "What do you remember?" "Oh, I think of all the women he's been running around with." "Is he running around with one right now, right here?" "No." So I say to the woman, "Then you are not really seeing him right now. You are seeing him in terms of your fantasy about him. See what happens if you just look at him now." There is much that can be done in regard to seeing people as they really are at the moment. When I zero in on one person, everyone else listens. So I might say, "Is there any other wife here who when she looks at her husband thinks, 'Oh, my God! All the garbage that is piled on me'?" Several women will hold up their hands. And I ask if there are any men who feel that way when they look at their wives. So we slowly weave the picture. What I am in effect telling them is that human problems are honorable; they do not have to be stigmatized.

Exactly what pattern the seminar takes depends upon how the particular group gathering develops and what evolves. Sometimes we work in special groups, such as all children together and then subdivided into the younger ones and the older ones. Sometimes we make groups of all men and all women. When enough time is available, like a week, we can differentiate a number of groups that can work together. By doing this, people learn more about their interactions and their particular family system, and they also have opportunities to open up their systems and expand interpersonal relationships.

Question: Do the groups of families go home at night and come back each day?

Virginia: No, when I get people together like this, I want to make use of the total time, so we stay together in some kind of residence or we can even camp out and use sleeping bags. It makes little difference what the facilities are so long as there are no blizzards or bad storms. We use whatever environment we have, however sparse. This learning and growth process can go on as long as there is enough food to eat, a place to lay our heads, and, of course, a place for the garbage.

This may give you the flavor of what I try to do. While I do make a lot of use of structure, it is always within the framework of trying to see whether it is true that, for example, you are the only one who thought your mother did not like you. There are millions of people who have that kind of experience, but before you find that out from others, you think you are all alone. People discover they are not alone in thinking, "I'd like to wring my father's neck!" They find that everybody has these kinds of thoughts and feelings, and not because they had parents but because people are people. They can then stop beating themselves and start building and growing.

Question: Could you point out some of the danger spots and supply some guidelines for working as change agents?

Virginia: The biggest pitfall has to do with the therapist's disappointment when he cannot make it work. When he has a captive family, such as those ordered to get therapy by a court, and the therapist himself does not understand about family systems and is following one of the communication stances without knowing it, the chances of making havoc of the family system are very great. One of the nice things about family therapy is that when people are free to leave—if they are not getting anything out of it, if it is not working—they just go. Thus chances of hurting a family in a voluntary situation are not great. If they are not helped, they do not come back. This is not true with individuals; they feel they have to continue. Another nice thing about working with families is that you do have the support of a system which is tight and strong—it may not be doing well with all its members but it is sustaining. However, with a captive family the going may be very rugged, and here is where a therapist who does not really understand systems can do harm.

In spite of this, let me say that I consider the most harmful result of therapy to be a suicide. Yet in the thousands of people that I have seen, only one person has suicided. It is not easy to take, and I am not sure to this day what went wrong. Always I have to remind myself that I am the leader of the treatment situation, not of the people in it. If you come to my office or my seminar, I will offer myself to you in that leadership role, but I will not take charge of your person.

Problems in the Practice of Family Therapy

Most of the pitfalls in family therapy are for the therapist, not the family. One is when the therapist uses the family as a laboratory for his personal growth. There is nothing wrong with that, unless it is done at the expense of the family. For instance, I have great concern about all the sexual acting out occurring under the guise of therapy. This is quite prevalent. I also am greatly concerned about the violence which occurs under the hypothesis that expressing hostility helps one grow. I think this is a "cop-out." Expressing anger is something completely different. Hostility is anger plus blaming the other person, just as depression is sadness plus blame of oneself. Angry feelings are honorable and sad feelings are honorable, but what worries me is the growing trend of therapists to profess that people become healthy by attacking other people with their hostility and hate. This kind of thing is quite common in some improperly conducted encounter groups, and I see it also in some work with families. I believe this is one pitfall not too many therapists are aware of.

Family therapy is not too different from working with individuals in one respect; that is, the therapist can hang on the backs of others his own problems and call them the family's problems.

Actually I see more pain than I do pitfalls in family therapy, because working with the family compels you to review every single experience of your own life, every conclusion you ever made, every pain you ever had, every good and bad thing in your own life. Everyone was brought up in a family and has ideas about how parents should treat children and how husbands and wives should treat each other. All manner of things cause struggle and turmoil for the therapist personally, and it is a sure bet that working with a family will activate these personal feelings.

I call anyone who makes his living by trying to change people a therapist. Some women therapists, when they work with a family in which there is a newborn child, may be so focused on that child that they forget the two adults. They may be so conscious of how the child ought to be brought up that they hover like a hawk over the parents. If you happen to be divorced and you deal with a family in the process of divorce, or you work with them while you are in the process of your own divorce, you identify and bring your personal experiences to mind in their situation. The result can be quite painful.

Utilization of Therapist's Family Experience

I am willing to undergo this pain because I realize that whatever has happened to me probably can be useful in my work with others. I am not through growing and I am not through making mistakes. The family I grew up in consisted of people who, under some circumstances, did horrible things and who also did some great things. I learned many things, some useful and some which had to be discarded. As I go along I may find more of both kinds of learnings from my past. For me, the pitfalls and pains are far overshadowed by the joy, the growth (with whatever pain accompanies it), and the results.

Probably there is nothing in any material a family presents to the therapist that he does not know something about. A group of us who work in family therapy got together and concluded that the best basic training was within our own families, the one we grew up in and the one we now have. Actually, we all have a lot more training than we may realize. Very few people can be aware of the whole family process, however, while they are growing up. They are only aware then of bits and pieces.

Mapping the Family Structure

If I were to map the family structure, what I am talking about would probably be a little clearer. At the beginning there are two people who have to find each other and get together to make the third person. The initial two people have three parts—me, you, and us. Then as soon as the child pops out of the womb he is related to the woman and she, willy-nilly, gets the label of "mother," and the man gets the label of "father." It has nothing to do with anything else, merely the physiological fact that the child was born. Then the family contains an adult female, adult male, a child, and three usses—three dyads, the marital dyad and two parental-filial dyads. We began with two individuals and one dyad. When the third individual is added we have the next order of family structure, which has three dyads and, in addition, three triads—the adult female regarding her husband and child, the adult male looking at his wife and child, and the child looking at the mother and father. Each triad has a life of its own and at least four lines of perception: how the individual sees himself, how he sees the other persons, how he sees the others seeing him, and how he sees the others seeing him see them. Also, there is a fifth perceptual process, which I seldom use, and it is how the individual sees the others seeing themselves. The minute the child comes into the family, the number of units increases from three to nine.

Not too many families have only one child, and, as they say in the English novel, as people have their wont, a second child comes along. Two more parental-filial dyads are formed, and another order of dyads is added, the sibling dyad, giving you all the orders of dyads contained in the family—marital, parental-filial, and sibling. With the addition of one person, making four individuals, three dyads are added, giving you a total of six dyads. When I illustrate this to family groups, I use clothesline rope to show all these relationships. If many members are added to the example of a family, you can easily imagine what a tangled web is woven. After the addition of the second child, let's look at what happens to the triads. The adult female takes a look at her husband and the new child, the adult male looks at what his wife is doing with the child, and the first child takes a look at what his mother is doing with the second child. We call it sibling rivalry when the child looks at a parent and the other child and says, "You like him better than you do me." The first child looks at what goes on between the father and the second child, and before very long the second child begins to notice what goes on between his mother and brother: "You let him go to bed later than me." The second child also looks at what goes on between the father and the first child, the father looks at what goes on between his two kids, and mother looks at what is going on between the kids. The triads are now increased to twelve, each with a life of its own, each subject to the perceptions I mentioned before, and the perceptual interrelationships become astronomical at this point. Each interrelationship is a valid part of the family system. Each can be seen entirely differently, and they are not always in harmony with each other.

What I could do is ask the father-husband how he sees himself, how he sees his wife, how he sees his first child, and how he sees his second child; how he sees his wife seeing him, how he sees his child seeing his wife, how he sees his wife seeing his child, and on and on. It can take all day to get through these perceptions, but they are the perceptions people function with.

This gives you some idea of the family map when there are only two children. When you add a third, the relationships go from twenty-two units, each with a life of its own subject to all these perceptions, to forty-five. If you draw a map on the wall of a family of ten, you could cover the whole wall. By the way, when I do this in working with families, they say that we do not need any more population explosion, with the problems it brings, because it becomes obvious with these multiple interrelationships that the present potential for problems is overwhelming.

A couple of things should be added. An increasing number of families have a second husband in the family unit, and the first husband has another family unit, so you have a whole new set of connections. There may even be two or three husbands or wives. Often a grandparent is in the family system and all the relationships are expanded to relate to the grandparent. This is the nuclear family network, otherwise known as the can of worms.

When you work with a family which has taboos against commenting, and you proceed by the role and stereotype method, you never really get into the family dynamics. You feel very much as though everything is slithering around like a can of worms.

In working with the family, I map out the network on a piece of paper. People can immediately see their situation. From the beginning of his life the second child in the family has had more lines of interaction than the first child did. If you can be in touch with this and know how each person perceives his lines, it will give you some idea of potential relationship collisions. The family maps are quite useful, and I do a lot with them.

Evolution of Family Therapy

In conclusion, I would like for you to think of family therapy's evolution. The early way of looking at families was to identify the symptom bearer. If it were a child, what you did was treat the mother and child. If you examine the whole network, however, the complete family system, you realize that there would not have been a symptom bearer without all the rest of the system's dynamics. The total picture has a graphic flow that stands out like a bas-relief. Some of you may remember the old stereopticons in which you could see one picture close in front of you but not the two, at a distance from the lens, which went into the composition of what you viewed. In therapy we used to see only what was in front of our noses and we did not know what was behind that view. Now we can know and we can better understand the family's system and the dynamics making up the picture it presents.

1. Gregory Bateson, Don D. Jackson, Jay Haley, and John H. Weakland, "Toward a Theory of Schizophrenia," *Behavioral Science*, 1 (1956), 251-264.

Chapter 8

Family Therapy in Action

by James Stachowiak

Introduction

Mr. and Mrs. J. came to the Mental Health Center seeking help for their marital difficulties. Their major complaint centered on their bickering, which often culminated in physical fights. They were seen for an initial interview and later agreed, along with their three children, to come for a demonstration family interview for a group of community care-givers.

The interview took place before approximately 140 onlookers. Such a situation undoubtedly influences the resulting interactions by affecting the ease with which the interviewer can approach his interventive task and the spontaneity with which the family can relate to him and to one another. Nevertheless, this interview shows that some productive work is possible under the handicaps imposed by such a situation.

Difficulties Unique to Demonstration Interviews

The interview was conducted with the therapist and family seated in a semicircle on a stage at the front of the meeting room in full view of the audience. The participants were arranged as follows: Dr. Stachowiak (Jim); Steve, age ten; Martha, the wife; Denise, age twelve; Scott, age fifteen; and Fred, the husband.

This session is characterized by a number of features which the reader may find of interest and to which he may wish to give some thought. One, of course, is the manner in which the therapist deals with his anxiety about interviewing before an audience. A related concern is the manner in which he deals with the family's feelings about revealing themselves before a group. Since interviewing families before groups is often part of a training experience, some thought needs to be given to the different ways in which the factors extrinsic to the family session may be managed so that they may be neutralized or, better still, integrated into the ensuing experience with the family. For example, is it possible to help the family feel at one with its onlookers so that the viewers are not experienced as alien and threatening?

Effect of Audience on Family

This demonstration interview poses, by implication, a concern the reader should keep in mind. Throughout the session the family showed little spontaneity. It may be helpful to speculate to what extent their constriction represented their basic interactional pattern and to what extent they may have held back because people were watching. We advise the reader, through an exercise of his imagination, to introject himself into this family, consider its culture, and visualize how he himself would have reacted within the interview.

Effect of Audience on Therapist

Another salient concern in this session involves the role of the therapist. In this interview the therapist not only seeks an understanding of the family but attempts to produce change. What are the advantages and disadvantages of the approaches he takes? Much may be gained if the reader clearly delineates the pressures in the situation that impinge upon the therapist and considers their impact on what he does. In attempting such an exercise the reader may better appreciate some of the complexities of family interviewing. As an example, it would appear on the surface that the wife dominates the family. However, the reader also needs to keep in mind the impact of the husband's sullenness, lack of apparent involvement, his construction, his vagueness, and what comes off as extreme guardedness. Because it is difficult to grasp the nature of his struggle in the interview, do we have an element of uncertainty (and, consequently, therapist anxiety) that directly affects what transpires? In this session the reader will note that the mother carries the family. To what extent does the convergence of forces in the family in front of an audience impel the therapist largely to engage her in change, and thus inadvertently reinforce her dominance?

Focus on Family Dynamics

Another important question worth considering relates to the substantial communications breakdown and role conflicts within the family. What is striking is the tendency of the spouses to persist in their maladaptive patterns despite the disruption it causes them. Because their behavior appears so resistive to change, the reader needs to ask what keeps it going? What's the payoff? To what extent are the forces that drive the family a part of external reality, and to what extent is external reality shaped by the family architects to resolve or at least cope with the unmet needs and influences of early childhood? How the therapist answers this question may determine what he opens himself up to in the family's experience and what he focuses his attention upon.

It is now well known in family dynamics that spouses tend to parentalize one another. However, spouses do not always serve as a stand-in for the same sex parent. For example, a husband may represent a mother to his wife at a far more basic level than he may represent her father. This interview touches on that point and offers a possibility for some interesting speculation about the wife's dynamics.

The reader should also consider the characteristic patterns of each spouse in dealing with marital frustrations. The behavior of each spouse undoubtedly has its precedents in his early learning experiences. How the spouse's parents dealt with conflict undoubtedly serves as a model that often is either emulated or rejected. In the latter event, the model nevertheless remains controlling because it is important to the spouse not to act as his parents did. The reader will note that the therapist does not engage the husband and wife in a discussion of their early role models for handling conflict. Another important question, then, is whether it would have been economical and advisable to do so.

In Chapter 7 Satir's focus on the "here and now" is productive and involving. However, when a family such as the J's engages in a perpetual and circular pattern of blaming from which there seems no extrication, how productive or manageable is a "here and now" approach? For example, the reader will clearly see how difficult it is for the family to talk to one another despite the therapist's efforts to get them to do so.

In this interview, as in all others, the therapist is confronted with the difficult challenge of finding a way to engage the family at the gut level of their emotions—to get at where the pain really is. There is no question that the interview which follows was a most difficult one to conduct. Those who interview families before groups will easily identify with the struggles of the therapist, as will those who have worked with constricted, largely nonverbal families.

Transcript of Interview

Jim: To begin, I know all your names and you have probably heard mine. I have a hard name to pronounce, so if it's all right with you, I would like to be called by my first name, Jim. And I would like to call you by your first names.

I have spent the last ten years trying to help families make changes in their life situation so that things will be happier and more satisfying for everybody. One of the ways I have done this is by trying to help other people who work with families to learn more about interviewing. I don't know how you all feel at this moment, but every time, right at the beginning, being in front of a group of people makes me nervous. You may be feeling that way too. I get sweaty palms and my heart beats fast, I shake a little and all that kind of stuff. What helps me is to take a couple of deep breaths, and you might want to do that too before we start talking. When we get started, though, I am sure that our attention will be here on one another and we will soon forget for the most part that we have an audience out there.

As I said, one of my interests is trying to help families find ways that they can live together so that everyone can be a little more happy. When families live together, there are times when one (or more) of the people feels hurt, and when one person in the family feels hurt, everybody shares in that. To begin with, I would like to ask each of you what it is in your family that you find hurtful. Who wants to start? (*Long pause.*) No one wants to start?

Martha: I suppose I will.

Jim: You suppose you will? Okay.

Martha: Well, what hurts me the most is when he goes off to hunt and never seems to think about the kids or I, either one. I mean, for instance, all this week he has been on vacation, and I had to get up and go to work and he never seemed to worry about breakfast or anything. If he wanted to go hunting, fine. If he wanted to stay in bed, fine. If he wasn't there when I got home from work, fine. I don't think he realizes how I feel, or does he try to even understand? We used to have the same thing—if he'd get mad he'd go drinking and it would be the same thing. Sure, I know I growl a lot and I gripe, but does he ever stop and think of why I do?

Jim: If I hear you right, what hurts you most right now is that you're not sure how Fred really feels about you and the family.

Martha: Well, I went to work so that the family could have more. We could get the bills paid. Does he repay it back? He don't seem to consider how much I got to do at home or what responsibility really lies on me.

Jim: These are all questions you'd like to be able to ask Fred and get an answer?

Martha: Yeah.

Jim: Well, Fred, you hear how Martha feels. What kinds of things are hurtful to you?

Fred (after a long pause, mumbles): What did you say?

Jim: What kinds of things are hurtful to you with Martha and the kids?

Fred (long pause, then mutters): Not very much of anything.

Jim: "Not very much of anything," did you say? Do you suppose, though, that the way Martha feels has some kind of effect on the way you feel? How would you put that into words?

Fred (very hesitantly, very low voice): Well, it's not very pleasant.

Jim: It's not very pleasant for you. How do you mean that?

Fred (long pause, low voice): Well, it's not very pleasant when two people don't get along.

Jim: When two people don't get along. What does it do for you? Does it get you here (*indicates his stomach*)?

Fred: No, not too much anymore.

Jim: Not anymore.

Fred: Not so much anymore.

Jim: So what you are saying, I guess, is that sometime in the past your way of trying to handle hurt was, what? To shut it off? Not let it hurt you?

Fred: Yeah, I suppose.

Jim: Well, what about the kids. How does this all affect you guys?

Martha: They're hurt whenever we're hurt.

Jim: Sure! Let's see. Scott, you are number one in age, aren't you? What hurts the most for you?

Scott: Well, not really anything.

Jim: Not really anything, Scott? I can tell when you say "not really anything" that there are some things. Is there anything that you would like to get talked about?

Scott: No, I don't think so.

Jim: You don't think so. Okay for right now. Let's ask your sister how she is feeling.

Denise: When Dad does something that Mother doesn't want him to do, then she gripes and it just makes everybody unhappy.

Jim: Uh-huh. When Dad does something that Mom doesn't

want him to do, she gripes—at whom, at Dad?

Denise: Uh-huh. And then she gripes at everybody.

Jim: So everybody gets unhappy, you think?

Denise: Uh-huh.

Jim: How do you handle that hurt? What do you do?

Denise: I don't know.

Jim: Well, like your Dad says, sometimes people try to close it off. Sometimes people will try to get out of it by going to their rooms or something like that. Do you do anything like that?

Denise (very low): I usually just read a book or something.

Jim: I didn't hear you.

Denise: I usually just read a book or something.

Jim: Just read a book. You try not to notice it, too. Steve, what do you do? (*Long pause.*) Did you hear what Denise said? What do you think about that? Do you see it that way too, or is it different?

Steve: Well, about the same.

Jim: You see it about the same. She says she tries to read a book. What do you do?

Steve (mumbling): I just go outside and play football or something.

Jim: Go outside and play football or something. Okay. You can see, just from talking about it a little, everybody in your family has some kind of hurt, even though it's hard at this point for Scott to talk about how it affects him. So far it looks to me like what you are saying is you really haven't found a way to talk about some of these feelings and to try to make changes.

To start with, maybe it would be a good idea to see how this family came to be in the first place. I am going to ask you, Steve, if you would change seats with your Dad so that we can talk about how the family got started. (*Father and Steve exchange places.*) There was a time, as you kids know, when none of you were here and your family got started with these two, Mom and Dad. So for a while I am going to take some time just to talk to these two. I want you kids to listen carefully to what we talk about. You may not have heard some of these things and you may want to ask some questions.

Now, Fred and Martha, out of all possible people in the

world, how did you two happen to meet and fall in love? Why don't you start, Fred?

Fred (low, very hesitantly, with lengthy pauses): Well, let's see. We lived not too far from them, and we got to visiting. A neighbor boy and me, we went to a Fourth of July in Chanute. *(Turns to Martha.)* Wasn't that when it was?

Jim: I don't know about others hearing you talk, but I can hardly hear you, Fred. Could you speak a little louder?

Fred: We went to a Fourth of July in Chanute and I didn't have a date with her or anything like that, then later I got a date with her.

Jim: And when was that, Fred?

Fred: In about '50. Let's see— '52 or '53, about '52.

Jim: About '52. That would have been about, what, nineteen years ago?

Fred: Yeah, that's pretty close.

Jim: Okay. How old were you at that time?

Fred: Twenty-two, I think.

Jim: Twenty-two years old?

Fred: Yeah.

Jim: Okay. And you went to this—on the Fourth of July—

Fred: Just as a group. All of us did.

Jim: But you were both in the group.

Fred: Yeah.

Jim: Had you ever seen Martha before? Did you know her?

Fred: Yeah. I had seen her before.

Jim: Where?

Fred: Let's see. She worked in a drugstore—I saw her there. And my folks and her folks visited together.

Jim: So your folks knew one another.

Fred:·Yeah.

Jim: Yours and hers. Right. But you had never asked her for a date, I guess.

Fred: No.

Jim: Okay. When did you know there was something about her that made your heart flutter a little bit?

Fred (long pause): Let's see . . . I don't remember. Oh, yeah. I had went to Oklahoma for a while, and I came back about seven or eight months later, and I didn't have nothing to do so I called her up and asked her for a date.

Jim: Uh-huh. Were you dating somebody else before that?

Fred: No.

Jim: No. So you came back and just decided to find out what would happen if you called her up.

Fred: Yeah.

Jim: Okay. You remember that first time you called her. What did you say?

Fred: Asked her if she wanted to go to the show.

Jim: What did she say?

Fred: Said she did.

Jim: Okay. What do you think it was, when you think back to that time, that made you want to get to know her better, get closer to her? What was there about her?

Fred: Oh, I guess I just started going with her, I don't know, to have somebody to go with, I don't know.

Jim: To have somebody to go with?

Fred: At first, yeah.

Jim: What I am trying to say is did you like the way her legs looked, or her pretty smile, or what was it?

Fred (slowly): Kind of the smile and the way she talked.

Jim: The smile and the way she talked. Okay. Let's ask Martha. You heard how Fred remembers this. How do you remember it?

Martha: Well, about the same way, I guess. I—to me at first he wasn't too interesting. I mean, he was always real nice to me and all this, but I was going with another boy.

Jim: You were going with another boy at the time he called?

Martha: Yes.

Jim: Ah-ha!

Martha: Yes. He was in the Navy.

Jim: You mean he was away from here, in the Navy?

Martha: Uh-huh. I didn't intend to fall in love with him, but I did.

Jim: With whom?

Martha: With Fred.

Jim: With Fred. Okay. Why? What is there about him that

turned you on like that?

Martha: Just cause he's him, I guess.

Jim: Yeah, but what is "him"? You know, I don't know him. You have to try to tell us.

Martha: I don't know. He just—he was always real considerate of me, before we was married.

Jim: Real considerate before you were married.

Martha: And he really never—I mean—I don't know. I really can't put it in words, I guess.

Jim: I think you're doing fine.

Martha: All this time I was telling myself not to fall in love with him because I had a ring from another guy. But I did.

Jim: But you did anyway. So what are you saying, then? That even with all these resolutions you made, he changed your mind?

Martha: He still won over. Yes.

Jim: He won over! Is he the strong, silent type? Is that Fred?

Martha: I suppose. He never was that silent before we were married.

Jim: Before?

Martha: I mean, he'd sit down and talk to me. Now he don't. He gets up and walks out.

Jim: So before you were married it was fun for you guys to talk, and after you were married, then what?

Martha: There was no *communication*.

Jim: I'd like to hear from both of you on this: How long did it take before you decided that you would get married?

Martha: Let's see. We started going together in May, I guess it was, and in August we decided to get married.

Jim (to Fred): Is that the way you remember it too?

Fred: Pretty close, yeah.

Jim: How do you both remember your deciding to get married? Martha says that she was telling herself, "No I'm not going to get married to this guy because I've got this other guy." But that changed. How did you go about deciding to get married?

Fred: We really never decided. We just kept going together more and more, and we could both feel that we loved each other, and we wanted to get married.

Jim: It just came up, like maybe one night when you were together?

Fred: It just gradually kept coming.

Jim: Did you talk about it some? Do you remember?

Fred: Yeah.

Jim (to Martha): How about you. How do you remember it?

Martha: Yeah, we talked about it. I wanted to wait until June to get married, and he wanted to get married in November, which we did.

Jim: You did what Fred wanted to do.

Martha: I still kept having this feeling that it *can't* be. And I wanted to go ahead and get married in November, but I kept thinking it just can't be.

Jim: Uh-huh. That it wouldn't happen, that it shouldn't happen? Is that what you are saying?

Martha: Something was going to happen to change it or something.

Jim: Yeah. Let's see, at that time nineteen years ago, how old would you have been, Fred?

Fred: Umm—twenty-two.

Jim: And how old were you, Martha?

Martha: I was seventeen when we started to going together, and I was eighteen in July.

Jim: In July, uh-huh. Now, how did your folks and your friends feel when they found out you were going to get married? Do you remember?

Fred: You mean my folks? They didn't care.

Jim: You said they knew her folks?

Fred: Yes.

Jim: Did you feel like they thought it was a good idea?

Fred: Yeah. I think they kind of expected it.

Jim: And what did you think her folks felt about her marrying you?

Fred: Well, I don't think they really cared.

Martha: They felt I was too young to get married, but they didn't say anything. My Mom kept saying that "she'll settle herself down."

Jim: I didn't hear you.

Martha: My Mom kept saying, telling my sister, that "if she'll settle herself down, well he's the man for her." Of course, I didn't know all of this until after I was married.

Jim: Then they told you?

Martha: Then my sister told me.

Jim: Uh-huh. But they wouldn't tell you that before?

Martha (with a giggle): Because I was kind of playing the field about that time, too.

Jim: Is that what they meant by "settling yourself down"?

Martha: Yeah.

Jim: So right at that time you had several guys that you were interested in.

Martha: Yeah. One in particular.

Jim: This was the fellow in the Navy?

Martha: Yeah.

Jim: Okay. But as far as you can remember, then, neither of you felt that your parents were against it. What kind of family did each of you come from? What was yours, Fred?

Fred: Farmers.

Jim: Farmers. And how many kids in your family?

Fred: Four, with me.

Jim: Four, with you, and what number are you?

Fred: Next to the oldest.

Jim: Did you have an older brother or sister?

Fred: I did have an older brother. He's deceased now.

Jim: When did he die?

Fred: Must have been, *(to Martha)* how many years ago?

Martha: It'll be ten years in July.

Jim: Ten years ago. Was this the brother you were closest to?

Fred (pause): No, not really. Not any closer than the other brother and sister.

Jim: Uh-huh. And who was the boss in your family, between your father and mother?

Fred: I suppose my father.

Jim: Your father. What was it like having an older brother? Did you like it, or did you fight a lot, or how was it?

Fred: Oh, I kinda liked him. We didn't fight too much. Had some fights.

Jim: Okay. And at the time when you were going to be married, what were you doing? What was your job?

Fred: Well, I went to work for the railroad before I— (*Pauses and looks at Martha.*) That was after I started going with you?

Martha: About July, I think it was.

Fred: Then my father and I was farming some together, too.

Jim: Okay. Now, Martha, in your family how many were there?

Martha: Three. There was a boy and two girls, and I am the youngest.

Jim: You're the youngest. Were you the "baby" of the family?

Martha: Well, there was only about sixteen months between us, so we just were all one group, seemed like.

Jim: Uh-huh, very close.

Martha: Uh-huh.

Jim: Okay. And it sounds like you never really felt like being the baby of the family.

Martha: No, not really.

Jim: As the youngest though—

Martha (interrupting): My Dad did kind of baby me some.

Jim: Babied you some?

Martha: My mother didn't.

Jim: Your mother didn't. Which one of them was the boss at your house?

Martha: It was kinda equal. I mean, Daddy had his things that Mother knew he liked and she did them, and vice versa.

Jim: Uh-huh. So how did it feel to get a little babying from Dad?

Martha: I don't know. I still feel closer to Dad than I do to Mom sometimes.

Jim: Are you saying that—

Martha (interrupting): Daddy could always understand when Mother couldn't.

Jim: Okay. Are you also saying that you wish that you and your mother were closer?

Martha: Well, I don't really miss it, I guess. There was times that I went to my grandmother and told her different things that should have been told to my mother.

Jim: Uh-huh. Are you saying that there was something that kept you from talking to her?

Martha: I always felt that she tended more to my sister than she did me.

Jim: Preferred your sister.

Martha: Yeah.

Jim: Which one was that, which number?

Martha: Next to me.

Jim: Next to you.

Martha: I have an older brother, then my sister, and then me.

Jim: Then if I hear what you are saying, you've always felt like more understanding came to you from a man?

Martha: From my Dad, yes.

Jim: From your Dad.

Martha: Or my grandmother was the same way, my Dad's mother.

Jim: And then I think I heard you say that when you and Fred got married, at least right before and maybe in the early years, you felt like he was very understanding toward you, considerate. And it meant a lot to you. (*Martha nods her head slightly.*) All right. I want to ask Steve and Scott, Denise, too, have you ever heard your folks talk about this? (*Negative responses.*) You never have? What do you think of it? Can you believe it, that it happened that way?

Steve (*very softly*): I suppose it did.

Jim: You suppose it did. If you have any questions about what you hear them saying, just let me know so we can ask them. Okay? So now we are at the point where you get married, and, Fred, you started working for the railroad, right? And what were you doing then, Martha?

Martha: I was working for a meat-packing company.

Jim: At the time you got married. Did you continue working there?

Martha: Yes.

Jim: Okay. You know, a lot of times when people get married they start thinking about what kind of family they're going to have. What ideas did you have about what you wanted your family to be like? What were your plans?

Fred (*very low and mumbling*): Well—I don't know—ordinary family, I do know that.

Jim: Ordinary family. Is that what you have? Did you ever think at that time when you were getting married that those three would be here with you (*indicating the children*)?

Fred: I didn't figure they would be as good as they are.

Jim: You didn't figure they would be as good as they are. So you are saying you're really pleased about being their dad? Okay. What did you think, Martha?

Martha: Well, I felt like when I got married that I gave my whole life to the family. I mean, you helped each other, and if one, just like the case now, where money didn't go around, the ends didn't meet, I went back to work, and I felt like he should step in and help me with my work at home, too.

Jim: You're talking about now, after you got married, or—?

Martha: Well, when I got married.

Jim: When you got married. If you were going to work, you thought Fred should help out.

Martha: Should help me at home, yes. And now I went to work to pay the bills, and it seems like sometimes he spends more on hunting and things like this than we actually pay on bills. I mean— (*falls silent*).

Jim: I kind of like the way you say that, because you don't say that is actually true; you say "it seems like" or "I feel like that's the way it is."

Martha: I feel like that's the way it should be, yes.

Jim: And you feel like maybe—

Martha: Maybe I'm wrong, yes.

Jim: You're not sure?

Martha: Well, that's the way I feel. I don't know whether anybody can change me or not.

Jim: Have people tried to change you?

Martha (bitterly): Yes, he has (*indicating Fred*).

Jim: Fred has tried to change you? Well—

Martha (interrupting): I mean, he feels like if he wants to go hunting, it shouldn't be— I mean, if he gets mad and he wants to go drink, I shouldn't say anything. Sure I gripe. I know I do.

Jim: Okay. You're getting a little bit ahead of me now. We'll come back to this later. What I want to ask is do you have the kind of family you planned to have?

Martha: I wouldn't mind having one more child, but it just didn't work out that way.

Jim: So you wanted to have—

Martha: Yes, I wanted a boy when Scott was born, a girl when she was born, and a boy when Steve was born.

Jim: How could you plan it that way?

Martha: I got just what I wanted.

Jim: Just what you wanted. Right. How do you think they are now?

Martha: I wouldn't trade them for life itself.

Jim: So each of you two are very pleased and happy that these three are your kids, right?

Martha: Yes.

Jim: Let's go back now to right after you were married. You, Martha, are working, Fred is working, and at that time during the first couple of years what is it like at your house? Can you remember how you felt? Were you then still talking to each other and understanding and being helpful to one another?

Martha: No, not really. Our first argument was over—he was working eleven to seven and I had to go to work at seven, and I came home from work and he wasn't there. I mean, quail season was on, so it didn't matter what time I got home. He wanted to hunt, fine. I shouldn't miss him.

Jim: This is eleven o'clock in the evening?

Martha: Well, when I got home from work in the evening. He would hunt all day, and then when he did come home, about eight o'clock or so, he wanted to go to bed and sleep before he went to work. That ended the communication. I mean, there was no time to talk.

Jim: Okay. Now, you say that was the first argument you had that you remember?

Martha: Yes, our first argument was over hunting.

Jim: And how long after you were married was that, do you remember?

Martha: About two weeks.

Jim: About two weeks. So did the honeymoon last two weeks for you?

Martha: I suppose it did.

Jim: Or did you get it back after that argument?

Martha: Not fully, no. There was distance between us.

Jim: That first argument was very important to you. (*To Fred.*) Do you remember that first argument? How did you see it?

Fred (*pause*): Well, I don't know. Maybe I looked at it wrong, but I just went out there to her folks' place and was hunting a little while in the evening. I think I stayed out there for supper. Her mother asked me to, and then I went to work at eleven o'clock.

Jim: Then you went to work. You mean at eleven o'clock at night?

Fred: Yeah.

Jim: You were working a night shift. And you, Martha, were working—

Martha: Days.

Jim: Days. When did you guys get together anyway at that time?

Martha: We could have in the evenings if he would have stayed home, because I got off about five o'clock.

Jim: Oh, I see. I thought you were saying that you didn't get home till eleven.

Martha: No, when I come home and got off work, he wasn't there.

Jim: Yeah. Now, let me check with you first, Fred. I think you're saying that you didn't expect Martha to get upset about that. Right?

Fred: Yes, that's right.

Jim: In your head this was just what a man does, and the wife's—

Fred: Well, it's—that one time was the only time I did it right then.

Jim: I'm not sure I understand. Can you tell me how you mean that?

Fred: Well, I just went hunting that one time that week. I don't know.

Jim: Oh, I see. You weren't doing it all the time. So she should have been able to accept that. Right?

Fred: I suppose.

Jim: I mean, is that what you felt?

Fred: Well, maybe I'm wrong. I don't see why she got so mad as she did. I don't know.

Jim: Okay. So even to this day you don't understand why Martha got so mad. Now one thing, and I guess this is true for both of you, is that when Martha acts mad, underneath that she's really hurt. Is that true? Would you see her that way?

Fred: I didn't—I never did. I don't know. I guess—yeah. I don't know. I never looked at it as her being hurt. I don't know.

Jim: You saw the madness, right?

Fred: Yeah.

Jim: Let me ask your kids at this point. Denise, what do you think about that? When your mother's mad, what's really going on with her?

Denise: She's just kinda hurt that he don't, doesn't take her out or something.

Jim: Doesn't take her out or something?

Denise: Well, the other night, you know, after he got done hunting, well, him and his friend went to eat at the cafe, and Mom thought he should take her in, you know, for supper. And she was kind of hurt because he didn't take her in. She was home from work.

Jim: Yeah. Tell me, Denise, how does your mother let your father know what she likes?

Denise: She gripes at him, and then tells him.

Jim: Ahead of time or later? For example, would she say to him ahead of time, "Hey, I would like to go out to eat tonight. Is that okay with you?"

Denise: Well, she kinda wants him to ask her. She doesn't want to tell him; she wants him to ask her.

Jim: Okay. You notice how hard it is sometimes for people to ask one another, even people who are close to them, for what they like? They'd rather have the other one recognize it without asking. Are you like that?

Denise: Yes.

Jim: How do you ask for what you want?

Denise: I ask her (*indicating her mother*) for it. Sometimes she gives it to me; sometimes she doesn't.

Jim: Yeah. What if you felt like you wanted to get a hug from your dad—how would you go about doing it?

Denise: I don't know.

Jim: Does he ever hug you?

Denise: Sometimes.

Jim: Like father-daughter hugs?

Denise: Yeah. I guess.

Jim: So you'd have trouble, I guess, asking him, too. Can you ever go up to him and ask him, or let him know that you'd like a hug?

Denise (low and hesitant): I don't know.

Jim: Does he like it, Denise, if you hug him?

Denise: I guess.

Jim: You're not sure. We have to find out about that, I think. What do you say, Fred? Do you like for your daughter to hug you?

Fred: What do you mean?

Jim: Do you like it when your daughter hugs you?

Fred: Well, yeah.

Jim: Do you think she knows that you like it?

Fred (very low): I don't know.

Jim: You see, so far what they are saying, and I have to check this out, is that these two gals in your family aren't too sure sometimes what is going on in your head. Right?

Martha: You were talking about me asking him to take me places. If I do, there's always an excuse of that he's got to do this or got to do that. But just as sure as when I am off to work, he can do the things he wants to do. There's time for this, but there's no time to spend with the family.

Jim: For now let's talk just about spending time with you, okay? You must wonder what Fred is really thinking about.

Martha: I never know. He pushes me out of his life!

Jim: That's the way you feel. (*To Fred.*) You know that she feels that way?

Fred: Yes, she says sometimes she does.

Jim: You believe her when she says that?

Fred: Yeah.

Jim: She says, "Fred is trying to get away from me and that makes me very nervous and hurt. Maybe he doesn't care about me." Is that what you read from her, too, that message?

Fred: No.

Jim: You don't feel that way?

Fred: No.

Jim: But she feels you feel that way. Did you know that?

Fred: I guess.

Jim: Now, how do you let Martha know that you don't feel that way? That is, how do you let her know that you do care about her?

Fred: Talk to her and (*long pause*) try to do things for her.

Jim: You try to?

Fred: Yeah.

Jim: Can you give me an example of something you would be likely to do to give her a message that you care about her?

Fred: Well, do dishes, or buy her a dress, or (*long pause*) something like that.

Jim: If you think back, in the last week or two, is there something that comes to your mind that you did just to show her how much you cared about her?

Fred: Well, yeah. Do dishes, and took her and went to Salina and tried to buy her some clothes Monday night.

Jim: You did, and I think you are saying that you do these things because it's one way you have of showing her that you care about her. Now, I noticed while Fred was saying that you were shaking your head, Martha. Why's that?

Martha (*bitterly*): I have come home every evening this week and found the breakfast dishes sitting on the table, except Monday evening, and Denise did them and we went to Salina. He hasn't picked them up the whole week. Just like I left them. I don't ever eat any breakfast before I leave. I get up and then I get her up or set the alarm so she'll get up. And they eat breakfast, and those dishes have been right there when I've come home every evening.

Jim: Does he sometimes do the dishes?

Martha: If I get up and start them and say, "Fred, will you help me?" Yes. But to take it on his own and go ahead and do it, no.

Jim: So, if you ask Fred in a situation like that—

Martha: Once in a while, yes. But if he doesn't want to he'll say, "I'm tired," as if I've not worked all day, too. This is, to me, this is a family deal. You do things for one another. That's the reason I went to work, so this family would have more.

Jim: Uh-huh. I hear you saying that you're getting a bad deal.

Martha: Well, it feels like it!

Jim: That's the way it feels to you. You went to work and you felt like that was your contribution. But you don't feel like you're getting an even shake.

Martha: I don't feel like that is my whole contribution, no. But I would like to have some help!

Jim: Okay. Let me ask you boys, because so far we've only been talking about Dad with females, how is it with you guys? How do you know how Dad feels about you, Scott?

Scott (very low): I don't really know.

Jim: You don't really know. If you wanted to ask him questions, you wanted to know something, how would you go about doing it?

Scott (very softly): Just go and ask him.

Jim: Can you think of a time you did that recently?

Scott (long pause): You mean, like—what do you mean?

Jim: Oh, what he thinks about things you want to do, or do you ever talk to him about dating girls?

Scott: No.

Jim: Are you interested in girls?

Scott: I guess.

Jim: You guess? You're not sure? Well, I am going to ask Denise? Is he really interested in girls, Denise?

Denise: Sometimes.

Jim: Sometimes.

Denise: I don't really know.

Jim: You don't really know, either! So here we have Scott, and we don't really know how he feels about girls, and you and your mother are saying that you don't know how Fred feels about girls. Are these two guys the same kind?

Denise: Well, Scott don't let us know about what girls he likes or anything else.

Jim: So he doesn't let you know what's in his head either!

Martha: He's a lot like his Dad. He's on the secret type. Once in a while he'll come to me and say something, but you never know what is going on in his mind either.

Jim: So he's a chip off the old block, you're saying. All right.

Martha: He does communicate more with me than Fred does, though. He'll come and ask me different things, if he can do different things, and I'll tell him a lot of times to ask Dad. And he says it won't do any good.

Jim (to Scott): To ask Dad? Is that true?

Scott: That's just like if I want to go to town or something, well, then she says go ask Dad first.

Jim: And you say that it won't do any good?

Scott: He'll just say—he'll just shrug it off. Maybe he'll say yes.

Jim: You're not sure what he'll do. It sounds like you're not too sure he is going to agree, so you go to Mom, because what? You think that you are more likely to get what you want?

Scott: I suppose.

Jim: So far, then, I don't know if you're hearing what people are saying, Fred. It sounds to me like they are saying they're not sure how to ask you about things, or what kind of an answer you're going to give.

Martha: You're really lucky if you get an answer. He'll turn around and walk off.

Jim (to Fred): Do you hear that? Even Scott is saying something like that. I get the feeling from the way you're talking here that you don't necessarily mean it to be that way. Did you know, though, that they feel that way?

Fred: That they feel that I won't answer them?

Jim: Yeah, or that you kind of walk away and don't deal with it.

Fred: No, I thought I always answered. I don't know.

Jim: So I am right that that's the way you'd want it to be?

Fred: Yes.

Jim: That they could come to you and ask you things and you'd want to give an answer if you can.

Fred: Yes.

Jim: Okay. Now, Steve, we got these two, Fred and Scott who's the chip off the old block, and it looks like the two gals go to-

gether pretty well. How do you fit into all of this? Which one
are you like?

Steve: More like Dad.

Jim: More like Dad. Does that mean that you feel like Scott,
too?

Steve: I'm like both of them.

Jim: You're like both of them. All right. Did you hear your
mother talking about being the baby in her family? Are you
the baby in your family? How do you like it? (*Long pause.*)
You're giving me what they say your father does, but I don't
know what that means.

Steve (*very low*): They get the same things that I do.

Jim: They what?

Steve: They get the same things that I do.

Jim: They get the same things you do. Do you mean Scott and
Denise? Hey, I'll tell you what, would you bring your chair
over here by me? (*Steve moves his chair between Dr. Stachowiak and Fred.*) Good. I figured, see, since we paired off these
others, two and two, that now you and I could pair off so that
we're even. Okay? Now, you said before that you feel like they
get the same things you do. What do you mean by that? What
kind of things?

Steve: Just toys or something like that. They get the same as I.

Jim: Okay. It's even, you feel. Sometimes the youngest in the
family can get away with stuff that the others can't. Do you
ever get away with stuff that they can't?

Steve: Once in a while.

Jim: Let me see if you can think of something that you might do.
(*Pause.*) That's really putting you on the spot, isn't it? If it's
okay with you, I am going to ask Scott if he thinks that's true.
All right? Is it true that he sometimes can get away with stuff?

Scott: Well, just little bitty things, nothing big he doesn't get
away with. Like if he takes something of mine, or something,
and busts it up or something, sometimes he goes and hides it,
and then I can't find it. Then he says, "I misplaced it," or
something.

Jim: Even though you think he took it?

Scott (*short laugh*): Yeah.

Jim: Okay. How do you guys handle that? Big brother, little brother.

Scott: I just tell him, and he usually gets mad and tries to beat me up or something.

Jim: Okay. And little brothers tend to do that, don't they? How do you handle that when he, who is smaller than you, wants to beat you up?

Scott: Well, he tries to bite me or something, pushes me down or something. Sometimes if there's something laying around, he'll pick it up and hit me with it (*with laughter in his voice*).

Jim: Uh-huh. I don't hear too much about what you do, though.

Scott: I usually make him quit. I try not to hurt him. We don't get in fights very often.

Steve: Me and Denise get in more fights than me and Scott.

Jim: You and Denise? Okay, tell me about those. (*Pause.*) What are they like? Who starts them?

Steve: Both of us.

Jim: Both of you? How do you start a fight? When's the last fight you had?

Steve (*long pause*): We haven't had one for quite a while.

Jim: You haven't. Let's ask Denise if she remembers. Do you remember a fight?

Denise (*laughing*): This morning we kinda had one.

Jim (*laughing*): Not for quite a while. Okay. Could you tell me about that?

Denise: Well, he was laying on the divan and I wanted to sit down there and cover up with the covers, and he had all of them, and he wouldn't give me any, so (*laughing*) I hit him and run.

Jim: You hit him and ran. He must be pretty tough. What are you afraid he'll do?

Denise: He may do anything.

Jim: Hit him and run. Yeah. Now, let's see if I understand how that works with Mom and Dad here. Do they hit and run?

Denise: I don't know.

Jim: Well, Fred, you take off, don't you, in these fights?

Fred: I try to avoid it.

Jim: Try to avoid it. You don't want to mix it up if you can avoid it, right? So when he takes off or tries to avoid it, how does that make you feel, Martha?

Martha: Well, I don't know what he means by "try to avoid them." He knows, just for instance this week, he knows how I feel about him taking the family car to go hunting. He puts a dog in it, and Wednesday night when he came home, her (*indicating Denise*) and I had to go into town, and there was mud all over the floor, pheasant blood all over the carpet in the back. It didn't worry him, I mean, and he tries to avoid it! He knows how I feel about that to begin with. We got a pick-up for such things.

Jim: Oh, I didn't think that's what he meant. What you're saying, I guess, is that if he really wanted to avoid them, he'd change the way he behaves.

Martha: He knows what— Why make payments on the car and then tear it up every month? I mean, these are the sort of things that—

Jim: I would imagine that Fred doesn't think that's what he's doing. Isn't that true, Fred? Are you tearing up your car?

Fred: I never hurt it any.

Jim: Never hurt it any.

Martha (angrily): It didn't hurt it to get—

Jim: But see where you're at now? You talk about the same thing but from different points of view. He is saying, "Didn't hurt the car much." You're saying, "He's tearing up the car and we're having to make payments on it." It's different.

Martha: I took the pickup and went up to the pasture and got stuck.

Jim: And?

Martha: He beat me up.

Jim: Beat you up?

Martha: I mean, I was tearing *it* up.

Jim: So he got—

Martha (interrupting): But I was going to look after our cattle. What was he doing? a-hunting!

Jim: Okay. Tell me, then, how did this happen? You took the pickup. Why?

Martha: Because I went up to see about the cattle.

Jim: And the car wasn't there, or—?

Martha: You just don't take the car up there anyway.

Jim: Okay. And you were doing that as a way, you thought, of being helpful?

Martha: Yes!

Jim: Okay. So you got stuck up there. What you mean is that it was muddy or something? (*Martha nods.*) Okay. And where was Fred at this time?

Martha: He hadn't gotten home from work yet.

Jim: So Fred comes home from work and—?

Martha: I didn't get home until about seven o'clock, I guess. I had to walk to get the tractor to pull me out. He met me in town. He was really mad. Said I was taking the pickup up there, tearing it up. We hadn't been up there all week, and I figured it was time we had better go see about them.

Jim: Right. We'll try to check what's going on in Fred's mind. How did you feel about all this, Fred?

Fred (*very reasonably*): Well, all I did was ask her where she had been, and she got mad.

Martha (*overlapping*): I said, "Are you mad?"

Jim: No, just a minute. We have to talk one at a time. We want the silent man over here to get some words in. (*To Fred.*) You just asked?

Fred: I asked her where she had been. I thought she might be stuck up there. I tried to get there but I couldn't make it, and I turned and went around the other way and met her in town.

Jim: Met her.

Fred: As she was coming home.

Jim: And what did she do?

Fred: I asked her where she had been, and she got mad.

Jim: Then what happened?

Fred: She came home, and I started in the house and she started arguing with me.

Jim: After you got home?

Fred: Yeah.

Jim: Okay. Now, were you mad at that point?

Fred: A little bit.

Jim: What were you mad about?

Fred: Well, she had been griping for about two or three days. That's part of it.

Jim: It was already building up in you.

Fred: Yeah. I was just going to go into the house and not—you know, just let it go.

Jim: You were going to try to avoid it?

Fred: Yeah.

Jim: Okay. But, as you saw it, Martha brought it up as soon as you got into the house.

Fred: No, she never let me get in the house.

Jim: Where was that, on the porch?

Fred: Outside the house.

Jim: Outside of the house. What did she say, do you remember?

Fred (pause): Just started griping, and picked up a pan there and hit me with it.

Jim: Picked up a pan and hit you with it.

Fred: Yeah.

Jim: Okay. And did it hurt?

Fred: Yeah, a little.

Jim: A little. Where did she hit you, by the way?

Fred: Just on the chest.

Jim: On the chest. Not on the head?

Fred: No.

Jim: So you don't have any scars from that, do you?

Fred: No.

Jim: Okay. So what did you do then after she hit you?

Fred: It kinda made me mad, and I pushed her back.

Jim: You pushed her back. From there on where does it go? Do you call a truce, or you just keep going?

Fred (very low): She picked up a piece of an old sink and cut my hand open with it.

Jim: I didn't hear you. She picked up what?

Fred: A piece of a sink and—

Jim: And cut your hand?

Fred: Yeah.

Jim: How did she do that?

Fred: Hit me with it!

Jim: You mean, she threw it, or—?

Fred: No, it had a handle on it, and she just hit me with it.

Jim: Okay. Then what was your next move?

Fred (*pause*): I just quit fighting.

Jim: You just quit fighting then?

Fred: Yeah.

Jim: Is there anything more that you can remember about that? Where did you go? Did you leave or what?

Fred: Yeah, I left.

Jim: You left the house then? Sometimes a guy will feel in a situation like that he wants to get a little "touch of the demon" to kind of calm himself down. Did you do that?

Fred: Yeah.

Jim: Yeah? Do you sometimes do that when you are upset?

Fred: Yeah.

Jim: Okay. Do you ever drink what you think is too much?

Fred: No.

Jim: Never? Never in your whole life?

Fred: Oh, maybe once or twice, maybe.

Jim: Yeah. Anytime recently?

Fred: No.

Jim: When would you most likely do that? When you were upset and hurt or mad, or when you were happy?

Fred: When I was happy.

Jim: When you were happy. Okay. Now, what do you think? Would Martha agree with you that you don't drink to get drunk?

Fred (*very long pause*): I don't know.

Jim: We'll have to ask her. Okay? I want to ask her now how she saw this fight. Did it happen the way Fred said from your point of view?

Martha: No, not really.

Jim: How did it happen, do you think?

Martha: Well, on Thursday night he came home and wanted to know if I had been up and seen about the cattle, and I told him no. And he kind of growled and said I didn't care if they were up to the pasture, or something like this. So I thought, well, it had been raining Friday and that road is muddy, and I thought I'd go Friday evening. We were wanting to go to

Wichita Saturday morning. I thought, "I'll go up and see about them," and there was a friend of ours there and he went with me. And we made it up there fine, but we got stuck coming back. But when we got out, when I met him in Wilcox— You want to know his exact words? What he said?

Jim: Whatever you think.

Martha: He says, "Where in the goddamned hell have you been?"!

Jim: Okay.

Martha: And I said, "I've been up to see about the cows." And he said, "You stupid bitch! You knew you couldn't make it up there!" And, "Get your ass home and get home now!" So I went home. Well, when he came up to the house, I got out of the pickup and he got out of the car, and I says, "If you got anything to say to me, say it now." And he turned around and started toward me, and I figured he'd probably hit me, because he has did it before. And then that pan was sitting there and I picked it up. It was a plastic pan, and I threw it at him. Well, he got me around the neck, and I *didn't* hit him with that sink—I *bit* his hand.

Jim: You bit his hand. Okay.

Martha: He had his arm around my neck, and then when he finally let loose, I did pick up the sink then and I was going to throw that at him, and then he left.

Jim: Now, if I hear you right, you're saying that you were expecting him to hit you because he had—

Martha (interrupting): Well, when he started toward me, yes, I knew he would!

Jim: Right. And so before he did that you were like defending yourself?

Martha: Yes. That's right.

Jim: Okay. Now, what did you do after he left?

Martha: I went in the house. I had supper in the oven, and Steve and the fellow who went up to the pasture with me ate. I couldn't eat anything. I was too upset. Scott and Denise was in town. They was having the homecoming football game.

Jim: Yeah.

Martha: I asked Joe if he'd take us in there to get the car. Fred had taken the pickup. And he did.

Jim: I'm sorry, I missed who Joe is.

Martha: He's a friend of ours, and he came over to pick up his shotgun. Fred had had his shotgun.

Jim: So you're upset after this. You can't even eat. Now, you two guys, Scott and Denise, weren't there, but you were, Steve. Right? Can you look at me a little because I can hear you better when I see your eyes. All right. Now, you heard what your Dad said and you heard what your Mom said. How did you see it?

Steve: I don't think Dad would have come at her if Mom wouldn't have said that. If Mom wouldn't have said, "Say what you are going to say."

Jim: If Mom wouldn't have said, "Say what you're going to say"? I don't know what you mean.

Steve: She just kind of griped at him—and—so he came at her.

Jim: What you're saying, I guess, is in that situation you feel like siding with your Dad. (*Steve shakes his head negatively.*) You don't?

Steve: Not really.

Jim: What do you mean when you say he wouldn't have done that if your Mom hadn't griped? Does your mother ever gripe at you?

Steve: Once in a while when I don't pick up my clothes.

Jim: When you don't pick up your clothes? (*Steve gives a short laugh.*) And what do you do about it?

Steve: Just go pick them up.

Jim: You just go pick them up. Do you ever gripe back?

Steve: Once in a while.

Jim: Once in a while? What would you say to her if you felt she was griping at you?

Steve: Just tell her not to gripe.

Jim: You'd tell her not to gripe so much. Do you know what would help her learn not to gripe, because that would make you feel better?

Steve (*laughs softly*): Pick up my clothes.

Jim: You learned that well from your mother, right? What she said is, let me check to see if I am saying this right, "If others would do the things they should, I, Martha, wouldn't have to gripe." Is that right?

Martha: Right.

Jim: Okay. Now then, who in this family does the things that they ought to do? I think both of you parents said that the kids do pretty much. Is that right?

Fred: Most of the time, yes.

Martha: I can't really complain about the two older ones. Scott never leaves his clothes laying around. Once in a while he'll leave something lay on the table that I tell him about. She will sometimes. And if Fred is not there, Scott generally goes and helps me with the chores. And if there's a load of feed to unload, which happens a lot of time, he'll say, "Mother, now don't be a-doing that. I'll do that."

Jim: So Scott does what he ought to.

Martha: Pretty much so. He gets rebellious, of course, any kid does. I mean, especially when we're arguing. He'll go to town and stay until one or two o'clock in the morning.

Jim: When you and Fred are arguing?

Martha: Yeah.

Jim (to Scott): You want to get out of it, right? Okay. It's unhappy for you to be around then. (*Scott nods in agreement.*) (*To Martha.*) You told us about these two older ones. What about this guy, the baby?

Martha: Oh, I'll pick his things up right, and a week later they're laying there again. So then I jump back on him.

Jim: Does that help? That griping?

Martha: I think if I'd blister his bottom it would help more than anything.

Jim: If you did. You mean you don't do that?

Martha: Not too often. I usually got him (*indicating Fred*) to whip too if I do.

Jim: So he's the protector. Okay. Now is that the same way that it was for you with your daddy?

Martha: No, not really. Because I had to mind my Dad or else I was in trouble, and I had to mind Mother too, because if I didn't I was still in trouble. Maybe this is the reason I got so much respect for him, because what he said went.

Jim: Did you always mind?

Martha: No. There were times when he slapped me and I got up and said, "Slap me again if it makes you feel better" (*laughs*).

Jim: Of the kids, who is most like that? Who would be most likely to act that way too?

Martha (*indicates Steve*): Him.

Jim: Okay. (*To Steve.*) So if she blisters your bottom, would you tell her, "Okay, now blister it again"?

Steve (*smiling*): I don't know.

Jim: All right now. It sounds like you parents feel the kids, except maybe for the baby who has protectors, are pretty responsible, pretty much the way you wish that they would be. What about the two of you. Does Martha do what she should?

Fred: Yes.

Jim: Yes, she does. And Martha, does Fred do what he should?

Martha: No.

Jim: Fred, do you do what you should? (*Steve makes a low comment.*) (*To Steve.*) I didn't hear you. What did you say?

Steve: Nothing.

Jim: I think I have a hint of what you said. I think you said, "Pretty often." Is that what you said? (*No reply.*) If you can tell me later, just give me a nod, okay? (*To Fred.*) Do you do what you should?

Fred: I think I do.

Jim: I think your littlest son thinks that. I guess there are times, though, because you've said it, that Martha thinks you are not doing a lot of things you should.

Fred: Yeah.

Jim: Are there times when she has a genuine beef?

Fred: Well (*long pause*). Well—maybe. I don't know. Not really, no.

Jim: Not really?

Fred (*not so hesitantly*): No, not really. If she would just mention it, well, that's the way I look at it. If she thinks I do something wrong, just mention it and go on.

Jim: She should just mention it. She shouldn't get on you too much.

Fred: Not just harp—keep harping on it.

Jim: Not keep harping on it. Okay. I think I hear you saying that you wished that Martha would be different about this, that you know there are things you perhaps have forgotten or haven't done and if she mentions it to you, that should be enough. She shouldn't harp at you.

Fred: Well, no, I don't— Yeah, if I do something wrong, that she thinks is wrong, she should have the right to tell me, sure.

Jim: Right. Then if she harps at you, I think what you are saying is—

Fred (overlapping): That just causes trouble. They never forget anything. They remember for twenty years all that stuff.

Jim: Who's they? Women?

Fred: Women.

Jim: Okay. Women have good memories.

Martha: Why I never forget is because he keeps reminding me of it. He keeps doing the same over and over every time!

Jim: He keeps doing the same thing. Are you saying to me that you have four "children" at your house?

Martha: That's just what it seems like.

Jim: That's what it seems like for one who—

Martha: I've got to worry about the bills and how they get paid and the whole thing. I mean, if they think there should be some extra money spent on something, they keep harping until they get it.

Jim: Who is "they"?

Martha: Well, the kids are as bad as he is.

Jim: All four of them?

Martha: I mean, if I say this much has got to go on bills, well, "I've got to have this or that." Scott is about my worst one on that.

Jim: You said they keep harping until they get it, right? Why? Why do you suppose they keep harping like that?

Martha (grimly): Because they know they are going to get it. Mother will give in.

Jim: Of course! So I wonder why you do that if you don't think you should?

Martha: I think it'll cease and it won't happen again, but it does.

Jim: Of course. But that's what you are teaching them. I think, from what I hear you saying, you're teaching them if they harp long enough, it might take a long time, but if they really harp long enough, to get them off your back you will go along with what they want.

Martha (mumbling): I imagine that's right. I don't know.

Jim: Now things have turned around a little, to where you think people harp at you, too.

Martha: Well, the money situation is—I mean, like for instance, now I am supposed to work six days a week until the end of the year, probably even seven days. You know what the answer was when I came home and said that now I'll have to be working every weekend? "You can get a new shotgun with your overtime money." I mean, never a word about, "Mother, I feel sorry for you because you are going to have to work them many hours." Scott says, "Maybe you can get Daddy a new shotgun for Christmas," and Fred says, "Maybe I can have a new gun before the first of the year."

Jim: And that makes—

Martha (overlapping): Never a word about, "Mother, you have all this to do at home," or "We'll help you with it so you can go ahead and won't be so tired." I mean, it's all a selfish reason.

Jim: And how did you respond to that?

Martha: I got mad.

Jim: You got mad. Okay. So here you are having been brought up the baby in your family—I'm talking now about how you must feel inside—having all these babies to take care of.

Martha: I don't know whether—

Jim: Four babies.

Martha: It seems like everybody puts the whole thing on me. I have to worry about the—

Jim: Right! Fantastic! How—

Martha (interrupting): How the bills are going to get paid, when, and—

Jim: Do you know how people get to be irresponsible in a family? For example, do you know why some kids don't make their beds?

Martha: They just don't make them do it, I suppose.

Jim: Cause *you* do it. So that every time—

Martha (overlapping): He's tried to take care of paying the bills, and the money don't go around.

Jim: Yeah.

Martha: It just, I mean, there's always somebody on our back for some bill that needs to be paid or something.

Jim: Are you saying if he tries to do it, he doesn't do it right?

Martha: He just doesn't do it! He will buy this or that, whatever he thinks that needs to be bought for hisself!

Jim: Uh-huh, and then—

Martha: And to heck with the bills.

Jim: And then what happens? How soon is it afterward that you take the bills over again?

Martha: About the first or second time we get a telephone call saying the bills are not paid.

Jim: Then you have to step in again, right? You know why, again, people behave irresponsibly? What you think is irresponsibly? Because somebody else in that family is super-responsible. How does it feel to be super-responsible?

Martha: Terrible.

Jim: What would you really like to get for yourself?

Martha: I don't think there's anything I really want for myself, except for the family to consider me and to get the bills paid. This is the reason I went to work in the first place was to get our creditors off of our backs.

Jim: It's hard for you to ask for something for yourself, isn't it?

Martha: Yes, it is. I don't feel like I need it. I'd rather for them to have it.

Jim: Yes, but do you know what happens to people after a while if they feel too much like that?

Martha: You feel like the whole world is caving in on you.

Jim: And pretty resentful too. Because what I hear you saying over and over again is, "I'm trying to do these things for them and getting nothing back for it!" Isn't that what you're saying?

Martha (hesitantly): Well, I feel like if I do it for them, they should voluntarily do it for me.

Jim: I know it. That's right.

Martha: They should feel about me just like I feel about them.

Jim: So you're saying that one of your really biggest hurts inside of you is that you're not sure how these people whom you care about a lot feel about you.

Martha: I feel the kids care about me, but I don't feel he does.

Jim: You know, I think I heard you say that sometimes you're not even sure that they do, like for example when Scott said, "Oh, good. Maybe you can get a gun with that." That hurts too.

Martha: This to me is just a kid. I mean, they think about their pleasures before they think about what the responsibilities of the family are.

Jim: So you can excuse it if it's a kid.

Martha: Well, sure he's got a grown-up mind, but not grown-up enough to consider what the family needs are. I mean, a kid that age thinks about pleasures for theirselves.

Jim: Their own pleasures.

Martha: Not what the family has to have.

Jim: You really think that these three here don't think sometimes at least about the family?

Martha: Yeah, they do. I know they do because different times Scott's asked for different things and he'd say, "Mother, if there's not money to get it, we can forget it."

Jim: That's being considerate?

Martha: Yes.

Jim: I just wonder how old these three are going to be before you expect them to behave like an adult.

Martha: Well, I expect it now, really. And they don't really disappoint me a lot.

Jim: Okay. But Fred does.

Martha: Yes.

Jim: Have you heard Fred saying today that when you get upset and ride him, he tries to pull away from that, or it makes him angry and he retaliates?

Martha (very softly): I suppose that's what he meant.

Jim: Have I heard you say that you do at times gripe at him?

Martha: I know I do!

Jim: Okay.

Martha: But why?

Jim: Does it get you the results you want?

Martha: Well, would just not saying anything about it get the results I want?

Jim: Let's stay with the other question first: Are you liking the results you are getting?

Martha: No. I wouldn't be here if I did.

Jim: Right. So you know there's something about the way you have been behaving that isn't working for your best advantage. Right?

Martha: It don't work that way and it don't work the other way either.

Jim: What other way?

Martha: For me not to say anything about it.

Jim: Right. Well, I didn't say that. But you know what gets people in trouble? This is for all of you. What gets people in trouble is when they can only see two sides, like you were doing. If you are either quiet or griping, those are only two ways. There are many others. There is a third one, one he even suggested. I don't know if it would work. He said, "Mention it, and that should be enough." That may not be enough, I grant you, but it is at least a third other way.

Martha: But when we make up after these arguments and what have you, he'll sit there and promise that he won't—now, like taking the car, he hasn't yet but he will—that he won't take it hunting and get it like that again, or he won't go hunting, and then turn right around the very next day and do it.

Jim: Uh-huh. Which means to you—what?

Martha: It means to me he is lying to me.

Jim: When he promises?

Martha: Yes.

Jim: That's interesting. (*To Fred.*) Is that right? Do you promise her?

Fred: She makes up most of that, or makes that up.

Jim: What do you mean "makes that up"?

Fred: She dreams I say that or something. I don't know.

Jim: She dreams that you said that.

Fred: I guess.

Martha: He does say it. We were going to get a new car in '59, and I didn't want to get it because I knew he'd just take it hunting. It wouldn't really be a family car. Denise was eleven days old, and the guy came down there about the new car, and I said, "I am not going to sign that much money away for you to take it out in the fields and get it stuck and ruin it!" And he said, "Do you think that's what I'm buying this car for? I am buying it for you." All right, we got it on Saturday. (*Angrily.*) On Sunday he took it out and got it stuck, and they pulled the front end out from under it, or something. Took it down to the garage and had it fixed before I seen it. All right, now. Was that a lie he told me to get his way?!

Jim: I don't know. Ask him.

Martha: Or did he actually have intentions he wasn't going to do it?

Jim: Ask him.

Martha: I've asked him and I haven't got any answers.

Jim: Well, let's see if you get an answer now.

Fred: Well, I don't remember me ever saying that even.

Jim: But ask him what you're asking him right now, which is what?

Martha: Do you really mean it or do you do it to get your own way?

Fred: Mean what?

Martha: That you won't do this, like taking the car.

Fred: Well, I never said I wouldn't.

Martha: He swears he never said it! I mean, when he goes ahead and does it, I'll ask him why he did it, and he'll swear he never said it at all.

Jim (to Fred): Do you sometimes feel like she's your parent?

Fred: I think she causes it to be that way.

Jim: She causes it to be that way. Doesn't it take two to tangle, though?

Fred: Yeah.

Jim: Do you have to help out a little?

Fred: Yeah.

Jim: It sounds like as long as she'll be the parent, that means you can be more like you were when you were a teen-ager. Did you ever get mad after you got married thinking that there's this kind of tendency to hold you back? That all of a sudden you're not supposed to go hunting and you're not supposed to drink, or you're not supposed to do this and that? Did that ever occur to you?

Fred (hesitantly): Well, yeah. I tried not to do it very often.

Jim: Tried not to do it very often.

Fred: Being's I'm married, yeah.

Jim: 'Cause you're married. That's something that a kid can do or an unmarried person, not a married person.

Fred: Yeah.

Jim: All right. And yet I hear Martha saying that she thinks you're doing it anyway. So then, where does that leave you?

Fred (pause): I don't know.

Jim (to Fred and Martha): You know, you guys sit here, and you've got feelings going on, but you don't look in each other's eyes much. I want to ask you to do something, if you don't mind, please. Just turn your chairs so you can face each other. Okay. Now, Fred, can you look at her eyes?

Fred: Yes.

Jim: All right. One of the things you're going to have to learn to do in your family, this includes the kids too, is to bargain, and also how to ask and talk more straight to one another. Now, Martha, I keep hearing you say that you're very tired of carrying the weight of the world on your shoulders. Your shoulders must get tired from doing that.

Martha (softly and sadly): I feel like everybody depends on me sometimes.

Jim: Everybody depends on you. Right? And part of you must like that.

Martha: I don't know. I'd like to get out from under the load sometimes and be a little kid again.

Jim: Okay. So you would like to get out of that and maybe be a little irresponsible at times, too. Why don't you?

Martha: Well, I feel like I am letting the family down if I do.

Jim: But you also feel that they, and especially Fred, are letting you down sometimes. You see, part of your anger toward this man, that you also care about, comes because there's a part of you which says, "I'm not doing any of that. How come he should do it? He ought to be more like me."

Martha: I tried doing the very thing that he was doing when the kids were little. Seemed like he was never home in the evenings with me or anything. All right, a few years ago I thought, "Well, I'll be the same way." So I went out and drank and did just like he did. (*Indignantly.*) I got accused of having an affair with another man, you name it. He even told me I didn't care anything about the family, or else I wouldn't do those kinds of things.

Jim: What about that, Fred?

Fred: That's the only time I ever know of I've not been there in the evening.

Jim: Let me ask you, Martha, is what you did something you really wanted to do, or did you do it because you thought that—

Martha: No, I did it out of spite more.

Jim: Okay. Now, that's never going to work for you. That will never pay off when you're not doing it because you want to, you're doing it—

Martha (*interrupting, very forcefully*): I don't enjoy going and doing things without the family with me, really. I mean, oh, to a certain extent, but to go drink without him, it's no fun.

Jim: Okay. What would you like to do?

Martha: I am the most happy when my family is with me or they're—like—well, I don't know how to put it.

Jim: Lordy, Lordy! Your shoulders are going to get even more loaded down.

Martha: It's not exactly when all the family is with me. If I know, like the kids, if I know what they're doing and where they're at, that they're not really getting into any trouble or anything, put it that way.

Jim: Yeah. Is there any moment in your lifetime when you don't have to be concerned about everybody?

Martha: When I'm at work I forget it.

Jim: When you are doing something else.

Martha: But (*pausing*), now like this week, he's been home. To me, he should have got up and helped the kids with breakfast and all this stuff. I mean, I feel like I'm cheating the kids by working to begin with.

Jim: Ah-hah! Now, I'm glad you brought that up because I missed that entirely, that you are cheating the kids. Okay, kids, is she cheating you?

Scott: I don't feel that way.

Jim: You don't feel that way.

Denise: Neither do I.

Steve: I don't either.

Jim (to Martha): You believe them?

Martha: Well, not exactly, because if something isn't ironed that they want right now, "Why haven't you got it done?" If something isn't sewed that they want, "Why haven't you got it done?"

Jim: Which makes you feel guilty?

Martha: Sure! It makes me—

Jim: All right!! Now—

Martha: I mean, that's my duty to do it!

Jim (gently): Should we, should we get a cross for you?

Martha (laughing softly): I don't know.

Jim: To really carry?

Martha: I don't know.

Jim: Good night! You know, here you are, burdened down to the ground, with all these people making you feel guilty. How are you supposed to manage that? What is one—tell me no matter what or how crazy it sounds—one thing that you want for you? Just you.

Martha (after thinking a few moments): I'd like to have a new home.

Martha: A new home.

Martha: Yes. That's one thing I'd—would like to work for and get it.

Jim: All right. Does it look like you will?

Martha: If we would work together, yes. I could have it.

Jim: And what would that mean? Working together?

Martha: That means that we'd all save money and one wouldn't have all the pleasures or— I mean like he don't realize how much money he spends in hunting.

Jim: What you are saying, I guess, is that both of you would have to be willing to put money away for that.

Martha: Well, yes, we would!

Jim: Have you told Fred about that? That that's what you'd like?

Martha: Yes, he knows that's what I would like to have.

Jim: And, Fred, what do you think about that?

Fred (long pause): Well—

Martha: He wants to build it ourselves.

Jim: Now, let's see what he says.

Fred: What I think about what?

Jim: What she just said. Did you hear what she said?

Fred: About saving for—? Yeah.

Jim: Okay. How do you feel about it?

Fred (pause): Well, yeah, I think that would be a good idea too —yeah.

Jim: You mean, you want to get a new house, too?

Fred (slowly): Yeah.

Jim: Do you think it is possible?

Fred: Yes.

Jim: What do you think that you two could do to work toward that?

Fred (long pause): Oh, just save some money along, and start doing it.

Jim: Yes, but now I feel a little bit like maybe you're making a promise, you know, that you really don't want to do. How would you do it?

Fred: How would I save the money, you mean?

Jim: How you would put the money away, right.

Fred: Just start a savings account, and just put so much in there every month.

Jim: Can you afford it?

Fred: You could if you'd start doing it.

Jim: You mean, instead of your new gun? That's what you would do with some of that money?

Fred: I don't know. I've never had a new gun for—well—oh, yeah, I did—one.

Jim: You did, one.

Fred (speaking faster and more distinctly): For about fifteen years. And she says that I spend money hunting. I know people that spend ten times more than I do. I don't spend any more for hunting than she does for jewelry or hairspray or all that other stuff.

Jim: So for you, it's the hunting to get even with her?

Fred: No, I don't do anything for revenge, or anything like that. Just go once in a while for a little enjoyment.

Jim: No, I meant you feel that it balances out what she spends on jewelry.

Fred: I guess, I wouldn't care if—I'm not thata way. If she'd want to spend more for that, it wouldn't make me any difference.

Jim: That's what I wanted to get at. Because I don't know if you understand this part or if you've heard it, Martha. The way I want to say it is I think I hear Fred say, "I'm okay. I'm Fred. I'm okay if I go out hunting. And you're okay, Martha, if you do something you want to do." Can you believe that, or do you think he's just giving you a story?

Martha (long pause): I don't believe it.

Jim: All right. How could you believe it?

Martha (bitterly): I mean he just leaves. And if the kids have got to be someplace at a certain time, he never thinks that he should be the one to stay there and take them and maybe I should go on. He goes first and does what he wants to do. Then if the kids have something they have to go to, which they most generally do, then it's me that has to stay and take them. Because there's never a thought of how they are going to get there or back or—

Jim: Is there one thing right now, today, in this moment, that you would really like to ask Fred?

Martha: I asked him this morning to get up and "Come on, let's go, we can eat breakfast on the road up here," and he wouldn't do it.

Jim: He wouldn't what?

Martha: He didn't get up till it was too late. We didn't have time to stop and eat breakfast on the road.

Jim: Oh! On the way, I see. Right. But how about right now, to-day, at this moment. What would you like to ask Fred?

Martha (*long pause*): To really consider how I feel.

Jim: Ask him.

Martha (*to Fred*): Consider how I feel.

Jim: Do you know what she means, Fred?

Fred: No.

Jim: Tell her.

Fred: That's most of—been the trouble all the time.

Jim: What? That you don't know what she means?

Fred: Yeah. I don't understand a lot of—most of that what she's talking about.

Jim: Okay. Ask her now what she means. See if you can find out what she means.

Fred (*to Martha*): What do you mean?

Martha: Well, the responsibility I got of working, keeping house, trying to make the money go around for the bills, the obligations I got to see that the boys get to baseball practice, football practice, and basketball practice and get home. (*Aside.*) Scott is real growly on that.

Jim: Uh-hum. That's okay. You're talking to Fred now. What are you going to say now, Fred?

Fred: Well, I think she crowds a guy out and thinks she's got to do it.

Jim: You're talking to her, though. Tell her.

Fred: She crowds you out. She— You think you're the one who is supposed to do it instead of letting somebody else do it.

Martha (*emphatically*): You don't do it.

Fred: I would!

Martha: When?

Fred: All the time.

Martha (*to Jim*): All right. I went to a—

Jim: Now, don't get me into this! It's between you two.

Martha: I went to a bowling tournament in Leavenworth about a year ago. I thought for sure he'd stay home and take care of the cattle—

Jim: Talk to Fred. "I thought sure *you* would stay home."

Martha: He went partying that night. He went to—

Jim: Fred went. Tell Fred, "*You* went partying, Fred."

Martha (to Fred): You went to Salina to Shriners; I stayed home and took care of the stuff. You went to Topeka to insurance school; I stayed home and took care of the stuff and the kids.

Fred: I took care of everything, too.

Martha: When I came home the chickens hadn't even been taken care of, nothing! He come home about two. Well, he didn't even come home, he went to a neighbor's about two o'clock in the morning. Nothing hadn't been taken care of or tended to.

Fred: They had and you know it.

Martha (gradually getting louder and angrier): Fred said a neighbor did it. The neighbor said Fred could have got home in time to do it, and he wasn't going to do it and he didn't do it! So they neither one did. Sunday night Fred *did* come home to see about stuff just before I got home.

Jim: Okay. Let me break in a minute, because I can see now while we are sitting here what you have gotten into over a long period of time. Any family does this. People get into ways of thinking about one another and not finding a way to work out where their differences are. This happens between you two I think when, for example, Fred, you seem to pull back from her. Do you like to get a hug from her?

Fred: Yeah.

Jim (to Martha): Do you know that he likes that?

Martha: Yeah.

Jim: And do you like to get a hug from him?

Martha: Yes, I do when he's— I mean, when he considers the family or something it makes me feel different to him altogether.

Jim: But you notice he didn't qualify. He just said, yes, he'd like to get it. But I think you're saying, yes, *if* he's a good boy.

Martha: Maybe that's it.

(Fred nods in agreement.)

Jim: He says that's right.

Fred: If everything suits her, and if it don't, why—

Martha: I mean, to me, he don't go hunting all day, come home, and expect—and me work all day, come home with still more work to do, breakfast dishes sitting on the table, and he expects me to have time for him!

Jim: So you're putting affection on the basis of, "*If* you're good we can have affection." Is that right?

Martha: No, not really. I—

Jim (to Fred): Do you feel that's right?

Fred: That's right.

Jim (to Martha): That's the way he feels. Did you ever hear about a little bit of honey helps the medicine go down? (*Denise laughs.*) What do you think that means, Denise? You know, 'cause you laughed when I said it. You know what that means, don't you?

Martha: I used to try that. One night he promised me if I'd just —just be there with him and—well, sex relations is what he was wanting—

Jim: Sure!

Martha: He would go with me to take Scott to the dentist the next day. What did he do? He got up about five-thirty in the morning, got the dogs, and went hunting. Forgot even what he had said the night before.

Jim: Okay. You know what that teaches you? That you shouldn't make bargains about affection. Did you want to make love that night?

Martha: No.

Jim: You didn't! So you participated on the basis of this promise, which later was broken. Right? Well, isn't that kind of bad faith? You guys are into this kind of thing! Did you know that she really didn't want to?

Fred (slowly and low): Yeah. I knew that was wrong.

Jim: I'll bet you when you were courting her, or in the early days of your marriage, you knew how to warm her up without that, didn't you?

Fred (very low): Yeah, I guess.

Jim: You guess. I'll bet you did. Do you know how to warm her up now? I mean without the promises.

Fred: No.

Jim: That's why you use the promises?

Fred: No, that's her idea.

Jim: You don't think you do that?

Fred: No. I don't believe in that way of doing.

Jim: Okay. Do you know, though, how to get her interested in wanting to go to bed and make love?

Fred: Well, I think I know how it should be, but that ain't—that don't work.

Jim: Would you be willing to tell her, today, now, how you feel about her.

Fred (long pause): What do you mean?

Jim: Well, you see, what she has actually been saying today is that she's not sure you care about her, that you love her. Do you?

Fred: Yes.

Jim: Can you tell her that, looking at her?

Fred: Yes.

Jim: Try it.

Fred (very ill at ease, muttering): I love you.

Martha: And I don't believe it.

Jim: You don't believe it.

Martha: No. (*Bitterly.*) You don't just love somebody by telling them. You love somebody by showing them.

Jim: But not, I don't believe, in the way you're asking. They don't—

Martha (interrupting): The little things he does for me shows me that he loves me, not just sitting there and telling me that.

Jim: So you are saying there are some things he does that tell you, right?

Martha (bitterly): Very few anymore, seems like.

Jim: Okay. Because you are really feeling bad, you know, and being let down. I think you have to realize that the two of you have gotten to the point where you are far apart and each one does something now more or less for spite against the other. That means you really aren't getting the happy times that you could get.

Martha: I do things for him, take care of his clothes, cook his meals, what he likes, to show him I love him, or for him because I do love him. And what is it he can say he does to show me he loves me?

Jim: He said before, but I think you're saying that isn't enough.

That's why you two have to learn to bargain, because you can't sit there saying, "I'm doing all this and you're not doing enough." What you have to do, if you really feel that way, is not do all those things.

Martha: As he says, "I'm working eight hours a day and bringing in a check. What more do you want?"

Jim: What more do you want?

Martha: Well, I want a little consideration and—

Jim: Do you know when you get it?

Martha: It don't seem to me like I get it.

Jim: Do you know why?

Martha: Uh—why?

Jim: You don't expect it at all!

Martha: Now this week everything was going fine until Wednesday. He went hunting all day.

Jim: Okay. And that ruins—

Martha: Then went to town and eat supper.

Jim: I get the feeling that ruins the whole thing even though part of the week has been going good.

Martha: He went hunting every morning anyway. I didn't say anything. He was there when I came home from work.

Jim: Do you remember when you were courting? You told me he was very considerate, loving, kind. What did you do to get it that way then?

Martha: Nothing really.

Jim: Nothing at all. Did you gripe at him?

Martha: There was no reason to.

Jim: No reason to. See your position is that you are in a circle, and it's got to be stopped either by Fred or you changing something about it, because you are both in it. The circle goes around and around. You expect him to behave like a little boy, he expects you to bitch at him, and when you do he says, "By God, I'm going to show that I am a real man and I can go out hunting if I want." Do you understand?

Martha: But why did he do it Wednesday? I wouldn't have minded if he'd a-went and been home when I would have got home!

Jim: Ask him why he did.

Martha (to Fred): Why did you?

Fred: Well, we had it planned for a long time we was going to go.

Martha: I didn't know a thing about it. I thought you'd be there when I got home from work.

Fred (hesitantly): We would have been, but we just—

Martha: It just makes me feel that he don't even want to be there.

Jim: Yeah, but, Fred, do you want to be there?

Fred: Well, yeah. That's the first place I go is home.

Jim: Do you want to be with this woman?

Fred: Yeah.

Jim: Do you want to be married to her?

Fred: Yes.

Martha: All right, then why wasn't you there?

Jim: Well, maybe he wasn't there that day but he's here now. What does that tell you?

Martha: It isn't because he wanted to really.

Jim: It isn't because he wanted to? Why is it?

Martha: No, because he growled all the way up here.

Jim (incredulous): What, Fred?! That's Fred's problem just like yours! You don't want to gripe either, do you?

Martha: No.

Jim: So both of you are acting in these ways that you don't really want to. But you are both here and that's enough for me to know that you both want to work on this!

Now, I think we are coming to the end of our time, and I want to share with you some of the feelings that I think are important about your family. One is that Dad and Mother, Fred and Martha, started out like all couples do. It was all nice and loving, and Martha felt Fred was very considerate, and you, Fred, liked winning her. Right? Okay. Then came the hard times of life—having kids, not enough money, wondering if Fred cares about you, Martha, and his wondering if you're going to be like a mother to him and chastise him—all the kinds of things you don't have when you're just going together. Along the way you forgot how you were when it was really good together. You got caught up in the responsibilities of the kids and the money, all of which is important, believe me. But you, Martha, took over too much. Fred let you do it, and partially resents it that you do it. So you have these hard feelings build up. Sometimes the kids have gotten in between you, also.

To begin with, what you need to do is remember what it was like at first, get back the way it was between just you two. Then sit down and start working out how you both want it to be. In other words, no more blaming between you two, because that just makes you get farther apart.

Now, let me ask you kids whether there are any questions you want to ask either your folks or me? What do you think of what has been going on here today? Is there anything you want to share with us? Is there anything from watching those two that you would like to tell either one or both of them? What about you, Denise? (*No response.*) How about you two fellows? (*No response.*) How about you two (*indicating the parents*)? Is there anything you want to ask or say?

Fred: I think she ought to give me some of that responsibility.

Jim: Tell her.

Fred: More responsibility.

Martha: Would he take it? Just like I was telling you on the money before—

Jim (overlapping): You listen to what he says, Martha. Say that again, Fred. You want what?

Fred: Give me more responsibility.

Jim (to Martha): Now, you can't say, "Will you take it?" Take him at his word.

Martha: What do I do if it's not done.

Jim: He will get it done. Can you wait, and let him get it done?

Martha: If he does it, yes.

Jim: Will you do it, Fred?

Fred: Yes.

Jim: Now, he may not do it exactly at the moment or time when you think he should, but if you want him to be more responsible, that is the road you have to go. Let me ask you, do you believe me when I tell you that?

Martha: I don't know. I've kind of lost trust in everybody and everything.

Jim: I know that. That's what really concerns me, Martha, because we have been sitting here and I have heard you say that you are the one on the bottom of all this, trying to take it all upon your shoulders. No wonder you are sad. No wonder you are angry. No wonder you think nobody cares about you. It's time to stop it. You *can't* take it all for this family. I like what Fred just said, because he is telling you, "I do care about you and I want to share some of that responsibility *if* you will let me." All you can do is take another chance. You think you can try?

Martha: Yes, if he'll take and worry about paying the bills and pay them.

Jim: If, schmiff. He said he would.

Martha: He said he would before, too.

Jim: I don't care about "before." The more you talk about "before," the more nothing is going to change for now. Now is now, and he is starting to change from this moment. (*To Fred.*) Right?

Fred: Yes.

Jim: What?

Fred: That's the way I always look at it, but they always bring up all the old back stuff.

Martha (interrupting): I could forget all that stuff in back *if* it didn't happen over again.

Jim: Well, I don't know about that, because I don't know about the past. But you are going to have to start, both of you, talking about how you want it to be now. Sometime either today or tomorrow; because it's the weekend, I hope you will sit down and talk about what we did here today and see where you can make a start.

It is time for us to stop, and I want to thank all of you for coming, for making the trip here and helping us demonstrate an interview for these people who are also interested in working with families. Thank you for helping us today.

Discussion Following the Interview

A panel consisting of Drs. James Stachowiak, the interviewer; Howard Williams, Director of Community Services of the Kansas Department of Social Welfare; and Mary Grohmann, a consultant from the agency, discussed the interview and responded to questions from the audience.

Howard: When one sees a painting on the wall, one often does not really know what the painter meant by his work unless one talks to the artist. I would like to ask our "artist" how he felt as he worked his way through the interview and as he began to understand what was going on in this particular family; and also what thoughts crossed his mind as he sought to bring some sort of closure to the interview so that the family would feel it was all right for them to have come here and they would be encouraged to come back and talk with someone another time.

Jim: It was, no doubt, obvious right from the beginning how anxious and nervous I felt. No matter how many times I have the opportunity to interview families with other people watching, it is always the same. I wonder if we are all going to go through the floor and what kinds of things will happen. There is an excitement and nervousness at the same time. Even though I tell myself that people who have come some distance, as these did, and have committed themselves to exposing their personal feelings in front of others, probably have good feelings toward the therapist, and though I'm sure we won't die, I still have that nervousness.

Progressive Stages of Family Therapy

At the beginning no one feels very comfortable, so I talk a little, explaining what we are doing. I don't know if they even hear too much of what I say, but it is a way to help us all relax some. With this family I felt at the outset that I wanted to accomplish at least three things: first, to give all of them a chance to talk about some of the things that were troubling them; second, I hoped I would get a chance to establish a warm relationship with each person; and third, I hoped we would have some time in which to experiment with ways in which change might be possible for them.

I pay very little attention to content per se as I meet with the family. What I pay attention to is the kind of reaction whatever I do gets from each person and, for example, what the son is doing when the father says something. I try to see out of the corner of my eye whether when I change they will change. All I am really doing is assessing how open and willing they are to consider making changes.

For each interview, or over a longer period of time if you continue to see the family in subsequent sessions, there is a pattern to the process, from ritual, to passing time, to games, and then to intimacy. When you meet people you start out with a ritual, like "How do you do. I am so and so," and you probably shake hands, the social ritual of our culture. Second, you have to pass the time a little and you give your orientation about what is going to happen, and everyone sits around and looks at each other nervously. Third, you get into what I call the games, which is like the wife saying, "See what a dirty s.o.b. my husband is," and his saying, "If it only weren't for you." That kind of game has to be played for a while, and I don't know of any way to circumvent it. Hopefully, if you get through these stages then maybe you can get to what is termed "intimacy," which means a mutual sharing and trusting relationship in which everyone feels it is possible for something to happen between you. Sometimes you never get that far—it just doesn't develop. The biggest errors I ever make, I think, are not recognizing where the people are in this progression and either trying to push them too fast into the next stage, or not noticing they are ready to go a little faster because I am nervous about some aspect and not responding to the flow.

Toward the middle of the interview I began to have very warm feelings toward everybody in the family. This is especially important to me. I was quite concerned about how I would be able to relate to Fred. When I met him here, I could see that he was very tense, expecting to be blamed, and he sat as far away from his wife as he could get. When I asked him and his son to change seats, I hoped that would go off all right. When it did, it gave me the clue that I could move farther, and while I did not touch him then, I could later on. One of the better things that happened was that although he started out speaking so softly I could scarcely hear him, he gradually became more relaxed and a little more talkative. All this culminated at the time I asked him to tell his wife he loved her. That was very emotional for him, and immediately afterward he had to get a cigarette. If I had asked him to do something like that earlier, it would not have worked, but I had hoped to get him to express his feelings for her before the interview was over.

At the same time I did not want to alienate the mother, because she has some very strong angry and hurt feelings. She said as much at one point near the end when she made the statement about feeling so bad for so long that she doesn't know whom she can trust or believe in. With someone like that, if you do not recognize those feelings, you get into a blaming attitude and switch things around to where she is the "bad guy."

Mary: I wondered how much you knew about the family before you started interviewing them. Had you seen them before or was this your first contact? And I also wondered about the hypotheses that went through your head as you worked with them. For instance, I found myself thinking about what various family members were really like, what they thought about things, what their reactions truly were, and so forth and so on, during the course of the interview. I had to revise my ideas at times, of course. This was the first time I had seen them, and I wondered how much you knew about them in advance.

Jim: Last night I received a brief description of the family and some information gathered at the time they approached the Center for help. They had come after the fight they talked about today. So that was all I knew. I had never seen them before. From what information I had beforehand, one thing which struck me as unusual was that all they were saying was that there was trouble in the marital relationship. There was nothing about the kids. This is quite unusual. When a family comes for help, they will usually pick out a child and focus on him. I wondered a little about this.

An important question is whether or not the kids would have been more actively involved if the interview had taken place in private. I think when a family like this one presents itself as being so oriented toward the marriage relationship, then you would expect the kids to behave as they did. In effect, both of the parents were excusing them from any kind of responsibility in the situation. It was only very late in the session when a few hints came out about the children's involvement. If I had the opportunity to see them longer, I believe the kids would take a more active part and could be very useful.

The hypotheses you spoke of, Mary, interest me, too. I also was continually revising my notions as I went along. I would go in one direction for a while and see where that led, and then discover that was the wrong track, and then I would try a different track. When I questioned them about their families, for example, I was really trying to get a picture of what their childhood families were like. I gave up on that, since at that point the father would not communicate very much. Then I tried to determine the pairs existing in the family. I probably overexaggerated, but I did it purposely. One reason was to give the father a chance to see that somebody might be on his side. The father seemed to beam a little when I referred to the older son as a "chip off the old block." At that point I was simply pairing them off, and also the daughter and the mother. One of my early hypotheses was that the little kid somehow didn't have a partner, so I would be a partner to him. Those were some of the thoughts I was having.

Howard: It seemed to me that one of the turning points in the interview was when you made the second shift in the seating arrangement. You brought the youngster in close to you so everybody had a partner. It was more than a shift of physical positions at that point, and I wondered if the slightly conspiratorial alliance of you and the youngest one did not relax the group's attitude toward you.

Jim: I am glad to hear you say that. It makes a lot of sense to me although I was not aware of it at the time. If it worked that way, that's good.

Mary: What particularly impressed me was the way in which

you were able to use yourself. It pointed out to me so clearly what can be learned from a session like this, which is not to imitate somebody else but to be yourself and use yourself in the best possible way. I felt you were obviously trying to ferret out where you could get into the emotional climate of this family, and that you were trying several ways of doing it. Then when you latched onto the little boy, that provided the entry. For someone else, it could have been some other person who would give the entry. To me, it was important to observe how you wove your way around until you found the entry.

Another important thing that happened at that point was that you became more relaxed yourself. Before that you seemed to me to be a little bit intellectual, asking sensible questions and getting information, but the really warm feeling toward the family did not come across until that moment. Suddenly your whole body, your facial expression and voice, everything about you became part of the whole interplay to a much greater extent than before. I think this was the major change of the whole interview. With a family you had not seen before, and one which obviously had a lot of rigid notions as to what one does and doesn't do, this was quite impressive, to my way of thinking. You may have noticed toward the beginning the little girl tucked her mother's skirt in place. She didn't get this idea of propriety out of the nowhere, yet at the end of the session the parents were talking openly about their sexual relationship. They could not possibly have done that until you became involved in a very total way.

Jim: Hearing you say that, I realize it happened just as you said. I was feeling much more relaxed at that point and as if somehow I had found an emotional breakthrough. What this illustrates is something I have said before: if you want to know what a family therapist does, don't ask him—watch him. In ten years' time I have had an opportunity to watch a lot of very good people, such as Nathan Ackerman, Virginia Satir, Jay Haley, and Don Jackson, and in the early stages I know what I used to go through. I thought I had to be like them, that somehow family therapists had a certain face. So I tried imitation and found it didn't work at all. Gradually I have se-

lected from among different aspects those that are meaningful for me. As I did this, I began to worry less about whether I
was going to screw up or say the wrong thing—because I did
have a chance to recover from that—and I became more con-
fident about using myself to the best advantage.

Howard: It seemed to me that one fine thing was your appreciation for the great amount of potential strength in this family,
and you indicated that to them—that they were vitally involved with each other, they did care, and that you would defend the family. Their willingness to be here was an actual affirmation of what the wife was complaining about. She was
the one who said that love is more than just saying the words.
But it was so difficult for her to go one step further and see
that an unwilling husband coming to this interview in front of
these people was showing that she meant very much to him. A
hard thing for me to understand myself is that if someone who
likes me does something for me which he really doesn't want
to do, it may be a greater expression of love than doing something for me that he thought of himself and wanted to do.

Mary: Toward the beginning as they were going along, I found
myself feeling irritated with the woman, wanting to say to her,
"Why don't you just cut it out!" How did you feel in that respect?

Jim: Well, for me one of the hardest things about working with
families is that we helpers bring to the situation the experiences we have had with our own families, and are bound and
determined to like some people and dislike others. It happens
very naturally at the beginning. That is why in a discussion
about the family the first tendency is to point out the "good
guy" and the "bad guy." I am very much aware of this and
can escape these inclinations. Perhaps a way of getting
around that for people who are less experienced is to have a
co-therapist work with you. It is best to have a
man-and-woman team so that the viewpoints of both sexes
will be understood. Since I am so much aware of the natural
inclination to respond to certain people in certain ways, I immediately try to determine, for example, which one makes me
anxious. In this case it was Fred, because I didn't know if he

would even talk to me. Then I look to see which one makes me feel angry so that I might starting blaming them, and here it was the wife. I am sure I slipped with her many times, but when I caught myself I tried to get my perspective back, saying "That ain't going to get you anywhere," and then I would back out of it and try a different approach. And it worked here, because I came to feel that I genuinely liked her. By the time the session was half over I really could feel tremendous compassion for her. She is playing this terrible role of having people dump on her. She is asking for it, almost begging for it, and doesn't know it. So the question is what can be done about it.

Question: What precipitated the wife finally calling for help, since the fight was typical of what was going on in the marriage?

Jim: This would ordinarily have been a track to explore, and I forgot all about it.

Comment: The main issue was the fight. She was most concerned about biting her husband's hand so hard she broke the skin. The main thing she focused on was wanting to do something to improve their relationship.

Howard: Would it sound awfully stuffy if I were to say she was panic-stricken at the realization of her own hostility?

Mary: I think that is exactly the point. She must have never realized before the tremendous emotion inside her. She finally found out that it can explode. I am sure she had never conceived of herself as being able to do a thing like that. When it suddenly happened, she was overwhelmed. That would be my guess.

Question: Jim, when you talked with her about doing what she wanted to do, she mentioned going out and drinking and being accused of having an affair. I wondered, then, if somehow she wasn't afraid that she was the sick one in the family.

Jim: It occurred to me as we were going along that there was a part of her which enjoyed, in a vicarious way, his acting-out behavior. On the one hand she would have liked to be doing that, and on the other hand she disapproved. She was married very young, and right away she had to get into the role of Mrs.

Responsibility. It may be that she does a lot of projection, putting unacceptable impulses of her own onto him. And I am sure neither of them would understand that. I just wanted to see if she would be willing to say that there was something she would like just for herself, and it is very difficult for her to do that.

Mary: I think it would have been interesting to find out what their ideas are of the masculine role and the feminine role and the type of responsibility each should take. I got a very strong impression that the wife sees herself as fulfilling her role to the best of her abilities, and if there is anything in which she is remiss, it is not her fault—it is because her husband does things that interfere with her being the perfect mother, the perfect wife, and perfect woman. If my speculation is correct, then the very fact that she stepped out of the role by being hostile and biting him has even more impact, because her whole image would be shattered. At that moment she might have felt that she was the sicker one.

Question: Jim, from your experience in working with families over a period of time, would you be willing to predict how much effect this one session might have on the family? What do you think will happen?

Jim: After the interview they moved to another place in the room, and I went over and sat down with them and talked to each one. The wife was much more relaxed than she had been before. I told them I was quite interested in how they get on. I asked them to write to me after about two weeks, and said that I would answer. Then it just clicked in my mind that Fred had stated he wanted more responsibility. My first reaction had been to give her my address, but I said, "Fred, I heard you say you wanted more responsibility, so I will give you the address and you see that the letter gets written, will you?" I was going to say "you write," but then I remembered that he has only about an eighth-grade education. I had a feeling he might have some qualms about writing himself, and I didn't want to put him in a bind. Anyway, she liked that a lot, and she said, "Very good, I'm glad," and he said they would write to me. If they are left alone now, I don't think too much is going to happen; but I do hope somebody will work with them on a regular basis, because I think a lot could be done with them. They would have to have a lot of very concrete teaching about how to behave differently. One idea I had, but there was not enough time to try it, was to say, "Fred, I am going to be you and I am going to talk with your wife," and then show him ways to talk differently to her. Then I would turn it back to him, and have him try these different ways. Then maybe the same thing could be done taking the wife's role, or having the kids enter into the role-playing. The actual teaching and practicing of different ways to say things should be of real benefit to them. It seemed that no matter what I tried today, they stuck with their own particular way of responding.

Question: During the follow-up would you have conjoint sessions every time?

Jim: Because of the way it went today, I really do not understand their roles too well, so for a while I would still want the whole family to come together. Then if I became convinced that the children truly were not much involved, I would focus more on the couple alone. One thing about having the children there, though, is that even spontaneously the parents brought up their sexual relationship in front of the kids, which gave me a feeling that things can be discussed relatively openly and easily in this family.

Question: What do you think is the mother's basic attitude toward the kids being more responsible?

Mary: I think this would amount to an abdication on her part, because she feels she has to worry. That's part of her role to worry, to know where they are at all times, and take them and go after them. I think she would have a big problem about letting go, of letting these kids grow up and take responsibility. To the degree that the children do that, her own role is diminished, you see. I think that would be very hard for her, and it would be one important aspect of her reeducation.

Jim: This is why it is so hard to work with a system. The strong tendency is to see things in terms of individuals, but there are interlocking, reciprocal systems in operation.

This reminds me of a play I saw several years ago, with

Gertrude Berg in the role of the mother who takes charge of the lives of everyone else in the family. The two oldest children are married and have moved as far away from the parents as they could. The last child, a daughter, is about to be married, but she is locked in a big identity and independence problem involving her mother; so unknown to the mother, she starts going to a psychiatrist. When the mother finds out about this, she visits the psychiatrist to let him know there is nothing wrong that the mother can't handle. However, in the process she reveals that her own life is completely tied up in managing other people's lives. The doctor asks her if there isn't something she would like to do just for herself, and she says, "Well, I used to play the piano and sing, but I haven't had time for that." The analyst tells her to go home, let the family take care of themselves, and play and sing. She decides that is what she will do. She will stop taking care of all the family because they don't like it anyway. Immediately the rest of the family starts putting it on her again, insisting that she help them with their problems. She is changing, but the rest of them switch around to try to get her back into her role. In the final scene the analyst has stopped by to see her at home, at her request. He tells her it is the kind of house he has always dreamed of living in, but his wife is an analyst, too, and she prefers an apartment. He looks very weary, and the mother is very solicitous. The doctor says he has a feeling she is going to start being his temporary mother-substitute. She says, "Why temporary? I'm available to be a mother on a full-time basis. Why don't you lie down on the couch, Doctor?" [1]

Types of Family Intervention

One point I want to make in conclusion is that there are three kinds of general interventions for families which we should consider. One is working with just the family itself. If you choose to do that, you have to make the assessment that they have the necessary resources to bring about changes. If they cannot carry it off themselves, with the support of weekly interviews, you may have to intervene directly in their system by going into the home and teaching them on the spot how to make some changes. Then there is the intersystem approach, as, for example, when one of the children is having difficulties in school. You may have to get the school and the family together, and act as a mediator or ombudsman to work out intersystem difficulties. Just seeing the family will not always provide the support needed for all families to change. With the family we just observed, weekly interviews may be all that are necessary, but you might want to consider going into their home to find out on the spot what is actually happening. Always you must keep in mind that each family system is unique in its own way, and there is no established pattern for family therapy. How you intervene for change, therefore, develops uniquely in each situation.

1. Leonard Spigelgass, *Dear Me, The Sky is Falling* (New York: Random House, 1963), p. 112.

INDEX

* Page numbers in italic type refer to material in interviews; the terms are meant to be suggestive only and neither definitive nor exhaustive.